Mainstream and Formal Epistemology

Mainstream and Formal Epistemology provides the first easily accessible yet erudite and original analysis of the meeting point between mainstream and formal theories of knowledge. These two strands of thinking have traditionally proceeded in isolation from one another, but in this book Vincent F. Hendricks brings them together for a systematic comparative treatment. He demonstrates how mainstream epistemology and formal epistemology may significantly benefit from one another, paving the way for a new unifying program of 'plethoric' epistemology. His book both defines and furthers the debate between philosophers from two very different sides of the epistemological spectrum.

Vincent F. Hendricks is Professor of Epistemology, Logic and Methodology at Roskilde University, Denmark. He is the author of many books, including *The Convergence of Scientific Knowledge, Feisty Fragments, Logical Lyrics* and *500 CC: Computer Citations*. Editor in chief of *Synthese* and *Synthese Library*, he is also the founder of Φ*LOG, The Network for Philosophical Logic and Its Applications*.

Mainstream and Formal Epistemology

VINCENT F. HENDRICKS

Roskilde University

CAMBRIDGE
UNIVERSITY PRESS

CAMBRIDGE UNIVERSITY PRESS
Cambridge, New York, Melbourne, Madrid, Cape Town, Singapore, São Paulo

Cambridge University Press
40 West 20th Street, New York, NY 10011-4211, USA

www.cambridge.org
Information on this title: www.cambridge.org/9780521857895

First published 2006

Printed in the United States of America

A catalog record for this publication is available from the British Library.

Library of Congress Cataloging in Publication Data

Hendricks, Vincent F.
Mainstream and formal epistemology / Vincent F. Hendricks.
p.   cm.
Includes bibliographical references and index.
ISBN-13: 978-0-521-85789-5 (hardback)
ISBN-10: 0-521-85789-9 (hardback)
1. Knowledge, Theory of.   I. Title
BD161.H35   2006
121 – dc22   2005029339

ISBN-13   978-0-521-85789-5 hardback
ISBN-10   0-521-85789-9 hardback

For

J *aakko*
ohan
ohn

Contents

Preface

Forcing epistemology is a trendy way of defeating the skeptics who since the days of old have cited *prima facie* error possibilities as some of the most devastating arguments against claims to knowledge. The idea of *forcing* is to delimit the set of possibilities over which the inquiring agent has to succeed: If the agent can succeed over the relevant possibility set, then the agent may still be said to have knowledge even if he commits many errors, even grave ones, in other but irrelevant possibilities.

Contemporary epistemological studies are roughly either carried out: (1) in a *mainstream* or informal way, using largely conceptual analyses and concentrating on sometimes folksy and sometimes exorbitantly speculative examples or counterexamples, or (2) in a *formal* way, by applying a variety of tools and methods from logic, computability theory or probability theory to the theory of knowledge. The two traditions have unfortunately proceeded largely in isolation from one another.

Many contemporary mainstream and formal epistemologies pay homage to the forcing strategy. The aim of this book is to demonstrate *systematically* that the two traditions have much in common, both epistemologically and methodologically. If they could be brought closer together, not only might they significantly benefit from one another, the way could be paved for a new unifying program in 'plethoric' epistemology.

Acknowledgments

I have on the way been aided and supported by much and many. I am particularly indebted to Professor Jaakko Hintikka (Boston University) for inviting me to Boston as a visiting professor in the spring of 2003. This book has benefited enormously from Hintikka's many insights and constructive criticisms. Other faculty members at Boston University also kindly discussed portions of the manuscript with me. I would like to thank Professor Klaus Brinkman, Professor Juliet Floyd, Professor Aaron Garrett and Dr. Troy Catterson for providing suggestive criticism and valuable advice. Sitting in on Hintikka's spring graduate course on 'Logic and Scientific Method' was an added bonus. I am also particularly indebted to Professor Horacio Arló-Costa (Carnegie Mellon University) for his extremely thorough reading of the manuscript and his very pertinent comments and suggestions for improvement. Professor Johan van Benthem and Professor Robert van Rooij (ILLC, Amsterdam) have likewise both encouraged me and suggested valuable improvements to the material presented here. The book has also benefited enormously from discussions with Professor Robert Stalnaker (MIT). I am grateful to Professor John Symons (University of Texas at El Paso) for reading the manuscript and making my own ideas about the subject matter much clearer. I'm also indebted to Professor Isaac Levi (Columbia University) and Professor Daniel Kolak (Rutgers) for discussing important portions of the manuscript with me. Professor Duncan H. Pritchard (University of Stirling) has likewise provided valuable criticism and constructive suggestions. Louise Westmark kindly subjected the manuscript to a thorough treatment, caught errors and provided many valuable suggestions for improvement. To Ditte Kiel

I am particularly indebted for *forcing* me to work really hard toward the end.

I thank the students of my epistemology seminar at the Humboldt University in Berlin in the fall of 2002 and the students of my graduate epistemology class at Roskilde University in the winter of 2002 for bearing with me and setting me straight while I was teaching and simultaneously developing the plethoric forcing epistemology program. I would also like to thank the Danish Research Council for the Humanities, which provided me with research grant no. 25-02-0355 through the 2003 academic year, allowing me to complete this book. My gratitude also goes out to Klaus Frovin Jørgensen (Roskilde University), who once again came to my rescue when I had LaTex problems. I am grateful to my publisher, Cambridge University Press, in particular, Beatrice Rehl for taking on this project.

My teacher, colleague and friend, Professor Stig Andur Pedersen (Roskilde University), is always there with his insight, support and good humor. This is yet another project that would not have gotten off the ground without him. Finally, I thank Henriette Kibsgaard for living life with me in the best of ways.

Vincent F. Hendricks
New York City
April 2003

1

Introduction

It is a curiosity of the philosophical temperament, this passion for radical
solutions. Do you feel a little twinge in your epistemology? Absolute skepticism is the thing to try . . . Apparently the rule is this: if aspirin doesn't work,
try cutting of your head.

Jerry Fodor (1985)

Humans are in pursuit of knowledge. It plays a significant role in deliber-
ation, decision and action in all walks of everyday and scientific life. The
systematic and detailed study of knowledge, its criteria of acquisition and
its limits and modes of justification is known as epistemology.

Despite the admirable epistemic aim of acquiring knowledge, humans
are cognitively accident-prone and make mistakes perceptually, inferen-
tially, experimentally, theoretically or otherwise. Epistemology is the study
of the possibility of knowledge and how prone we are to making mistakes.
Error is the starting point of skepticism. Skepticism asks how knowledge
is possible given the possibility of error. Skeptics have for centuries cited
prima facie possibilities of error as the most substantial arguments against
knowledge claims. From this perspective, epistemology may be viewed
as a reply to skepticism and skeptical challenges. Skepticism is the bane
of epistemology, but apparently also a blessing, according to Santayana
(1955): "Skepticism is the chastity of the intellect, and it is shameful to
surrender it too soon or to the first comer" (p. 50).

Skepticism is a tough challenge and requires strong countermeasures.
In set theory, a powerful combinatorial technique for proving statements
consistent with the axioms of set theory was invented by P. Cohen in the

1960s. The technique is called *forcing*. In particular, Cohen developed forcing in order to prove that the negation of the Axiom of Choice and the negation of the Continuum Hypothesis are consistent with the axioms of set theory. Today, there are various ways of using the forcing technique. One way is to construct an object with certain properties or to construct a model in which there are no objects with certain properties, thus forcing what you want directly – either constructing the object or iteratively destroying any such object.

Contemporary epistemologies have developed a family of countermeasures for standing up to the skeptical challenge; these exhibit a type of 'bluntness' similar to that of set-theoretical forcing.[1] The idea of epistemological forcing is as follows: whenever skeptics cite possibilities of error as arguments against knowledge claims, the strategy is to show that, although they are possibilities of error, they fail to be *relevant* possibilities of error. Some possibilities of error are simply not genuine – they are too remote, too speculative, or too much. These possibilities may accordingly be *forced* out and are henceforth not to be considered during the knowledge acquisition process. If the agent can succeed over the possibilities deemed relevant, then that is good enough for knowledge – knowledge will, or should, exhibit all the classical characteristics under forcing.

The influential *epistemic reliabilism* of Goldman, Nozick's elegant formulation of the *counterfactual epistemology* and Lewis's new *contextual epistemology* are all informal epistemological proposals observing the forcing relation.

Epistemic reliabilism (Goldman 1979, 1986) and especially the recent versions outlined in Goldman (1992, 1996) acknowledge the agent's limited cognitive abilities and accordingly deflate the agent's epistemic responsibilities. The idea is to replace the rather demanding requirements typically proposed by skepticism for justified knowledge possession with more lenient conditions. In principle, a particular justified belief may be false; however, its method or mode of acquisition must in general lead to true convictions. For knowledge to come about, besides the truth of the belief in question, its method of acquisition must rule out all relevant possibilities of error. The forcing technique is included in the method of acquisition. The method may not be able to exclude the possibility that Descartes' devious demon is feeding the agent systematically misleading sensations. Then again, this is not a relevant possibility of error. Or so

---

[1] Otherwise set-theoretical and epistemological forcing bear little resemblance to one another. In a certain sense one may even call them opposites. The term 'forcing epistemology' was coined in Hendricks 2001.

it is claimed. According to epistemic reliabilists, infallible methods are not required for knowledge. The development of epistemic reliabilism up to the current versions is scrutinized from the forcing perspective in Chapter 3.

Nozick's (1981) counterfactual reliabilistic knowledge definition, an adapted and supplemented version of a proposal put forth by Dretske (1970), is likewise a forcing proposal. The goal is to show that knowledge is in fact possible. The inherent decision procedure in Nozick's definition of knowledge, together with the counterfactual semantics, requires the agent to succeed in all possible worlds sufficiently close to the actual world. The agent may not know that he is not a brain in a vat – a famous thought experiment suggested by Putnam (1981) – but that possibility of error is so remote, and the semantics governing the counterfactual conditional guarantees the long distance. This counterfactual epistemology is the topic of Chapter 4.

Whereas both epistemic reliabilism and Nozickian counterfactual epistemology begin by confronting the skeptical challenge, Lewis's (1996) contextual epistemology, in contrast, assumes knowledge of a great many things in a variety of different contexts, particularly conversational contexts. 'Contextualists' hold the view that the standards for knowledge acquisition, possession and maintenance fluctuate with what is at issue – and at stake – in the particular linguistic context. The current interlocutors determine which possible worlds are real or relevant and also why and when. The knowledge that you are currently wearing sneakers may evaporate into thin air once you set foot in an epistemology class because in this new context you may doubt whether you even have feet to put your sneakers on. Be that as it may, we have knowledge, and epistemology starts from there – not from ignorance or demonstrations of the mere possibility of knowledge. Considering brains in vats and Cartesian demons is to 'epistemologize', which may make knowledge 'elusive' especially in an epistemology class. What is needed for obtaining knowledge are regulatives to rule out possible worlds dictated by the current (conversational) context and then describe how we avoid error and gain truth in the ones that are left. Contextual epistemology is discussed in Chapter 5.

It turns out that a host of *formal* epistemological proposals also share the forcing heuristics. Knowledge claims may be restricted by algebraic constraints defined for the accessibility relation between possible worlds, which is the forcing foundation for *epistemic logic* or *logical epistemology*. Logical epistemology originates with Von Wright (1951) and was propounded most notably by Hintikka (1962). The algebraic properties of the accessibility relation between possible worlds may sometimes be defined in such a way that the skeptic has nowhere to go. The forcing characteristics and the (often neglected) epistemological significance of epistemic logic are the topics of Chapter 6.

Formal learning theory, also dubbed *computational epistemology* by Kelly (1996), focuses on the intrinsic solvability of inductive epistemic problems for both ideal and computationally bounded agents (Kelly 2000). The basic idea is that when an agent is faced with an epistemic learning problem, the problem determines a set of possible worlds in each of which the agent has to succeed to solve the problem and acquire knowledge. This is also forcing. Brains in vats sever the connection between knowledge acquisition and reliable inquiry, but short of that, agents may have quite a bit of reliable inductive knowledge. Although it is a logical paradigm, in that it utilizes tools from mathematical logic, it is also a procedural or effective paradigm, as it concentrates on learning and knowledge acquisition issues rather than modal operators, axiomatics and validity, as logical epistemology does. Computational epistemology is the topic of Chapter 7.

The last epistemological proposal to be considered is called *modal operator epistemology*.[2] Modal operator epistemology is a mixture of epistemic, tense and alethic logic and a few concepts drawn from computational epistemology. It was developed in order to study the validity of limiting convergent knowledge (Hendricks 2001). To obtain limiting convergent knowledge, the agent has to converge to the true hypothesis only in the possible worlds consistent with what has been observed so far. This approach also pays homage to the forcing relation. Brains in vats are as devastating here as elsewhere, but if blocked, knowledge may in the limiting end have a certain strength measurable by a yardstick devised by logical epistemology. An outline of the modal operator theory of knowledge, together with an analysis of its epistemological importance, is provided in Chapter 8.

Epistemology may be pursued in different ways:

- 'Mainstream' epistemology (which encompasses epistemic reliabilism, counterfactual epistemology and contextual epistemology) seeks necessary and sufficient conditions for the possession of knowledge using largely common-sense considerations and folksy examples and counterexamples (see Fig. 1.1).

---

[2] Elsewhere the paradigm is also known as *modal operator theory*, since the paradigm is flexible enough to study other modalitites than knowledge.

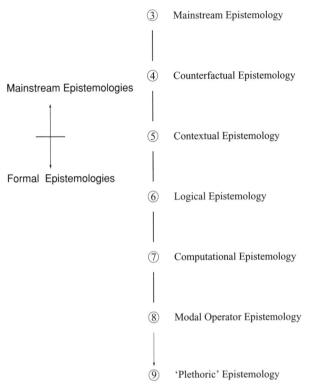

FIGURE 1.1. Epistemologies covered in this book and the chapters in which they are discussed.

- 'Formal' approaches to epistemology (which include logical episte-mology, computational epistemology and modal operator epistemol-ogy) either proceed axiomatically or concentrate on learning and knowledge acquisition using toolboxes from logic and computability theory.

The two traditions have regrettably not paid much attention to each other. But both approaches, or rather their current exponents, employ the reg-ulative forcing principle to combat skepticism. Based on this common denominator, the fundamental epistemological similarities and differ-ences of the six paradigms may be cashed out in terms of how they each determine the set of possible worlds required for successful knowledge possession or acquisition.

The two approaches to the theory of knowledge share something else as well. One of the primary debates in contemporary epistemology concerns the justification condition of the standard tripartite definition of knowledge as justified true belief. Time and time again, philosophers attempt to remedy the justification condition in order to avoid 'Gettierization' (Gettier 1963) and other epistemic unpleasantries. The justification condition is supposed to ensure that the belief and the truth conditions of the tripartite definition are 'adequately connected', that is, that the reasons for believing are truth-conducive and, insofar as they are, indicate what is meant by rational inquiry. Philosophy of science includes a subdiscipline concerned with exactly the same thing: methodology.

Methodology may crudely be characterized as the study of the methods by which science arrives at its posited truths. Methodologists and formally minded philosophers have a large technical toolbox available for analyzing and hopefully ensuring the truth-conduciveness of the methods of science. These techniques range from various inductive and nonmonotonic logics to Bayesianism, game theory and belief revision theory to formal learning theory, and so forth. When mainstream philosophers talk about justification, formalists speak of methodology. A philosopher may choose to invoke reliability; the formalist then asks how reliability is to be defined and what it can do for you methodologically. The mainstream epistemologist calls for a defeasibility condition, and the philosophical logician starts to think about default rules and nonmonotonic logics; the mainstreamer wants to get to the truth sooner or later, the computational epistemologist, say, begins to consider solvability and criteria of successful convergence; accumulating evidential support the mainstream community decides for and the Bayesian community will start conditionalizing; minimum mutilation of the web of beliefs and the belief revision theorists will work on revision functions and entrenchment relations; an epistemologist may worry about rationality, the game-theorist will start to consider, say, strategies for winning noncooperative games of perfect information. What the mainstream epistemologists are looking for may to some extent be what the formal epistemologists have to offer. But what the formal epistemologists have to offer the mainstream community, and vice versa being a two-way street, may also be quite sensitive to the perspectives on inquiry that the different approaches adopt.

The general prerequisites for studying these epistemo-methodological affinities are outlined in Chapter 2, then applied systematically in the subsequent chapters. Finally in Chapter 9, they are used for the purpose of outlining a program of 'plethoric' epistemology.

2

Priming the Pump

The epistemo-methodological prerequisites for comparing mainstream and formal epistemologies concentrate on the following items: the modality of knowledge, infallibility, forcing and the reply to skepticism; the interaction between epistemology and methodology; the strength and validity of knowledge; reliability; and the distinction between a first-person perspective and a third-person perspective on inquiry.

> If knowledge can create problems, it is not through ignorance we can solve them.
>
> Isaac Asimov

2.1 Modal Knowledge, Infallibility and Forcing

Agents inquire to replace ignorance with knowledge. Knowledge is a kind of epistemic commitment or attitude held toward propositions or hypotheses describing some aspect of the world under consideration.[1] Agents may in general hold a host of different propositional attitudes, such as belief, hope, wish, desire etc. But there is a special property that knowledge enjoys over and above the other commitments. As Plato pointed out, a distinct property of knowledge is truth. Whatever is known must be true; otherwise it is not knowledge, even though it very well may qualify as belief or some other propositional attitude.

Contemporary notions of knowledge are often *modal* in nature. Knowledge is defined with respect to other possible states of affairs besides the actual state of affairs (Fig. 2.1). The possibility of knowledge seems ruled

---

[1] The terms 'hypothesis' and 'proposition' are used interchangeably unless otherwise stated.

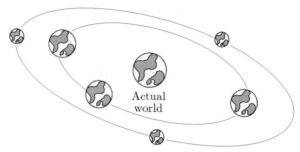

FIGURE 2.1. Modal knowledge is defined with respect to other possible worlds.

out when it is possible that we err. Introducing other possible state of affairs is an attempt to preclude exactly these error possibilities. Knowledge must be *infallible* by definition. As Lewis (1996) puts it, "To speak of fallible knowledge, of knowledge despite uneliminated possibilities of error, just *sounds* like a contradiction" (p. 367). A fallible notion of knowledge is not much different from a concept of belief potentially allowing the agent to 'know' a falsehood, severing the connection between knowledge and truth.

Plato also observed that knowledge, as opposed to mere true belief, is stable in nature. Knowledge has steadfastness and indefeasibility attached to it. True belief is quite useful as far as it goes, but in the light of true evidence, it may vanish. In the light of true evidence, knowledge will not evaporate. Inevaporability makes for the robust usefulness of knowledge compared with beliefs that are simply true. True belief in the actual world is not necessarily preserved if circumstances were to change but slightly. On the other hand, knowledge in the actual world is assumed to be stable across quite radically varying circumstances. Thus, among both informally and formally minded epistemologists, there is an agreement that knowledge is defined with respect to other 'possible worlds'. As Hintikka (2003a) notes,

In order to speak of what a certain person *a* knows and does not know, we have to assume a class ('space') of possibilities. These possibilities will be called scenarios. Philosophers typically call them possible worlds. This usage is a symptom of intellectual megalomania. (p. 19)

There is an immediate difference between a philosophical logician and a philosopher. The logician typically remains agnostic about the ontological significance of the possible worlds and may refer to them as scenarios, situations, states, contexts or conceptual constructions. The philosopher is usually quite concerned with the metaphysical baggage that comes along with the notion.[2]

Be that as it may, the stability and robustness of knowledge over other possible worlds leaves open the question of which space of worlds should be considered relevant for epistemic success. The classical conception of infallibilism is taken to require that an agent, in order to have knowledge of some hypothesis, must be able to eliminate *all* the possibilities of error associated with the hypothesis in question. The set of *all* worlds is considered. This set of possible worlds is too big for knowledge to have scope over. The set includes some rather bizarre worlds inhabited by odd beasts ranging from demons to mad and malicious scientists who have decided to stick your brain in a tank of nutritious fluids to systematically fool you. Or worlds in which contradictions can be true and tautologies can be false, like 'impossible, possible worlds' (Hintikka 1975). If these worlds were to be considered relevant all of the time, skepticism would have the upper hand all of the time. Epistemology may just end up with a fallibilistic notion of knowledge after all: there may not be a way for an agent to determine that he is not in the world of the beast or the brain. But then again, a fallibilistic notion of knowledge hardly qualifies as knowledge at all. At most, it amounts to a description of knowledge-seeking practices. Consequently, *if infallibilism is to be a viable reply to the skeptic, then infallibilism cannot be defined with respect to all possible worlds.* This is where epistemological forcing comes in.

The bizarre and extravagant possibilities of error may, under the right circumstances, be ignored even though they are logically possible, for all the agent knows. Knowledge may accordingly remain infallible but with world restrictions imposed. Forcing is more of an heuristic principle than an epistemological thesis proper:

> Whenever knowledge claims are challenged by alleged possibilities of error, the strategy is to show that the possibilities of error fail to be genuine in the relevant sense.

---

[2] To stay with currently adopted jargon, other scenarios, situations, states or contexts will be referred to as 'possible worlds' but nothing metaphysical is necessarily implied by the usage. Possible worlds are not to be understood as ontological or semantical totalities complete in their spatiotemporal history. Later it will become apparent that possible worlds may be endowed with enough formal structure to actually facilitate the achievement of important epistemological results.

Contemporary epistemologists choose to speak of the *relevant* possible worlds as a subset of the set of all possible worlds.[3] The philosophical logicians and other formal epistemologists consider an *accessibility* relation between worlds in a designated class within the entire universe of possible worlds. It will become apparent that there is no principled difference between relevance and accessibility. Informal epistemologies differ by the way in which relevance is forced given, say, perceptual equivalence conditions, counterfactual proximities or conversational contexts circumscribing the possible worlds. Formal epistemologies differ by the way in which the accessibility relation is defined over possible worlds. For example, philosophical logicians obtain different epistemic modal systems valid for a knowledge operator by varying (adding, dropping or relativizing) the properties of the accessibility relation, which might change from being reflexive and transitive to being reflexive, symmetric and transitive, for example.

Computational epistemology also forces as inductive epistemic problems to be checked for solvability specify a set of possible worlds for the agent to succeed over. Modal operator epistemology assumes that limiting convergent knowledge is restricted to possible worlds that are consistent with what has been so far observed.

> An informal epistemological paradigm may be a forcing strategy, and a formal one may be too. The task is then to find out how they each force so they can be put on a par for comparison.

Following Lewis (1996), one may say that it is a basic epistemic condition for agents to force for knowledge. The technically minded theorists of knowledge choose to formalize this basic epistemological condition.

2.2   Skepticism

The unstated premise of epistemology is, of course, that agents are seekers of knowledge or information – that is the whole point of conducting inquiry. Skepticism argues that even though gaining truth and avoiding error is the point of inquiry, the acquisition of knowledge is impossible given the standing possibility of error. In the end, we are left with ignorance rather than insight. Skeptics often cite two lines of argument in favor of their pessimistic conclusion.

---

[3] Explicit forcing proposals in the epistemological literature are sometimes referred to as 'relevant alternatives proposals'. Cf. Bernecker and Dretske 2000.

A great many skeptical arguments rely on the notion of *underdetermination*. In antiquity, skeptical arguments were molded around the possible fallibility of sense perception. The world is secretive in the sense that it does not always directly reveal what it is about. If the world does reveal what it really is like, this is not inconsistent with receiving scrambled signals. Any knowledge claim put forth by the agent about some aspect of the world is not guaranteed its truth if the truth depends on the 'underlying reality' or some other aspect transcending the immediate experience and evidence. Recent instances of such an argument may be identified in the well-known Cartesian demons, Hume's hidden springs of nature, the Duhem-Quine thesis, Kuhn's incommensurability, Putnam's brains in vats and Rorty's edification over inquiry.

The systematic underdetermination of a hypothesis by any available evidence is referred to as *global underdetermination* by Kelly (1996):

A hypothesis is globally underdetermined if there are two possible worlds such that one of the worlds assigns the truth-value true to the hypothesis while the other assigns false in such a way that the evidence received by the agent remains the same forever independently of which of the two worlds is the actual world. (p. 17)

Global underdetermination leaves inquiring agents with two possibilities: one may either retreat to the Academic skepticism in which ignorance is bliss à la Carneades' and Arcesilaus's *ataraxia* (peace of mind) or invoke forcing to stay on the knowledge acquisition track. Forcing is obviously a way to deal with global underdetermination because global underdetermination only amounts to a skeptical objection if success is required in all possible worlds.

Skepticism plays on more than one string. Ever since the Pyrrhonian skepticism of Sextus Empiricus, the problem of induction and its various derivatives have presented a series of problems pertinent to knowledge possession and acquisition. The ornithologist may want to investigate whether all ravens are black. If he sets out to investigate by examining ravens one by one, there may not exist any finite specifiable time after the which the ornithologist can safely decide that all ravens are black. The next raven in line for observation could be white. By this argument, Sextus Empiricus was taken to have demonstrated the unreliability and consequently the untenability of inductive inference. Michel de Montaigne agreed with Sextus although Hume was awarded credit for the discovery, despite discussing causality rather than enumerative induction. A philosopher such as Popper identifies Hume as the one responsible for intellectual insight.

Skepticism about induction is the result of the *local underdetermination* possibly obtaining between evidence and hypothesis:

A hypothesis is locally underdetermined by the evidence in a possible world if there is an infinite sequence of evidence possible for all the agent knows, such that each initial segment of this evidence sequence could arise independently of whether the hypothesis is true or false. (Kelly 1996, 24)

This definition implies the lack of a determinate finite time after which the agent can reach a decision concerning the truth or falsity of the hypothesis in question. An inductive skeptic, in turn, concludes that beliefs acquired by induction are locally underdetermined and cannot be justified.

Forcing is not going to come to the rescue either, or at least it should not. Eliminating the odd worlds does not preclude generalizations in those remaining unless one aspires to use forcing not only to dodge global underdetermination but also to boil down the set of relevant worlds in such a way that inductive inference essentially becomes deductive inference or something close to it (see Chapter 7).

There are sometimes cures for the problem of local underdetermination. If induction is unreliable, it may be the result of imposing a particularly demanding criterion of success for inductive inferences: *decision with certainty* demands that the agent, after having inquired for some period of time, will *halt*, conjecture the truth and do so in every possible world allowed by the forcing clause. This criterion of success looks like the one advocated by Plato in the *Theatetus*. Platonic inquiry has the agent stop after having inquired for some finite time. No matter what the truth will turn out to be, the agent will come to know what the truth is and will also know that he knows it. There is a finite time after which, for each later time, the agent has stabilized to the truth of some hypothesis. 'Eureka!' the agent halts, outputs the truth and does not change his mind about it independently of the turn of the world. Not changing one's mind again during inquiry is referred to as *convergence*, and subsequently stopping inquiry as soon as convergence has arisen is called *convergence with certainty*.

Peirce (1958) thought that science in the long run may converge to the truth without ever producing an unequivocal sign of convergence. An agent may stabilize to the truth at some point but be unable to tell when stabilization occurred. There is convergence but no halting. Such a situation is referred to as *limiting convergence*. Given the evidence and forcing assumptions of the epistemic problem under consideration, computational epistemology has provided results to the effect that an inquiring agent may be logically reliable and guaranteed limiting arrival at the truth for notions of successful assessment clearly weaker than decision with certainty (see Chapter 7). Epistemic problems of knowledge possession, assessment and acquisition may be reliably solvable for weaker notions of success and convergence. Beliefs acquired via inductive methods may sometimes be justified after all.

2.3 Epistemology

Both informal and formal epistemologies combat skepticism and the possibilities of error, but along different lines or paths. Since Plato's *Meno* and *Theatetus,* informal epistemology went down the path of identifying the defining ingredients of knowledge. Implicit in the works of Plato and in Kant's *Critique of Pure Reason* and explicitly described by C. I. Lewis (1946), knowledge is characterized by three individually necessary and jointly sufficient ingredients: truth, belief and justification. The *standard tripartite analysis of knowledge* still largely entertained in mainstream epistemology pays tribute to the idea that an agent Ξ, or an agent applying a method of inquiry, knows a hypothesis h insofar as the following conditions are satisfied:[4]

Ξ knows h iff
1. Ξ believes h,
2. h is true,
3. Ξ is justified in believing h.

The three distinct ingredients of the standard definition have not all enjoyed the same philosophical limelight. Believing is typically considered to be a psychological primitive or a dispositional psychological state. The state may exist independently of manifestation. Belief has not raised any serious eyebrows as an ingredient of knowledge. This first condition is essentially a condition hooking up the agent Ξ to hypothesis h. Knowledge presupposes belief that h, but meeting condition 1 alone is not sufficient for knowledge of h. The belief may turn out false. Humans are free to believe something which is in fact false, but knowledge is not such a lenient commitment. This paves the way for condition 2. The tripartite analysis accordingly suggests, as an additional necessary condition, that knowledge of h entails the truth of h. Truth has already been discussed as a necessary ingredient.[5]

---

[4] 'Agent' and 'method' are treated as one and the same unless otherwise stated.

[5] It should be observed that some philosophers, notably Williamson, have argued that the concept of knowledge is primitive. Knowledge is not composed of truth, belief and

To qualify as knowledge, not only must the belief be true but it must be held true in a *justified* or robust way. The justification condition has usually been in the limelight, from Plato to contemporary epistemology. It is not easy to define what is meant by justification. As Lenzen (1978) argues,

> Though there is basic agreement that *something* must be added to true belief to obtain knowledge, what precisely this 'something' is, remains far from being evident. Because of the vagueness of such notions as 'having sufficient reasons for believing', 'being justified in believing', it is difficult to make a decision concerning the adequacy of (5), *i.e.* that knowledge implies justification. (p. 28)

A claim to knowledge requires that the connection between the belief condition and the truth condition is 'adequate'. Yet the two conditions alone are jointly insufficient for the attainment of knowledge. True beliefs may be the result of blind luck, clairvoyance, random guessing, etc. Beliefs generated by such procedures do not amount to knowledge. The reason is that such procedures are rather obscure and seemingly unreliable, even if true beliefs have actually been produced. The adequate connection of condition 1 and 2 is severed, and condition 3 must therefore be instated. The condition is intended to provide supportive reasons explaining why the first two conditions are suitably connected. Only furnished with such supportive reasons, together with the satisfaction of the other two conditions, may the agent be said to have the necessary and sufficient testimony required for knowledge.

The term 'mainstream epistemology' refers to the *modus operandi* of seeking necessary and sufficient conditions for the possession of knowledge based on the standard definition or some close derivative thereof. The methodology involves advancing folksy and intuition-based examples and counterexamples, or if needed, less folksy and less intuitive examples and counterexamples. Reasons for the possession of knowledge may be undercut by 'suitable' counterexamples; these counterexamples may again be undercut by suitable counter-counterexamples, restoring knowledge, and so on. It is a dialectical and sometimes even 'diabolical' process that by its very nature balances between the theory of

---

justification but rather is a primitive (mental) state in the following sense: 'If the content of a mental state can depend on the external world, so can the attitude of that content. Knowledge is one such attitude. One's knowledge that it is raining depends on the weather; it does not follow that knowing that it is raining is not a mental state. The natural assumption is that sentences of the form "*S* knows *p*" attribute mental states just as sentences of the forms "*S* believes *p*" and "*S* desires *p*" do' (Williamson 2002, 6). I am indebted to Lars Bo Gundersen for pointing this out.

knowledge and skepticism. As odd as this way of conducting epistemology may seem, it should, to make sense, be viewed from the heights of a greater philosophical ambition: global conceptual understandings of various epistemic notions. These understandings are allegedly often gained by the delicate use of fictions, intuition pumps and thought experiments (Baggini and Fosl 2003).[6]

Some formal formats for epistemology may very well subscribe to the standard definition of knowledge. Others may not but may still have something epistemically pertinent to say. A logical epistemologist may agree that something must be added to belief to obtain knowledge. Whatever has to be added in terms of justification is, however, abundantly unclear, as Lenzen argued in the passage quoted earlier, so drop it because it is not pertinent to the aim of logical epistemology (other's like Hintikka [2003a] would disagree). Computational epistemology may be affiliated with a view of knowledge as reliably inferred stable true belief. It is forced neither to such a view nor to any other theses pertaining to the nature of knowledge. If knowledge, however, is about reliably extending truth with more truth, then computational epistemological investigations are of great relevance to such an epistemic conception, as Kelly (1996) noted. A final example: insofar as knowledge acquisition is construed as winning a game against nature or winning against a collective of other agents, game theory has something significant to offer pertaining to rationality as it relates to winning strategies. A winning strategy does not necessarily presuppose some particular understanding of knowledge, although a winning strategy may be sensitive to what knowledge (information) is available to the player about the other players (Osborne and Rubinstein 1994; van Benthem 2000).

Instead of pursuing a global conceptual understanding of knowledge, formal epistemologies proceed in a more piecemeal fashion. A certain amount of conceptual understanding is presupposed, or a certain set of conceptual parameters are fixed. The fixed parameters may be anything: the epistemic goal, the attitude, the method, the strength (validity) of knowledge/belief, the forcing relation, and so on, or some combination thereof. Such a fixation and the additional structure imposed by the

---

[6] Hintikka (1999a, 1999b) recently attacked the extensive use of 'intuitions' in contemporary philosophy. He tracks its recent history back, not to Gettier (see later), but nevertheless to the same period, when philosophers methodologically misunderstood Chomsky's transformational grammar program. Another source of misguided use of 'intuitions' around the same time was Kripke's determination of rigid designation, according to Hintikka.

formal apparatus of choice (logic, learning theory, probability theory, game theory, belief revision theory, etc.) give rise to a formal model of inquiry. In such a model, particular notions are naturally singled out for formal analysis, such as validity, reliability, computability, and rationality. The idea is then to study what follows from the model with respect to the concepts of interest. Although the results of the piecemeal conceptual analyses in a formal framework may not add up to a global concept of knowledge, they may all the same reveal something about the structure of the ingredients making up such a concept.

There may also be an initial operational difference between the mainstreamers and the formalists: whereas the former often remain quite vague about the tacit assumptions and presuppositions of their conclusions, which are based on intuitions and folksy examples, the latter use intuitions and examples only to illustrate results obtained within a framework. If intuitions are used for more than this, formal epistemologists are always required to state these usages explicitly as definitions, assumptions and lemmata. The explication is needed to evaluate the plausibility of the results subsequently obtained. Coming to terms with the operational discrepancy between mainstream and formal epistemologies is important for the realization of a plethoric epistemology. Neither the operational discrepancy nor the difference in local and global ambitions is an impediment to interactively glueing mainstream and formal epistemology together (see Chapter 9).

One may object that the endeavour of comparing mainstream and formal epistemologies based on a unilateral forcing heuristics is flawed from the outset. Let an operational difference between mainstream and formal approaches be granted. The real difference is that while formal epistemologies force by slamming the door shut on skepticism as a matter of initial assumption, mainstream proposals force by using 'possible but however unlikely' clauses.[7] This makes for a fundamental difference pertaining to how seriously the overall skeptical challenge should be taken and prevents the two epistemological approaches from being put on a par for comparison.

There are examples from formal epistemology to support a claim about the categorical dismissal of skepticism from the outset. Epistemic logicians sometimes assume no false beliefs and infallible knowledge for

---

[7] I am indebted to Charles Griswold, Juliet Floyd and Troy Catterson for bringing this objection to my attention during the discussion after my lecture at the Boston Colloquium (Boston University, February 21, 2003).

certain applications. There are other applications for which knowledge of knowledge is assumed but not infallible knowledge in terms of knowing one's ignorance. And there are yet other applications for which logical epistemology assumes knowledge to be even weaker, leaving the door open to skepticism more and more. It is dependent on the application, or rather the *context*, as to how strong knowledge is taken to be. This is, however, exactly Lewis's point in his mainstream contextualistic epistemology. Sometimes the door can be slammed shut on skepticism if the context is right. Nozick's mainstream counterfactual epistemology virtually subscribes to this when the demon world is too far off. Also to be taken into account is the fact that a formal approach like computational epistemology is to some extent skeptical in flavor, as underdetermination and the possibility of reliable inquiry are intimately connected (see Chapter 7). Mainstream and formal epistemologies seem to be on a par for comparative forcing analyses after all.

2.3.1 Interlude: Bayesian Epistemology

As opposed to the mainstream preoccupation with knowledge, some versions of Bayesian epistemology consider knowledge epistemically overrated and unnecessary for decision and action; measures of opinion are good enough as long as they are strong enough. Jeffrey (1992), for example, propounds a radical sort of Bayesianism that deflates the notion of knowledge and embraces only degrees of beliefs. Acceptance rules are rejected in part due to skeptical motives, and there is no certainty about anything save for logical laws (or rather, only probability 1 on these laws, and no certainty about anything at all). As radical probabilists reject certainty in any form, they shun knowledge as well. Less radical Bayesians make certainty and knowledge indistinguishable.

Bayesian epistemology may initially also be read as a formal forcing paradigm: it requires the agent to succeed in possible worlds with high prior probability and disregard sets of possible worlds with low probability (Earman 1992; Howson and Urbach 1989). If the truth is in a world ascribed 0 or infinitesimally small prior probability, the truth is never to be found. Bayesian epistemology does not alter the nature of the forcing relation. On this construal, Bayesian epistemology simply provides yet another argument for dumping error possibilities.

It is one thing to determine what knowledge is, its mode of justification and its potential resistance to skeptical challenges, it is another to study how knowledge or information may or should rationally change in light of what is already known and new evidence. Van Fraassen (1989) has outlined the tenets of what he calls a 'new' epistemology, and he recommended a shift in epistemological focus from the 'defensive' *statics* of the classical definition of knowledge to the 'offensive' *dynamics* of epistemics and doxastics based on probabilities:

> What I hope for is some reconciliation of the diverse intuitions of Bayesians and traditionalists, within a rather liberal probabilism. The old we might call defensive epistemology, for it concentrates on justification, warrant for, and defense of one's beliefs.
>
> The whole burden of rationality has shifted from justification of our opinion to the rationality of change of opinion.
>
> This does not mean that we have a general opinion to the effect that what people find themselves believing at the outset is universally likely to be true. It means rather that rationality cannot require the impossible. We believe that our beliefs are true, and our opinions reliable. We would be irrational if we did not normally have this attitude toward our own opinion. As soon as we stop believing that a hitherto held belief is not true, we must renounce it – on pain of inconsistency! (p. 10)

This view, minus its inherent probabilism, is also shared by many contemporary pragmatists, from Levi to Putnam (in recent pragmatist incarnations) to authors influenced by cognitive science, like Gärdenfors. A common denominator for an instrumentalism like van Fraassen's and the pragmatism of, say, Levi is their joint emphasis on the idea that what is in need of justification is not static belief but the methods for changing it. This is what is common to various strands of this 'new' epistemology.

The central idea is to deny as irrelevant something that may seem presupposed by the very forcing metaphor, namely, that epistemology is largely conducted by engaging in a justificational game with the skeptic. The forcing metaphor may be taken to suggest that this is the essence of epistemology. Playing the game against the skeptic – which van Fraassen dismissively calls 'defensive epistemology' – is not to be understood as monopolizing all types of epistemological activity. Rather, one may have it both ways: 'forcing' and the 'new' epistemology are not mutually exclusive. Van Fraassen says that some of the new trends in epistemology focus on justifying the strategies for changing beliefs rather than on defending the beliefs that one happens to endorse at a certain instant. Reflecting on the methods for changing beliefs presupposes that one has some tools for representing belief and knowledge to begin with. Arguing for the appropriateness of this or that representation for solving one epistemic problem or the other may lead to interesting foundational issues, some of which might be connected with skepticism. Forcing may sound defensive in this respect, but it comfortably leaves room for, endorses, and encourages the great variety of modern studies of dynamic epistemics and doxastics characteristic of a 'new' epistemology. In fact, by the end of the day, forcing may be viewed as a methodological feature rather than an epistemological one encompassing the statics as well as the dynamics of knowledge and other epistemic and doxastic attitudes relevant to epistemology (see Chapter 9).

Treating Bayesianism as another excuse for dismissing error possibilities is too simple a construal. It ignores a corpus of recent work based on nonstandard probabilities or on conditional probability. Arló-Costa (2001b) has argued that the most promising form of Bayesian epistemology is based on the idea of taking conditional probabilities as primitive. The resulting acceptance rules are capable of avoiding the lottery paradox (by implementing ideas inspired by the work of De Finetti and van Fraassen) and similar problems, and the conditional logic arising out of this form of unified probabilism seems to improve on other forms of radical probabilism.[8]

The literature on mathematical economics registers a great deal of work in this direction, regarding not only rules of acceptance but also rules of decision. Arló-Costa (2001b) recently made a distinction between 'monist' and 'pluralist' strategies in Bayesian epistemology. While the monist strategies only allow one probabilistic primitive (monadic or dyadic probability), the pluralist strategies accept doxastic primitives not reducible to probability (De Finetti, Levi, and others). These pluralist strategies in Bayesian epistemology are not immediately concerned with dumping error possibilities. They start with a notion of belief given as a primitive, which determines the space of probability carriers. This is a way of focusing on what Levi would call 'serious possibilities', but here the primary motivation is not 'defensive' but pragmatic. As stated by De Finetti (1974):

In almost all circumstances, and at all times, we find ourselves in a state of uncertainty. Uncertainty in every sense. ... It would therefore seem natural that the customary modes of thinking, reasoning and deciding should hinge explicitly and systematically on the factor uncertainty as the conceptually pre-eminent and determinative element. The opposite happens however: there is no lack of expressions referring to uncertainty, but it seems that these expressions, by and large, are no more than verbal padding. The solid, serious, effective and essential

---

[8] One can show that this form of unified probabilism is mappable to non-standard probability via the extension of a result first presented by McGee (1994) and Arló-Costa and Thomason (2001). I am indebted to H. Arló-Costa for pointing this out.

part of arguments, on the other hand, would be the nucleus that can be brought within the language of certainty – of what is certainly true or certainly false. It is in this ambit that our faculty of reasoning is exercised, habitually, intuitively and often unconsciously. (p. 24)

De Finetti makes clear that his set of certainties contains more than mere tautologies and that its main role is to determine or fix a space of possibilities:

Thinking of a subset of truths as given (knowing, for instance, that certain facts are true, certain quantities have given values, or values between certain limits, certain shapes, bodies or graphs of given phenomena enjoy certain properties, and so on), we will be able to ascertain which conclusions, among those of interests, will turn out to be – on the basis of the data – either certain (certainly true), or impossible (certainly false), or else possible. (p. 25)

When it comes to probability as such, De Finetti holds that 'probability is something that can be distributed over the field of possibility'.

Using a visual image, which at a later stage could be taken as an actual representation, we could say that the logic of certainty reveals to us a space in which the range of possibilities is seen in outline, whereas the logic of the probable will fill in this blank outline by considering a mass distributed upon it. (p. 26)

The initial certainties that reveal this space are not the propositions that can be defended against the skeptic. This body of certainties would be way too thin to engage in any kind of useful form of inquiry. They are the 'practical certainties' needed for everyday interaction and scientific inquiry. The agent considers himself as infallible at every instant about their truth. How to reconcile this with the need for changing views has been the main topic of an epistemology of authors like Levi.

2.3.2 *Getting Gettier*

A particularly devastating blow was directed at the established epistemological view in 1963. In a three-page paper, 'Is Knowledge Justified Belief?', Edmund Gettier gave the now legendary and quite scandalous counterexamples to knowledge as true justified belief. Russell (1956) had anticipated the counterexamples in the late 1940s:

It is clear that knowledge is a subclass of true beliefs. ... There is a man who looks at a clock when it is not going, though he thinks that it is, and who happens to look at it at the moment when it is right; this man acquires a true belief as to the time of day, but cannot be said to have knowledge. There is the man who believes, truly, that the last name of the prime minister in 1906 began with a B, but who believes this because he thinks that Balfour was prime minister then, whereas in fact it was Campbell Bannerman. (p. 170–1.)[9]

Even a stopped clock shows the right time twice a day. Looking at it just at one of those two moments does not suffice for knowing what time it is. Thus, Russell anticipated these problems, but the explicit formulation of the counterexamples are due to Gettier. The counterexamples have partly fixed the agenda for mainstream epistemological research since.

The Gettier paradoxes often involve the derivation of something true from something false. Smith may have in the past collected firm evidence that, together with other relevant background information, Γ, furnish supportive reasons for or perhaps even deductively entail the following hypothesis about Jones's possessions with respect to automotive vehicles:

h_1 : Jones owns a Ford car.

Suppose Smith has an acquaintance, Brown. Smith does not know where Brown is. For no particular reason Smith uses his internal randomizer and chooses a location, say, Boston, as Brown's current location. Then by applying the introduction rule for the disjunction, Smith concludes,

$$\frac{\Gamma \vdash \text{Jones owns a Ford car.}}{\Gamma \vdash \text{Jones owns a Ford car} \ \lor \ \text{Brown is in Boston.}}$$

If the derivation is valid for Boston, it will be valid for Barcelona and Brest-Litovsk as well. Smith constructs the following three disjunctive hypotheses immediately entailed by h_1:

h_2 : Jones owns a Ford car $\lor$ Brown is in Boston.
h_3 : Jones owns a Ford car $\lor$ Brown is in Barcelona.
h_4 : Jones owns a Ford car $\lor$ Brown is in Brest-Litovsk.

Let Smith accept h_2, h_3 and h_4 based on his solid belief in h_1. Given the standard tripartite definition of knowledge, Smith is then justified in his belief in h_2, h_3 and h_4. He is cleared to consider them as instances of knowledge. Odd, since by randomizing Smith has no clue as to Brown's whereabouts, though that does not matter for the disjunctive truth. Gettier then tells this story: Jones in fact drives a rented car from AVIS so it is not his own Ford. By accident, however, Brown is in Barcelona. This information is still not available to Smith. It follows nevertheless that Smith is justified in believing h_3, but he does not know that h_3 is true. Smith has

---

[9] I am indebted to Robert van Rooij for bringing Russell's anticipation of the Gettier-examples to my attention.

gotten things right but for the wrong reasons: He claims to have knowledge because he apparently has reasons to believe that Jones owns a Ford, which he does not. All the same, truth is preserved because, unknown to Smith, Brown is in fact in Barcelona. Smith's original reasons for believing and being justified are undercut. According to the standard definition of knowledge, however, Smith may still be accredited with knowledge.

The other counterexample discussed by Gettier is based on two other celebrated logical principles – substitutivity of identicals *salva veritate* and the introduction rule for the existential quantifier. Suppose that Smith and Jones are applying for the same job. Suppose, once more, that given relevant background information and evidential support Smith is justified in believing

h_1 : Jones will get the job.

Smith is also justified in believing another hypothesis:

h_2 : Jones has $10 in his pocket.

Given h_1 and h_2, the introduction rule for the existential quantifier and the principle of substitution of coreferential terms, Smith derives:

h_3 : The person who will get the job has $10 in his pocket.

In the end, it turns out that Smith himself will get the job and, by the way, Smith himself has $10 in his pocket. Smith is justified in believing the *de facto* true hypothesis h_3, but once again he is right wrongly.

One way to solve the Gettier paradoxes would simply be to reject the counterexamples and claim them defective on the basis that they rest on a questionable, perhaps even false, principle that false hypotheses can justify the agent's belief in other hypotheses. That is probably a bit too easy, and examples similar to the original ones contrived by Gettier have been produced that do not rely on this allegedly dubious principle.

The standard strategy has been either to put some more meat on the justification condition or supply a fourth condition to the standard definition to keep Gettierization from surfacing. A host of different fourth conditions have been proposed some of which have been able to solve the original Gettier problems, some of which have not, but either way they have usually occasioned yet new Gettier derivatives, some of them plausible, some of them less. In fact, the epistemological community has turned the production of Gettier derivatives into an industry; thus, only a few influential ones will be reviewed later. Finally, attention is also restricted to the additional conditions that in one way or the other attempt to solve the Gettier paradoxes by appealing to *reliability*.

The Gettier paradoxes are like a disease that is both virulent and primitive. They point to a fundamental flaw in the classical conception of knowledge and do so by using quite simple means, like the introduction rules for disjunction and the existential quantifier. A particularly malignant feature of the paradoxes is that they allow one to remain comfortably in the actual world. Given the truth conditions for the two disjuncts, one may extensionally compute the truth-value for the entire disjunction. One is not required to invoke intensional measures and other possible worlds for this computation. The same goes for the introduction rule for the existential quantifier and substitution *salva veritate*. In other words, the Gettier paradoxes do not require modal universes for their formulation, not even much tampering with the agent's local epistemic situation. Solutions to the Gettier paradoxes, however, most often rely on modal notions of knowledge. Though the paradoxes are virulent but primitive, the cures are often modal and complex, involving rather strong medicine. Both mainstream and formal approaches alike are licensed to prescribe such medicine.

2.3.3 From Justification to Methodology

Some mainstream epistemologists have attempted to account for the notion of justification in terms of *reliability* in order to solve the Gettier paradoxes. The idea is to block 'knowledge' for the wrong reasons by a reliable procedure that ensures knowledge for the right reasons:

- Goldman argues that the belief in some hypothesis is justified if and only if the method by which the belief is formed is reliable. Reliability means producing more true convictions than false ones in the actual world, sometimes in other worlds as well.
- Nozick insists on a 'heavier' strategy by appealing to a strongly reliable recursive procedure with a halting condition imposed in all nearby worlds.
- Lewis in his modal epistemology speaks of a rule of reliability to be enforced in all worlds deemed relevant by the current context. He refers in a footnote to a type of nomic sufficiency account of reliability à la Armstrong.

Regardless of what reliability is supposed to mean in the end, *it is a criterion imposed on the inquiry method or agent* responsible for producing the belief:

The justification condition of epistemology ends up in methodology as the study of how science arrives at its posited truths, that is, how beliefs are justified by the canons, norms or recommendations and internal workings of the method applied or the agent in question.

Justification may be vague and is in need of clarification. Clarification may come from consultations with methodology, as Sankey (1999) recently noted:

These are questions about the truth-conduciveness of the method. While they relate directly to the epistemic status of the method, they bear *indirectly on the nature of rational justification.* For if use of method conduces to truth, then, given the relation between method and justification, the warrant provided by the method is warrant with respect to truth. (p. 1)

Bonjour (1976), a mainstream epistemologist, expressed the same view:

An adequate epistemological theory must establish a connection between its account of justification and its account of truth: *i.e.* it must be shown that justification, as viewed by that theory, is truth-conducive, that one who seeks justified beliefs is at least likely to find true ones. (p. 75)

Methodological recommendations for 'rational' scientific inquiry, truth-conduciveness, reliability, convergence, strategies for winning games, changing beliefs economically and reliably, and the like, are at the very *core* of many formal epistemological proposals. Computational epistemology scrutinizes the feasibility of recommendations for getting to the truth reliably for both ideal and computationally limited agents; game theory models rationality among agents; belief revision theory concentrates on informational economy and the agent's rational change of beliefs; and so on.

An illustrative example of where formal epistemology meets mainstream epistemology occurs when Stalnaker (1996a) suggests using belief revision (and epistemic logic) to get out of the Gettier-cases [Stalnaker 1996a]: Milton knows that *h* iff Milton believes *h* and learning no further true information would lead him to change his mind. Given the standard analysis of belief revision, the analysis gives rise to an account of knowledge which validates the modal system **S4.2**.[10]

---

[10] I am indebted to Robert van Rooij for suggesting Stalnaker's solution as an example. Hintikka (1962) embraces a similar understanding of knowledge when he explains, 'If somebody says I know that *p* in the strong sense, he implicitly denies that any further information would have lead him to alter his view' (p. 21). Changing one's mind about *p* implies that one did not know *p* from the outset. This point about how knowing *p* implies that one would not change one's mind about *p* (which one may also find in some of Unger's skepticism-friendly early work) is what led Kripke to complain that if this were so, knowledge would demand doxastic intransigence – that is, if the agent knows *p*, then he must regard all information that suggests ¬*p* as misleading. Kripke never

Mainstream epistemologists have usually been quite unimpressed by the epistemological results of the formal approaches. For instance, the results of modal validity for knowledge operators in epistemic logic have not been considered pertinent to the primary justificational concerns of mainstream epistemology. This is odd indeed, since epistemic and doxastic logics *are* the logics of knowledge and belief. Admittedly, some philosophical logicians have also been of the opinion that there is no, or should not be, any connection between epistemic logic and general epistemology and have accordingly blurred the connection even more.

Knowledge is to be justified, and by being justified, it may also attain a certain epistemic strength. Modal logic has devised a sliding scale of epistemic strength, since the modal systems that a knowledge operator may validate exactly says something about how strong knowledge is over other possible worlds. When justification may be accounted for in terms of belief revision, as Stalnaker suggests in the earlier example, knowledge attains a certain strength on the order of **S4.2,** which is demonstratively stronger than **S4** but weaker than, say, the modal system **S5**. Similarly in modal operator epistemology, if knowledge is defined as limiting convergence, then knowledge may be proved **S4** strong on the condition that the agent behaves in accordance with certain methodological recommendations (of justification). From the mainstream epistemological perspective, the formal validity of an epistemic operator is a yardstick for how strong a *modal* knowledge concept may become, how infallible it may be and how good a response epistemic strength is to skepticism. Some of the 'formal' mainstreamers, like Lewis and Nozick, actually discuss the modal systems, epistemic axiomatics and the modal strength of knowledge explicitly in their theories of knowledge. By way of example, Nozick views some of the closure conditions for knowledge, which are actually axioms of epistemic logic, as untenable because acceptance of these closure principles puts skepticism right back into play. Lewis then counters by claiming that knowledge is closed under implication and that one may all the same still leave the skeptic out of the game in a given uniform context.

2.4 Methodology

Methodology was described as the study of the methods and methodological recommendations by which science arrives at its posited truths.

actually committed his thoughts on this matter to print, like much of his thinking on epistemology, in fact, but others have cited them. I am indebted to Duncan H. Pritchard for directing my attention to this latter point.

A pertinent question in science and epistemology is *when* a method of inquiry is expected to have an answer ready on epistemic problems. In a previous section, two convergence criteria were introduced: (1) *convergence with certainty*, and (2) *convergence in the limit*. The first criterion requires the agent to succeed by some finite time and clearly signal this success by halting. The second criterion is weaker. It requires the agent to succeed by some finite time, but halting is not demanded.

A crisp formulation of certainty convergence may be found in Kelly (1996). Suppose Ξ is an arbitrary inquiry method that the agent applies, and let h be a hypothesis:

> Ξ *converges to h with certainty iff there is a time n such that*
> 1. Ξ *signals at n that it is ready to conjecture,*
> 2. Ξ *conjectures h at n + 1, and*
> 3. Ξ *does not signal earlier than n that it is ready to conjecture.*[11]

Convergence with certainty is viewed as the hallmark of convergence in epistemology and methodology. Due to Hume's problem of induction, hypothetico-deductivism is, for instance, committed to the bold formulation of universal hypotheses and to waiting for the incoming evidence to refute them. When a counterinstance is encountered, the hypothesis in question could not possibly be true. It is accordingly refuted with this type of certainty. An existential hypothesis has a similar property, but instead of being refutable, it is verifiable with certainty. Conjecture the existential hypothesis and wait for the first collaborating instance in the observed evidence. Eureka! The hypothesis is verified with certainty, so stop inquiry and output the truth.

As attractive as certainty convergence may be, it is not always possible to obtain this kind of security. Real epistemological and scientific problems are not always amenable to convergence with certainty. In these cases, one may choose to drop the stop condition but not the requirement of convergence. Limiting convergence emerges, as the agent is free to oscillate regarding his conjecture some finite number of times. This number is not specifiable in advance. At some point, nevertheless, the agent must reach a convergence modulus and stabilize his conjecture, even if he does not

---

[11] Note that immediately prior to the certain conjecture the method of inquiry is required to produce a *signal* (say, Eureka!) of certainty. This is due to the fact that the method may produce the sign of certainty more than once. Therefore, the certainty conjecture is taken to be the one following immediately after the first occurrence of Eureka!. Subsequent signals of certainty will be 'ignored, as though the method has finished its job and is merely producing irrelevant noise thereafter' (Kelly 1996, 48).

know, nor is required to say, when stabilization has occurred. American pragmatists like Peirce and James are sympathetic to this idea. As already briefly noted, Peirce held the view that it is impossible to say anything about the direction of science in the short run but that science may all the same asymptotically approach the truth in the long run. Similarly for James (1960), as knowledge of universal laws may become impossible to acquire if one is obligated to say when science has got it right.

Limiting convergence has become a more and more respected convergence criterion in philosophy; recent arguments for scientific realism in the philosophy of science rest on limit assumptions (Boyd 1984); computational epistemology utilizes limiting convergence for a variety of purposes, including the acquisition of certain characterization theorems for the inductive solvability of epistemic problems (Kelly 1996); and Bayesians apply a limiting convergence criterion to obtain 'almost sure' convergence theorems (Earman 1992).

Philosophy, of course, is a rather abstract field. Perhaps it is not too much of a surprise that limit considerations are to be found here. Computability theory and computational linguistics, say, are less abstract, but limit criteria nevertheless enter here as well. Gold (1965) observed that there is an interesting class of problems in computability theory that only can be solved:

by infinitely long decision procedures in the following sense: An algorithm is given which, for any problem of the class, generates an infinitely long sequence of guesses. The problem will be said to be solved in the limit if, after some finite point in the sequence, all the guesses are correct and the same. (p. 28)

Limiting convergence may be defined in the following way:

Ξ *converges to h in the limit iff there is a time n such that for each later time n′ Ξ conjectures h at n′.*

An immediate question pops up: Why entertain a notion of convergence but no certainty of when convergence has occurred, as Kitcher (1993) asks:

To be sure, there are [Bayesian] convergence theorems about the long run – but as writers from Keynes on have pointedly remarked, we want to achieve correct beliefs in the span of human lifetimes (p. 293).

The problem posed by local underdetermination is that one may not be sure to get it right in the 'span of human lifetimes'. To weaken convergence is not a way of cheating epistemology and science, for if the limit is what it in essence takes for truth, then rather wait around for it. The short-run performance does not make us any better off. Peirce's asymptotic considerations pertaining to scientific progress are exactly intended to determine whether science is in progress. In the short run, no answer to this question can be had. Limiting convergence is actually also a condition of real scientific practice, as computational epistemologists like Martin and Osherson (1998) explain:

> The general point is that Ψ is not required to recognize or signal in any way that its conjectures have begun to converge. In this respect our paradigm is faithful to the situation of real scientists, whose theories remain open to revision by new, unexpected data. It is, of course, possible to define paradigms that require scientists to signal convergence. The prospects for success, however, are then diminished. (p. 12)

Using computational epistemological means, Schulte (2000), for instance, proves that the identification of conservation principles for particle reactions is a limiting tractable problem, not one tractable with certainty. To criticize a limiting solution for not being a solution with certainty is like criticizing an apple for not being an orange.

Whether a given epistemic problem is amenable to a solution depends not only on the convergence criteria used but also on what sort of success is envisioned. Convergence criteria by themselves say little about being right or wrong, correct or incorrect. Epistemic concepts like verification, refutation, decision and even discovery determine senses of cognitive success for methods of inquiry. Confirmation theorists have favored assessment methods of verification, falsificationists have preferred refuting assessment methods, and recent results of computational epistemology show how the discovery of new hypotheses from evidence may be successful.

If criteria of convergence are mixed with criteria of success, criteria of successful convergence are obtained, and these specify the senses in which epistemic problems could (or should) be solvable. Many mainstream epistemological paradigms seem to favor assessment in terms of decision with certainty. Goldman's epistemic reliabilism (Chapter 3), Nozick's counterfactual epistemology (Chapter 4) and Lewis's contextual epistemology (Chapter 5) all hold, for different reasons, that the agent's local epistemic environment suffices for deciding the truth status of the beliefs under scrutiny with certainty. The situation in logical epistemology is a bit trickier, since methods and successful convergence criteria are hardly discussed due to the initial inactive nature of the agents involved in the inquiry process. All the same, the philosophical motivations furnished for logical epistemology likewise indicate a tribute to certainty convergence (Chapter 6). Computational epistemology concedes to the epistemological tradition that knowledge acquisition may indeed be possible for a variety of successful convergence criteria weaker than decision with certainty and also for discovery engines (Chapter 7). On these grounds, modal operator epistemology in turn utilizes limiting discovery as a success criterion for convergent knowledge (Chapter 8).

2.4.1 Methodology: Categorical or Hypothetical

James (1960) is responsible for the insight that there is a significant difference between avoiding error and gaining truth. One may avoid error while at the same time not necessarily gain truth. Some logical positivists thought they would gain the truth via their confirmational program without really checking. Worse, perhaps, it seems to be the case that many early proponents of confirmation theory, like Hempel, did not insist on convergence to a true hypothesis. Confirmation was end enough in itself. It follows, then, that one may, with or without a worry, confirm forever but at the same time head nowhere near the truth.

There exists a result due to Putnam (1963) but hardly noticed among philosophers of science that backs a worry. Putnam provided one of the first computational epistemological results: for any algorithm of extrapolation based on a Carnapian theory of confirmation, there is an epistemic problem that the Carnapian extrapolator cannot acquire knowledge of even when fed all possible instances of the problem. Using confirmation theory is not necessarily a truth-conducive methodological strategy. Computational epistemology has since then provided many striking results showing how norms of inductive rationality may interfere with reliability (see Chapter 7).

Epistemologists and methodologists are in the business of advocating guidelines for rational scientific inquiry in terms of truth-conduciveness. One has to make sure that the guidelines have the intended truth-conducive property, which is not always the case, as Swinburne (1968) demonstrates:

Compatible with any finite set of phenomena there will always be an infinite number of possible laws, differing in respect of the predictions they make about unobserved phenomena. Between some of these ready experimental tests can be made, but experimental tests between others are less easy and between them we provisionally choose the simplest one. Evidence that a certain law is simpler than any other is not merely evidence that it is more convenient to hold that suggested law than any other, *but evidence that the suggested law is true.* (p. 51)

Swinburne's approach seems to exhibit an indifference to the question of whether proceeding in accordance with the prescription of simplicity is truth-conducive. It is stipulated but not demonstrated. One may argue that simplicity is a guide to truth under special forcing stipulations such that all worlds are eliminated save minimally complex worlds consistent with the evidence. To ensure that simplicity is truth-conducive under these forcing clauses requires an analysis of reliability, but none seems forthcoming.

Arguing that principles of rational inquiry are normative in terms of getting to the truth should be done cautiously. The principles advocated may just be in the way of the truth, as shown by the existence of a method that violates the principles and could have gotten to the truth. One should accordingly distinguish between two types of methodology;

- In a categorical methodology, a methodological recommendation is advanced for its own end regardless of finding the truth.
- In a hypothetical methodology, a methodological recommendation is advanced with the aim of finding the truth.

2.5   Reliability

Reliability is a methodological property, not an epistemic goal as such. First, an inquiring agent may strike upon the truth in the actual world or relevant possible worlds without being reliable. Second, try replacing truth with reliability in the second condition of the standard tripartite definition of knowledge. It makes little sense to say that the hypothesis is reliable. It makes sense to say that the agent is reliably forming a hypothesis, but then it is a property an agent may enjoy and hence a justificational and accordingly a methodological concern.

One particularly important methodological concern is what the definition of reliability amounts to or should amount to. The community of epistemologists seems to be greatly divided on the issue. If knowledge is to be modal, infallible, and reliable to ensure truth-conduciveness, then reliability must be *categorical* in the following sense:

> A concept of reliability is **categorical** if defined in terms of unequivocal success for some convergence criterion in the actual world or relevant possible worlds.

Reliability is defined with respect to two parameters: sense of success and range of possible worlds. A familiar argument for categorical reliability is the following. If success is not unequivocal success, then one could end up in either one of the following situations: a situation in which there are uneliminated possibilities of error or a situation in which a belief is 'reliably' formed but in fact false. The former is a situation in which reliability has scope over other possible worlds whereas the latter is a situation in which the forcing conditions may be strong enough to admit only the actual world. Unequivocal success implies an infallible notion of knowledge acceptable to both Nozick and Lewis, for instance.

On the other hand, a fallibilistic notion of knowledge is not unacceptable to Goldman, since he entertains a *stochastic* understanding of reliability:

> A concept of reliability is **stochastic** if defined in terms of a success to failure ratio for some convergence criterion in the actual or relevant possible worlds.

Goldman's primary reason for advocating a stochastic concept of reliability and possibly a fallibilistic notion of knowledge is simply that he considers categorical reliability to be too strong. It is an inadequate notion of reliability for actual epistemic practice. Nozick is perhaps less worried about describing actual epistemic practice and more concerned with prescribing medicine capable of curing recalcitrant diseases in epistemology, like the Gettier paradoxes (and other serious skeptical challenges). Lewis wants to have it both ways – practically executable prescriptions.

Categorical and stochastic reliability are linked to two sets of the distinctions: the distinction between descriptive and normative epistemology, and the distinction between a first-person and a third-person perspective on inquiry.

2.6   First- and Third-Person Perspectives

Contemporary epistemology often draws a distinction between descriptive and normative theories of knowledge. There is a similar distinction in moral philosophy between descriptive and normative ethics. The former attempts to describe actual moral behavior whereas the latter sets the standards for correct moral conduct.

Similarly, descriptive epistemologies account for actual epistemic practice whereas normative epistemologies prescribe rules of inquiry, including mechanisms for avoiding error and gaining truth, truth-conducive justification criteria, learning and winning strategies, procedures for revising beliefs, and so on. The distinction is sometimes blurred by the fact that when describing actual epistemic practice, one may have to define

various notions such as knowledge itself, justification and reliability, bringing normative aspects into the picture. Introducing a weak version of reliability like the stochastic one allegedly still rules out certain cognitive
mechanisms – such as 'intuition', 'hunch' and 'clairvoyance' – as reliable
means for getting to the truth. All the same, the agent in the environment
may still cite them as reasons for holding convictions. Normative proposals may also exhibit descriptive characteristics if the means for solving
some problem actually are available to the agent in his natural epistemic
environment.

Both descriptive and normative epistemologies usually subscribe to the
common premise that epistemic practice is in some sense 'rational'. What
separates the two is their stance on whether epistemology is to simply describe epistemic practice or to try to optimize it. It would be irrational
epistemic behavior to follow some practice demonstrated *a priori* to be
en route to error (when this practice is available course of conduct to the
agent in the environment). It is not necessarily irrational, on the other
hand, not to follow some prescription if the natural epistemic milieu sets
the standards for what the agent is able to do and this prescription is not
among the available courses of action. The local epistemic circumstances
may for one reason or the other bar the agent in question from choosing
the best means for an end. The constraints could even be such that they
reward 'irrational' behavior. Calling such situations irrational would undermine the common premise to which the two approaches subscribe.
Not only may the environment limit the agent's behavior, other agents
may as well. This is, for instance, illustrated by game theory's distinction
between cooperative and noncooperative games.

Sometimes agents would be able to have more knowledge than they
actually have if they were not constrained by their local epistemic milieu.
Then they could freely pursue the optimal means for obtaining some
desirable result, whether truth, epistemic strength or winning in some
other sense. Thus, one may rightfully ask why epistemologists sometimes
are in the business of means-ends prescriptions that no local agent is able
to abide by. There are two related answers to this question:

- Epistemologists are in the business not only of ascribing knowledge
  to themselves but also of ascribing knowledge to other agents. Lewis
  (1996) has pointed out that there is a significant difference between
  one agent ascribing knowledge to himself in his local epistemic situation and others ascribing knowledge to him given the situation they
  are in. The two situations do not always coincide. Different persons
  do not share the same real world in many contexts. There are rules

to follow under knowledge attribution to oneself and others to know what we think we know.

- Rather a principled answer in the long run, than no answer in the short run; and rather, principled information about what it would take to solve the epistemic task at hand, than no information at all. Epistemology is about whether knowledge is possible and about what agents can and cannot know insofar as knowledge is possible. The problem is that it is not always clear from within whether something is knowable or not. One recurs to an outside perspective for a principled answer that may then spill over into the local circumstances.

According to Lewis, the agent may actually know more than we are able to ascribe to him. On his account, this is due to the fact that the attribution of knowledge is highly sensitive to which world is considered the actual to the agent in a given conversational context.[12] An agent in his environment is more likely to be aware of what the relevant possibilities are given the world considered actual by him than the knowledge ascriber standing by him or even outside. Lewis refers to these two stances as a *first-* versus a *third*-person perspective on inquiry.

Observe that an agent is free to be prescribe recommendations for himself to follow as long as the means suggested are available to him where he is. An outsider may also freely prescribe recommendations for the agent as long as they are available to the agent. If the outsider decides to prescribe a course of conduct to solve an epistemic problem for the agent in the environment but that course of conduct is unavailable to the agent, then the situation changes. What then becomes emphasized is what it would take to solve the epistemic problem regardless of whether the agent is capable of actually performing the necessary action(s).

The distinction between normative and descriptive and the distinction between first-person versus third-person perspectives are not mutually exclusive. The distinction between descriptive and normative theories of knowledge and a modified version of Lewis's first-person and third-person perspective dichotomy are subsumed in the following formulations:

A perspective on scientific inquiry is **first-person perspective** if it considers what an agent can solve, can do or defend given the available means for an end and given the epistemic environment he is sunk into.

---

[12] What is also troublesome is that 'actual' is an indexical for Lewis (1984) in his modal ontology so there is not necessarily a real question of considering 'a world' actual. I am indebted to John Symons for reminding me of this feature.

Goldman's epistemic reliabilism and Nozick's counterfactual epistemology are thoroughly first-person perspectives, on this definition. Lewis's contextual epistemology encompasses both perspectives, as does logical epistemology, surprisingly enough, while computational epistemology and modal operator epistemology are more thoroughly third-person perspectives on inquiry.

> A perspective on scientific inquiry is a **third-person perspective** if it considers what an agent could solve, could do or defend given the best means for an end independently of the epistemic environment he is sunk into.

Just as with convergence criteria, one should be careful not to conflate the two different perspectives. Criticizing some position, whether mainstream or formal, without noticing that the criticism is based on a third-person perspective and that the position advocated is based on a first-person perspective may again turn out to be criticizing an apple for not being an orange. For example, distinguishing between the two perspectives can be of extreme importance for a formal epistemology like epistemic logic. The dichotomy has a significant bearing on the epistemology's general plausibility and its way of dealing with skepticism (see Chapter 6). Finally it will later become apparent that the distinction between the two perspectives is a *philosophical distinction that entails a formal difference.*

Distinguishing between these two perspectives on inquiry and observing, the other prerequisites highlighted in this chapter are the parameters with respect to which selected contemporary mainstream and formal theories of knowledge will be analyzed, assessed and compared. The parameters, at the same time, form parts of a program in 'plethoric' epistemology.

3

Mainstream Epistemology

Mainstream epistemology seeks necessary and sufficient conditions for the possession of knowledge. The focus is on folksy examples and counterexamples, with reasons undercutting reasons that undercut reasons. According to epistemic reliabilism, reasons may be sustained, truth gained and error avoided if beliefs are reliably formed, sometimes in the actual world, sometimes in other worlds too. But the stochastic notion of reliability unfortunately backfires, reinviting a variety of skeptical challenges.

> FORCING   On the present rendering, it looks as if the folk notion of justification is keyed to dispositions to produce a high ratio of true beliefs in the actual world, not in 'normal' worlds.
> Alvin Goldman (1992)

Mainstream epistemologies emphasizing reliability date back at least to the 1930s, to F. P. Ramsey's (1931) note on the causal chaining of knowledge. The *nomic sufficiency* account developed by Ramsey and later picked up and modified by Armstrong in the 1970s is roughly as follows: If a connection can be detected to the effect that the method responsible for producing a belief is causally chained to the truth due to the laws of nature, then this suffices for nomologically stable knowledge and keeps Gettierization from surfacing. Causality through laws of nature gives reliability (Armstrong 1973).

Armstrong draws an illuminating analogy between a thermometer reliably indicating the temperature and a belief reliably indicating the truth. Now a working thermometer is one that gives accurate readings in a range of temperatures. This is not a coincidence. A thermometer is successful because there are laws of nature that connect the readings to the very temperature itself. As a thermometer reading can be a successful indicator

35

of the temperature, noninferential beliefs can likewise be successful indications of facts about the world. The condition is that the occurrence of the beliefs is lawfully connected to the facts of the world themselves. A belief in turn qualifies as knowledge if and only if it has the properties that are nomically sufficient for its truth. The truth of beliefs is thus guaranteed via laws of nature. Reliability on this account is categorical given the lawlike connection (either it obtains or it does not) and is restricted to the actual world.[1]

According to nomological epistemology, knowledge is considered to require an appropriate response to the conditions of the agent's immediate environment. This proper response is the production of the beliefs about the environment that the agent in fact possesses. Knowledge is acquired when the agent produces those beliefs in a way that reflects the way the environment into which he is sunk really is. So the nomic sufficiency account has a thoroughly first-person perspective on inquiry.

In agreement with its first-person perspective, Goldman embraces the nomic sufficiency account in 'A Causal Theory of Knowing' (1967). He subsequently abandons nomological epistemology exactly because he considers the reliability constraint unrealistically strong and impossible to meet for mortal inquiring agents and their actual cognitive faculties. Not only has nomological epistemology been abandoned on grounds of the untenability of actual categorical reliability, other obvious problems for the causal proposal have often been cited in literature (Everitt and Fisher 1995). While the theory may work well for perceptual knowledge of objects in which a straightforward causal relation obtains between the generated beliefs and the perceptual objects, it is significantly harder to argue that a similar causal relation holds between abstract objects and the beliefs about them. Numbers, lattices, algebras and sets are abstract mathematical objects, agents have beliefs about them, but they are not the results of causal connections in any obvious way.

In 'Discrimination and Perceptual Knowledge' (1976), Goldman develops a more lenient theory of justification and knowledge called *epistemic reliabilism*. He subsequently modifies the theory in 'What is Justified Belief' (1979) and in *Epistemology and Cognition* (1986), then revises it in once more in 'Epistemic Folkways and Scientific Epistemology' (1992)

---

[1] The nomic sufficiency account may be expanded with a many-world view of reliability such that the lawlike connection stands categorically in all worlds in which the nomic condition obtains (see Chapter 5). The original version of the nomic sufficiency account suggests a nonmodal concept of knowledge.

and 'Reliabilism' (1996).[2] As Armstrong's nomological criterion is considered too strong, the idea of epistemic reliabilism is to weaken the connection between belief, method and truth. Utilizing a reliable method no longer guarantees true beliefs on every occasion. There will be occasions on which the belief-generating method fails to output the truth. Even on these occasions, the beliefs are still justified as long as the method of production in general outputs more truths than falsehoods:

> The justificational status of a belief is a function of the reliability of the process or processes that cause it, where reliability consists in the tendency of a process to produce beliefs that are true rather than false.
> ... Again, the degree of justifiedness is a function of reliability.... Returning to the categorical conception of justifiedness, we might ask how reliable a belief forming process must be in order that its resultant beliefs be justified. A precise answer to this question should not be expected. Our conception of justification is vague in this respect. It does seem clear, however, that perfect reliability isn't required. (Goldman 1979, 10, 11)

A belief in some arbitrary hypothesis is justified insofar as the method by which the hypothesis is generated is reliable in the stochastic sense for a first-person knowledge operative. The stochastic reliability of the belief-forming method provides necessary and sufficient conditions for justification.

Epistemic reliabilism uses a cardinality measure for error, as the theory ignores 'small' sets of mistakes rather than, say, distant or bizarre ones. The cardinality measure allows for occasional mistakes, so there may be justified beliefs that are in fact false. From Smith's perspective, either he marched down the wrong road, as he did not use a reliable method from the outset, or he made a mistake owing to the betrayal of his otherwise 'reliable' method, on this special occasion related to Jones's ownership of a Ford. It follows that this mainstream epistemology does not unequivocally solve the paradoxes put forth by Gettier.

An odd consequence it seems, as reliability is typically launched to exhaust justification and hopefully block these paradoxes. Reliability in terms of the ratio of true beliefs to false beliefs allows a reemergence of the Gettier paradoxes. This is under the assumption that the reliability condition is to serve as the justification condition in the standard definition of knowledge. Epistemic reliabilism is perhaps first and foremost concerned with justification, not knowledge. Exhausting justification in

---

[2] Other variants of epistemic reliabilism have been presented by Swain (1981) and Talbott (1990).

stochastic reliability may nevertheless be extended to cover the definition
of knowledge, as Goldman (1996) explains:

A similar reliabilist account is offered for knowledge, except that two further
conditions are added: First, the target belief must be true and, second, its mode
of acquisition must rule out all serious or 'relevant' alternatives in which the belief
would be false. (p. 3)

The reemergence of the Gettier paradoxes is due to ignoring possibilities of error, which in turn undercuts the reliabilist solution to the
paradoxes.[3] Consider a case in which an arbitrary hypothesis h is a reliable indicator of yet another hypothesis h' in the following way:

$$P(h' \mid h) = .95 \text{ and } P(\neg h' \mid \neg h) = .95 \qquad (3.1)$$

Now a method that bases its conjecture about $h \vee h'$ on h' alone will
be reliable. The probability of an error when h occurs is 0 because h
again entails $h \vee h'$ due to the introduction rule for disjunction. The
probability of an error when h' occurs is .05. This means that the overall
unconditional probability of a mistake pertaining to $h \vee h'$ is given by

$$P(h) \cdot 0 + P(\neg h) \cdot .05 \leq .05 \qquad (3.2)$$

The method is accordingly highly reliable. Nevertheless (3.2) is exactly
a Gettier case. The strategy of weakening the nomological and necessary
relation to a stochastic relation for the purpose of achieving a more realistic description of agents and their actual cognitive faculties simply invites
the paradoxes back in. It also implies a fallibilistic notion of knowledge.
    This is additionally emphasized by the fact that the theory embodies
an element of luck. As a matter of definition, epistemic reliability is not
necessarily on the truth track all the time: the worst case is a ratio on the
order of .51 over .49. This is as bad as it gets, but it still is good enough for
stochastic reliability. The doxastic generator fails on virtually every other
occasion on which it is applied. Your eyes are reliable even if they produce
images of flying toasters virtually every other time you open them. The
best case puts the success ratio in the neighborhood of 1, but 'perfect
reliability isn't required', and so a success ratio of 1 is not required either.
    Epistemic reliabilism faces other problems. Some counterexamples
have been designed to disprove the sufficiency of the reliability condition
for justification and knowledge. A clairvoyant deliverance may *actually* be

----

[3] I am indebted to Kevin T. Kelly for the example.

reliable for generating noninferential knowledge if it meets the requirements set forth by the stochastic definition. As far as the agent is concerned, he may not have supportive reasons for considering clairvoyance reliable or he may have supportive reasons for thinking that clairvoyance is highly unreliable. Either way, intuitively it seems that the agent would not be justified in adopting a belief based on this cognitive faculty.

Here is a rather speculative example taken from the epistemological literature.[4] Suppose a particle physicist is led to the belief, by means of clairvoyant deliverances, that the force between protons and neutrons responsible for the existence of the nucleon is caused by the presence of meson particles. Meson particles are exchanged between protons and neutrons. Imagine that the physicist continues to believe the hypothesis while reasonable evidence nevertheless suggests it is false. The fact of the matter is that meson particles are responsible for the force. This means that the particle physicist applied a reliable belief-forming method to begin with. He is justified in believing the hypothesis. It is a case of noninferential knowledge regardless of the intuitively dubious clairvoyant method.

Different strategies have been suggested to deal with both the alleged insufficiency of reliability and the Gettier paradoxes. One strategy is to eventually add on a nonundermining clause to epistemic reliabilism adopted from defeasibility theories of knowledge. In general, mainstream defeasibility theories, like the one once advocated by Klein (1971), claim that a Gettier proof analysis of knowledge requires adding a fourth condition of *defeasibility* to the standard definition of knowledge:[5]

A hypothesis h is defeasible for agent Ξ if there is some alternative justifiable hypothesis h' such that if h' was believed, then Ξ would not believe h.

True beliefs qualifying as knowledge are not defeasible beliefs. Knowledge is epistemically stable if there are no defeaters. A warranted belief in terms of justification must be such that there is no truth that, if placed with the pool of reasons justifying the belief, is of such a nature that the belief could no longer be held justified. Defeasibility theories of knowledge tackle the Gettier paradoxes. The example presented next, suggestive of

---

[4] See Bonjour (1980), although his case does not involve particle physics.
[5] See also Levy (1977), Lehrer (1970b) and Johnsen (1974). Formal epistemological approaches use nonmonotonic logics like default logic, belief revision and dynamic doxastic logic to model defeasibility. See also Chapters 6 and 9.

the mainstream epistemological Gettier industry, concerns Aston and his identical twin Martin and eventually a deranged mom.

Suppose Ξ knows Aston fairly well and saw what appeared to Ξ as Aston winning at the Aqueduct racetrack Thursday of last week. Ξ now entertains the belief that Aston did win at the racetrack on that Thursday. For the sake of the argument, suppose that Aston indeed did win. Also suppose, that, unknown to Ξ, Aston has an identical twin, Martin, who is a horserace lover and was at the racetrack on Thursday of last week. Martin also won at the very same racetrack. Though Ξ arrived at his true belief through sound reasoning based on true information, Ξ does not know that Aston won at the racetrack. From a cognitive point of view, it is strictly accidental that Ξ arrived at the truth. Ξ could as easily have based his true belief on the fact that he saw Martin winning. Ξ believes the truth for reasons that are wrong or at least accidental enough to undermine knowledge as true justified belief.

Defeasibility theorists can respond thus: The belief that Aston won at the racetrack is undermined. If the true hypothesis about Martin was to be added to Ξ's pool of beliefs, Ξ would no longer have a sufficient justificational basis for believing that Aston won this Thursday last. By the theory of defeasibility, accidental true beliefs lose their warranty given their incapacity to stand up to the truth at the end of the day.

Epistemic reliabilism may utilize defeasibility as applied to methods of doxastic acquisition. The agent must then neither hold the belief nor have evidence to the effect that the belief is unreliably produced:

If Ξ 's belief in hypothesis h results from the application of some reliable method Ξ', and there is no alternative method Θ' at the agent's disposal such that, had Θ' been used by the agent in addition to the method actually applied, Ξ' would have resulted in the agent not believing h, then Ξ's belief in h is justified.

Return to the particle physics example: If there is an alternative reliable method available that is 'the proper use of evidence', as Goldman (1992) suggests, such that the physicist would not be led to believing that there were mesons, then the belief in their existence on basis of applying the first method would be unjustified. As reality will have it, there is an alternative method: the method that contributed to H. Yukawa's winning the Nobel Prize in physics in 1946. Obviously, Yukawa never used clairvoyance. Utilizing Yukawa's method of estimating the mass of the claimed meson by identifying the distance traversed by the particle when emitted from the nucleon actually supports the hypothesis that meson particles are real. But then the alternative method is only a witness to the fact that the original clairvoyant deliverance was reliable. Believing in the existence of mesons by reference to the latter method is more justified, considering 'the proper use of evidence'.

Undermining counter-counterexamples to the restated condition are to be found: Let there be an alternative belief-forming method that is in fact reliable, but suppose the physicist has no reason to think so. Had the alternative method been used, the particle physicist would not come to a belief in h. On this restated condition, the physicist is not justified in his belief in h. This is counterintuitive, for the physicist has no reason to be convinced that the alternative method is reliable.

Proponents of defeasible epistemology have their own problems. Leave everything intact in the scenario concerning the racetrack, with one exception: Aston does in fact not have a twin brother. Aston has a mother, however, and she persistently claims that Martin exists. Given the sincere avowal of the mother, Ξ is led to believe that the hypothesis regarding Martin's existence is true. This then defeats the original justification. The belief that Aston won at the racetrack would be undermined. Suppose Aston's mother is totally deranged and believes in a Martin who in fact does not exist. In these circumstances, it seems that Ξ knew that Aston won at Aqueduct all along.

Defeasibility theorists have suggested resolving this problem by enforcing a distinction between *misleading defeaters* (the sincere claim of Aston's quite deranged mother) and *genuine defeaters* (Aston's possession of an identical twin called Martin, Klein 1979). Among these theorists, there is no unilateral agreement as to which conditions should be satisfied in order to uphold the distinction. Stabilization of the truth is severely threatened if no such clear distinction is forthcoming. The genuine defeaters should guarantee reliable stabilization to the truth, because apparently the misleading ones lead right into error.

The counterexample of clairvoyance is based on the accountabilistic *internalistic* Bonjourian assumption that the justificational support for a belief is accessible to the agent and fits into a coherent framework of beliefs (Bonjour 1980, 1988). The agent must be capable of accounting for what it is that provides the justification. Epistemic reliabilism is typically viewed as a species of epistemological *externalism,* as it cashes out justification and knowledge in truth connections, truth tracking, truth ratios, and so on. These features are outside the agent's mind and not necessarily accessible to him. If agents always were required to have a cognitive grasp on the justificational reasons for their adopted beliefs, then a multiplicity of agents would lack knowledge. It is not immediately clear that the requirement of grasp is needed for knowledge; 'Don't children know?' as Nozick (1981, p. 196) polemically puts it. Milton is six years old and comes home from school to tell his father that he knows that $2 + 2 = 4$. Whatever the justification, it seems fair to ascribe this knowledge to Milton even if he is not aware that what really justifies his knowledge are the Peano axioms of arithmetic.[6] Similarly, for empirical hypotheses.

Clairvoyance is supposed to demonstrate that reliability is insufficient to guarantee justification and knowledge. If clairvoyance is a faculty that always generates the truth, then independently of whatever intuitions one may have about it, it is what it is. One might not like it any day of the week and hate it two times on Sunday, but if clairvoyance eventually and always guarantees success, then it is reliable by definition – categorically and then trivially stochastically. On top of that, it would even be a great discovery if there was something to it, according to a physicist like Weinberg (1994):

Alongside the mainstream of scientific knowledge there are isolated little pools of what (to choose a neutral term) I might call would-be sciences: astrology, precognition, 'channeling', clairvoyance, telekinesis, creationism, and their kin. If it could be shown that there is any truth to any of these notions it would be the discovery of the century, much more exciting and important than anything going on today in the normal world of physics. (p. 48)

Yet other internalistic examples are cited to show that reliability is not a necessary condition for justification, nor for knowledge possession either: A Cartesian demon may deceive someone totally. The agent victim of deception is fed the exact same sensory inputs as the agent who is not deceived by the demon. All the resulting beliefs of the deceived agent are wrong. Independently of the unreliability of the deceived agent's belief-forming methods, his beliefs are justified to the same extent as the agent who is not the victim of deception. Viewing the matter from a subjective point of view, the grounds for belief are the same. In conclusion, only subjective features and internalistic factors are significant for justification and knowledge. Externalistic factors are not.

It is an exercise to track Goldman's responses to the skeptical objections. The nature of the envisioned forcing relation changes as epistemic reliabilism time and time again attempts to cope with the demon. Under the assumption that reliability of the method of acquisition is to be evaluated with respect to the world of the demon, epistemic reliabilism does seem to entail the unjustified nature of the beliefs in question in the

---

[6] It is probably a bit too much to require Milton, at age six, to reproduce, let alone understand, the Peano axioms.

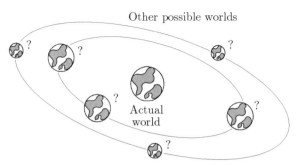

FIGURE 3.1. Epistemic reliabilism currently requires stochastic success in the actual world only.

diabolical world. One open strategy, apparently currently entertained, is to 'force for life' and thus restrict reliability to the actual world, hoping for the best in other worlds (Fig. 3.1):

For example, a reliabilist might propose that what counts is reliability in the *actual* world. Since perceptual belief-formation is reliable in the actual world, use of the same process or processes would yield justified beliefs even in the demon world. (Goldman 1996, 2)

The idea appears to be this: Suppose that cognitive skills like visual perception of medium-sized physical objects, accurate memory and culturally instilled skills for deriving square roots and taking integrals are reliable in the actual world. Their utilization will also yield justified beliefs even in a world where some diabolical creature is calling the shots. The beliefs may be justified but not necessarily true, neither in the actual world, nor in the demon world.

The tactical move creates graver problems than those it was designed to solve. The world in which you have accurate memory and skill at deriving square roots could be the demon world. Many mainstream and formal proposals hope that the real possibilities are determined by the agent's local epistemic circumstances. The view just described definitively buries this hope. Like the global skeptical challenge would have it, what is at stake now is which world is actual. In turn, the set of real possibilities involved in the forcing relation is at stake as well.

On the present rendering, it looks as if the folk notion of justification is keyed to dispositions to produce a high ratio of true beliefs in the actual world, not in 'normal' worlds. (Goldman 1992, 301)

This quotation from Goldman is a bit earlier than the previous quotation and refers to an idea developed fully in *Epistemology and Cognition* (1986), under the heading 'Normal Worlds Reliabilism'. Normal worlds are worlds consistent with the agent's general beliefs about the actual world. In all possible worlds, the demon world included, a belief is justified just in case the method by which the belief is produced has a high truth ratio in the range of normal worlds. The diabological world problem is supposedly resolved because the truth ratio of the method is not to be assessed with respect to the demon world itself but with respect to its truth-ratio performance in normal worlds. Since the truth of a reliable method ratio is apparently very high in normal worlds, the method succeeds even in the demon world, and accordingly beliefs formed there are justified as well. So knowledge is, from this earlier point of view, belief whose truth is forced by local epistemic circumstances over the possible worlds accessible from the actual world.

One may track a different version of epistemic reliabilism in terms of forcing in even earlier writings. There, Goldman's view is that one should gain truth in the actual world but at the same time avoid error in the relevant possible worlds under criteria of perceptual equivalences:

A person knows that *p*, I suggest, only if the actual state of affairs in which *p* is true is distinguishable or discriminable by him from the relevant possible state of affairs in which *p* is false. If there is a relevant possible state of affairs in which *p* is false and which is indistinguishable by him from the actual state of affairs, then he fails to know that *p*. (Goldman 1976, 88–9)

The 'reliable discriminative mechanism' is intended to solve, if not the original Gettier paradoxes, then what are called 'Gettierized' examples: In a dark room, an agent sees directly in front of him what appears to be a candle. Really what he sees is the *reflection* of the candle, though the candle, as a matter of fact, is in front of him; the reflection he sees is caused by an ingeniously devised system of mirrors. Because the circumstances in which he sees the light in front of him are indistinguishable from the circumstances in which the light is reflected (i.e. there is a perceptual equivalence), the agent fails to have knowledge of the light in front of him.[7] Admittedly, the possibility of error due to the mirror-installation is extraordinarily small, but:

even in the ordinary cases, of course where *S* sees a candle directly, the possibility of reflecting mirrors constitutes a perceptual equivalent. In the ordinary case,

---

[7] The identical twins example and the famous papier-maché barn examples (Goldman 1976) also rest on the premise of perceptual equivalence.

TABLE 3.1. *Goldman's Views on Forcing over a Thirty-Year Period*

	Gain Truth	Avoid Error
1a. Goldman 1996	w	—
1b. Goldman 1996	w	w'
2. Goldman 1986	w, w'	—
3. Goldman 1979	w	—
4. Goldman 1976	w	w'
5. Goldman 1967	w	—

however, we would not regard it as a serious possibility. The Gettierized case impels us to take it seriously because there the actual state of affairs involves a devious system of reflecting mirrors. So we have an explanation of why people are credited with knowing in ordinary perceptual cases but not in the Gettierized case. (Goldman 1976, 100)

One may try to argue that what is 'Gettierized' by the candle example is not Gettier but something more like a devious demon, a mad scientist or the cooperative effort of a glazier and a glass cutter with too much time on their hands to fool around. Again, reliable inquiry is made impossible by global underdetermination, and global underdetermination is exactly what the candle example amounts to in the moment of perception. This is probably not a correct complaint insofar as the underdetermination of the case in question does not stay around forever as required by the definition of global underdetermination in Chapter 2. What Goldman seems to suggest is that knowledge may get Gettierized from time to time. Instead of trying to solve the Gettier paradoxes definitively, as both of the subsequent mainstream proposals attempt, one might just admit that Gettierization occurs either because of the pledge to stochastic reliability or because of mirror installations. If knowledge is to be Gettierized, then better for this to occur as the unfortunate consequences of entertaining stochastic reliability than as a result of a devious but dubious story like that of the mirrored reflection.

Goldman over the years has apparently held a series of different viewpoints pertaining to the forcing and reliability conditions, sometimes including other possible worlds, sometimes not; sometimes emphasizing gaining truth in the actual world w while avoiding error in other (normal) worlds w', and then again sometimes not. Table 3.1 is a (probably incomplete) compilation of the various positions entertained over the years. In this table, the first entry denotes the current stance, which actually may embody more than one view of the forcing relation. The current view suggests either: (1) gaining truth in the actual world and hoping for the best in other possible worlds, the diabolical world included, or (2) gaining truth in the actual world and avoiding error in other 'relevant' worlds. The fifth entry denotes the nomic sufficiency account adopted from Armstrong.

New 'virtue-theoretic' versions of reliabilism have recently been proposed, such as Greco's (1999) *agent reliabilism* and Sosa's (1985) *perspectival reliabilism*.[8] The basic idea is to merge objective as well as subjective features of justification into a unified theoretical structure. Two related features stand out as particularly pertinent: the attempt to explain how contingently reliable methods may be knowledge producers and the attempt to show how agents then may become aware of, or sensitive to, the reliability of the employed methods. One of the advantages of such views is that they are capable of dealing with certain kinds of demon cases that face reliabilism while also giving a clearer account of how the reliabilist might respond to the single-case problem (see below). Humans have a better conception of how to individuate cognitive faculties and intellectual virtues than how to individuate methods. In any case, given that the 'methods' are, presumably, supposed to be cognitive faculties and intellectual virtues anyway, this should be a natural way of reading the reliabilist thesis. Indeed, in recent work, Goldman seems to want to explicitly ally his view with this type of position.[9]

There are more objections to epistemic reliabilist epistemology based on demonology. One objection is that the demon example demonstrates that reliabilism's evaluation of cognitive processes is extremely sensitive to the epistemic, cultural and technological environment in which the processes are performing their job 'reliably'. There is epistemic relativism inherent in epistemic reliabilism.[10]

Given the possibility of an infinitely powerful deceiving demon, not much escapes relativism. Relativism may, however, mean different things. Radical epistemic relativism relies on total arbitrariness of the evaluation of cognitive processes. All epistemic parameters in the evaluation

---

[8] I am indebted to Duncan H. Pritchard for suggesting these new versions of reliabilism.

[9] But as is common in mainstream epistemology, 'virtue-theoretic' versions of reliabilism have also been challenged. See, for instance, Kvanvig 2003.

[10] Plantinga (1993) has argued that epistemic relativism is all to the good and should be incorporated as a constitutive part of any epistemological theory. By way of example, perception is a reliable method of knowledge acquisition relative to the actual world but not other possible worlds.

process are dependent on the particular cognitive, cultural and techno-logical circumstances. A more moderate and plausible version of epistemic relativism holds that the evaluation relative to whatever standards are finally fixed is not an arbitrary affair. The scale may be arbitrarily fixed and even calibrated. Whether the agent's cognitive processes measure up to the scale in the end is a sound question for which an answer may be expected. Some epistemic parameters are beyond the powers of the agents, and others are not. In conjunction, these parameters add up to the local epistemic environment into which the agents are sunk. From this first-person point of view, the agents then try to do the best they can. Epistemic reliabilism 'smoothly' describes what the agent's behavior is in an environment that mostly suffices for the agent to decide and to know with certainty.

Forcing is introduced to ensure that a demon is not waiting around in the actual world or relevant worlds. According to one of the current trends in epistemic reliabilism, the mode of acquisition apparently fixes stochastic success in the actual world but does not necessarily avoid error in other worlds. According to the earlier quotation by Goldman, reliability in the actual world also yields reliability in the demon world.

Consider again the issue of determining which world is actual from a contemporary reliabilist's point of view. The reliabilist would have to know which world is actual by consulting the method of inquiry. The method may not be able to determine this, and it is not known *a priori* that the method is reliable. In turn, the demon world is not ruled out as a serious possibility. As far as we know, it may be the actual world, and the method would not be in a position to determine that we, agent and method, are not in that world.

Both forcing and reliability are gone. Stochastic reliability reinvites the Gettier paradoxes. Reliability was introduced to provide justification in a way descriptive of actual epistemic practice. The agent should not be overly responsible epistemically, so the agent's cognitive responsibilities are deflated by dropping the infallible methods. The conclusion seems to be, however, that either the agent is *immensely* responsible beyond all possible cognitive powers or just sometimes *extremely* lucky in the actual world.

Cardinality is a matter of quantity rather than quality. The demon world is a qualitative issue rather than a quantitative one. A qualitative problem that a cardinality measure cannot deal with and should not deal with, as it should be forced out. Global underdetermination is the impossibility of reliable inquiry anyway, so there is no need to demonstrate it twice.

Epistemic reliabilistic theories of knowledge are allegedly best viewed as instances of the program in naturalistic epistemology. Many reasons have been given; here are two: (1) normative epistemic properties may be reduced to natural and nonepistemic properties, and (2) agents are to be viewed as physical systems for which knowledge possession and acquisition are to be understood as the successful result of a natural process (Goldman 1996). Goldman's tactical maneuvers in responding to the demon arguments seem to run counter to the very foundation on which Quine (1975) envisioned the realization of naturalized epistemology:

Epistemology is best looked upon, then, as an enterprise within natural science. Cartesian doubt is not the way to begin. Retaining our present beliefs about nature, we can still ask how we arrived at them (p. 68).

A final problem that crops up for some versions of epistemic reliabilism is called the *single-case, range* or *reference class* problem. The problem shows something about what sort of convergence criteria are envisioned by epistemic reliabilists for the assessment of epistemic reliability.

Suppose only a single hypothesis or belief is produced by the method the agent applies. When the belief is in fact true in the actual world, the method is categorically reliable. In case the belief turns out to be false, the belief-forming method is totally unreliable in the actual world. Feldman (1985) notes that 'this is plainly unacceptable, and in the extreme case, where every relevant type has only one instance, (RT) has the absurd consequence, that all true beliefs are justified and all false beliefs are unjustified' (p. 161).[11]

The single-case problem appears if the reliability of the method is considered to be the actual frequency with which the beliefs turn up true. Schmitt (1981) has made an attempt to resolve the situation by substituting frequentism for propensitism: 'the optimal approach is to let a process be a concrete, completely specific event, and let its reliability be its propensity to produce true beliefs' (p. 413). A method is reliable if it has the propensity to produce true beliefs. There are different understandings of propensities: (1) Single-case theories of propensity consider propensities to be physical dispositions of a singular execution of the method to come up with a true belief; (2) Long-run theories of propensities consider propensities to be dispositions that give rise to certain relative frequencies of true beliefs in long runs of method execution which manifest the propensities. The strength of a propensity is then

[11] 'RT' refers to Goldman's notion of reliability.

given in the unit interval $[0; 1]$ by some real valued frequency r. In contrast, single-case theories hold that the disposition of a single execution of the method to bring about a true belief is evidence of the existence of the propensity rather than some measure of its strength.

Schmitt's proposal does not make it clear whether a single-case or a long-run understanding is envisioned. Feldman wisely seems to read off a long-run interpretation: The method is reliable when it has a propensity to lead to true beliefs on assumption 'that it would generally lead to true beliefs if tokens of it occurred frequently' (Feldman 1985, 168). In case the method generates one belief that turns out to be false, the method may nevertheless have a genuine propensity to lead to more true beliefs in the long run. If this interpretation is the right one, the single-case problem can be said to be accounted for in modal terms.

With a single-case theory of propensity, the problem unfortunately remains the same. If the single belief is in fact false, it follows that there is no evidence of the method's propensity to yield true convictions. If the single belief is in fact true, then there is evidence of reliability. Adopting a single-case propensitism to solve the single-case problem does not resolve the single-case problem at all. It basically leaves untouched what was taken to be the original problem: Either there is evidence that the method is categorically reliable or there is evidence that it is not.

The success of the long-run interpretation of propensities implies the existence of a hypothetical collective of beliefs relative to which the method would succeed. Now, when the viable interpretation of propensity is the long-run one, it seems to follow that the way back to relative frequencies is relatively short. According to von Mises's (1956) frequentistic interpretation of the probability calculus, 'The principle which underlies the whole of our treatment of the probability problem is that a collective must exist before we begin to speak of probability' (p. 56). Classic frequentism does not encounter the single-case problem. The reason is quite simple: The problem does not exist for a frequentistic interpretation of probability. For much the same reason, the single-case problem should not bother epistemic reliabilism any more than it does frequentism: If there are no collectives, there are no probabilities and no problem.

4

Counterfactual Epistemology

In counterfactual epistemology, knowledge is characterized by tracking the truth, that is, avoiding error and gaining truth in all worlds sufficiently close to the actual world given the standard semantic interpretation of counterfactual conditionals. This conception of knowledge imposes a categorical conception of reliability able to solve the Gettier paradoxes and other severe skeptical challenges.

> FORCING   Knowledge is a real factual relation, subjunctively specifiable, whose structure admits our standing in this relation, tracking, to p without standing in it to some q which we know p to entail.
> Robert Nozick 1981

Epistemology begins with facing the beastly skepticism that arises from the possibility of an evil demon. Any talk about knowledge possession, acquisition let alone maintenance before skepticism's claim about the impossibility of knowledge is defeated, is absurd. To get epistemology off the ground it must be demonstrated that knowledge is in fact possible:

> Our task here is to explain how knowledge is possible, given what the skeptic says that we do accept (for example, that it is logically possible that we are dreaming or are floating in a tank). (Nozick 1981, 355)

This is the starting point for the counterfactual epistemology developed by Dretske (1970) and later refined by Nozick (1981).[1]

The often cited premise supporting the skeptical conclusion that agents do not know much of anything is this: If an agent cannot be guaranteed the ability to know the *denials* of skeptical hypotheses, then

---

[1] For a thorough investigation of the relationship between Dretske's and Nozick's approaches to counterfactual epistemology, see Gundersen 2002.

knowledge regarding other issues cannot be ascribed to the agent. The traditional understanding of infallibilism (see Chapter 2), which counts every possible world as relevant, supports this pessimistic premise. Some arbitrary skeptical hypothesis is a possibility of error, and its falsity must be known to the agent for him to acquire knowledge regarding some other common hypothesis. The agent's inability to know that the skeptical hypotheses are false prevents him from knowing the truth or falsity of ordinary hypotheses.

To get skepticism off the ground, skeptics mobilize the set of all possible worlds – weird worlds included. However, there is a thesis that is logically weaker than traditional infallibilism but that suffices as support for the pessimistic premise, namely, that knowledge is *closed* in the following sense:

$$\text{If } \Xi \text{ knows } h \text{ and knows that } (h \rightarrow h'), \text{ then } \Xi \text{ knows } h'. \qquad (4.1)$$

The epistemologically optimistic idea is that if the weaker closure condition can be denied, infallibilism may be rejected as a matter of assumption.

The classical thesis of infallibilism supports the skeptical premise by demanding that Ξ should be capable of knowing the denials of all the possibilities of error. The closure condition (4.1) demands only that Ξ is knowledgeable of the denials of those possibilities of error that in effect are known logical consequences of Ξ's knowledge.[2] Suppose Ξ knows that he is currently sitting reading this book on forcing epistemology. Let it also be the case that Ξ knows that if he is sitting reading this book, then he is not being fooled by the Cartesian demon. Then Ξ must also know that he is not being fooled by the demon.

If Ξ does not know that he is not being deceived by the demon, then, given that Ξ knows the implication, Ξ in turn lacks knowledge that he is sitting reading forcing epistemology. Now, this is exactly what the pessimistic premise pushes for. But Ξ can know that he is sitting reading this book without knowing that there is no demon of deception seducing him into the false belief that he is sitting reading this book. Being seated reading this book implies that no Cartesian demon is leading Ξ to falsely believe that he is reading this very book. It follows that knowledge is not closed in the sense of (4.1) according to counterfactual epistemology.

---

[2] Or perhaps rather known logical consequences of Ξ's knowledge, including denials of all possibilities of error (the so-called 'contrast consequences' [Dretske 1970]).

Even if the condition of closure is denied, the epistemological mission is still not completed. An explanation must still be provided describing how knowledge of common hypotheses is possible, joined with an explanation of the failure to know the denials of skeptical hypotheses. This also goes for the situations in which it is known that the common hypothesis at issue implies relevantly rejecting the skeptical hypothesis.

Dretske's solution is to install a modal condition for knowledge, imposing truth-conduciveness by *sensitivity*:

$$\text{If } h \text{ were not true, } \Xi \text{ would not believe } h. \qquad (4.2)$$

A belief qualifying as knowledge is a belief that is sensitive to the truth: The hypothesis h is true in accordance with the standard definition of knowledge. Had h been false, the agent would not have been led to the belief that h.

Condition (4.2) readily explains why closure fails. Proximity relations between possible worlds are introduced due to the semantics for the inserted subjunctive conditional (see later discussion). One may know both antecedents h and $(h \rightarrow h')$ relative to one set of relevant worlds accessible from the actual world and yet fail to know the consequent h' relative to a different set of possible worlds. Now, relative to a set of possible worlds in 'close' proximity to the actual world, one knows h and simultaneously knows that h implies the denial of the skeptical hypothesis, say h'. But one may, all the same, fail to know the consequential denial of the skeptical hypothesis itself, for knowledge of the skeptical hypothesis is relative to possible worlds distant from the actual world. These possible worlds are radically different from the actual world. 'Way-off' worlds are accordingly forced out, skepticism far away because closure fails, and the possibility of knowledge prevails.[3]

In *Philosophical Explanations*, his monumental book on knowledge, skepticism, free will and other pertinent philosophical issues, Nozick formulates a definition of counterfactual knowledge along Dretskian lines. The proposal furnishes virtually the same answer to the skeptic and also solves the original Gettier paradoxes.

Nozick's idea is to use condition 4.2 to efficiently solve the paradoxes: If it were not the case that Jones owns a Ford car, then Smith would not believe that Jones indeed does. In contrast, suppose now that Jones in

---

[3] Dretske (1970) does also have an explanatory story to tell about why closure might fail independently of the point about sensitivity, in his discussion of 'semi-penetrating operators'. I am indebted to Duncan M. Pritchard for reminding me of this.

fact has a Ford. Hypothesis h_1, regarding Jones's ownership of a Ford car, would be true. It may be the case that Smith in fact believes h_1. It does not follow, however, that Smith's believing h_1 in any way is connected or sensitive to the truth of h_1. The proposal is augmented with yet another subjunctive conditional to the effect that if it were the case that Jones has a Ford, Smith would be led to believe that Jones does own one such automotive vehicle. Nozick's definition of counterfactual knowledge may be formulated as follows:[4]

Ξ *knows h iff*
1. *h is true,*
2. Ξ *believes that h,*
3. $\neg h \mapsto \neg$ (Ξ *believes that h*), *and*
4. $h \mapsto$ (Ξ *believes that h*).

The truth and the belief conditions of the standard tripartite definition of knowledge are retained, but the justification condition is dropped. Then again, not exactly. Conditions 3 and 4 of the definition actually provide justification when justification is understood along reliable methodological lines, as will become apparent.

To see how the definition works, consider the manner in which possible world semantics provides truth conditions for the subjunctive conditional. A subjunctive conditional such as $A \mapsto B$ (for arbitrary statements A and B) is true insofar as, in all those worlds in which A is true that are 'closest' to the actual world, B is also true. More specifically, of three worlds w, w', and w'', if w' is closer to w than w'', then $A \mapsto B$ will be true in w iff A is not true in any world or there exists a world w' in which A and B are true that is closer to w than any world w'' in which A is true but B is false.[5]

The criterion of closeness or proximity in possible worlds semantics is, in general, troublesome. It hinges on a notion of *similarity* between possible worlds. The more similar one world is to another, the closer it is. Usually, similarity is cashed out in terms of *ceteris paribus* clauses: The less tinkering with a possible world, everything else being equal, the more similar that world is and, accordingly, the closer it is to the actual world. From this perspective, floating around in a tank on a planet called Alpha

---

[4] '$\mapsto$' denotes the subjunctive conditional.

[5] This semantic account of the subjunctive conditional follows rather closely Lewis (1973). Nozick is, however, not committed to a particular understanding of the semantics and also discusses Stalnaker's (1968) subjunctive semantics. See also Nozick 1981, 680 n. 8.

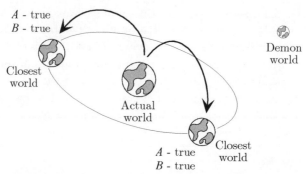

FIGURE 4.1. Counterfactual epistemology requires categorical success in *close* possible worlds.

Centauri requires *ceteris paribus* more conditions to be changed than the world in which one was born in Copenhagen rather than New York City. In effect, the beliefs an agent would have on Alpha Centauri would be a far cry from the beliefs the agent would have if he had been born somewhere closer to home.[6]

For knowledge possession, one does not have to consult all possible worlds, as the skeptic would insist: Given the standard semantical analysis of the subjunctive conditional, it is enough that the consequent *B* holds in those possible worlds closest to the actual world such that the antecedent *A* holds (Fig. 4.1). In terms of forcing, a subjunctive conditional is true just in case the consequent is forced among the worlds closest to the actual world in which the antecedent holds.

The third condition of the definition above is included to avoid error. The fourth is included to gain truth. The two conditions are collapsible into one condition: Ξ's *belief tracks the truth of h*:

> To know is to have a belief that tracks the truth. Knowledge is a particular way of being connected to the world, having a specific real factual connection to the world: tracking it. (Nozick 1981, 178)

The method for resolving the question of whether *h* is true is a combined verification and refutation procedure and thus a *decision* procedure: Ξ must output *h* if *h* is true and must output ¬*h* if *h* is false. The justification condition is absent in Nozick's definition of knowledge. When

---

[6] Some attempts have been made to specify what is meant by similarity and closeness. But it remains an open problem in philosophy and possible world semantics. Lewis (1973) has argued that our notion of similarity is notoriously vague and by its very nature resists specification.

methodology exhausts justification (see Chapter 2, sect. 2.3.3), the justificational condition is reintroduced in terms of a recursive procedure in all close worlds.

This methodological feature of justification is emphasized by the weak version of counterfactual epistemological truth-tracking, which is somewhat Popperian in nature. Suppose one is of the opinion that methods of scientific assessment (should) fare well with respect to avoiding error. This conviction does not conversely entail that the methods in question are good at gaining truth. Suppose one also entertains the idea that there is no method of scientific inquiry for formulating new laws or concepts required for an advanced and complicated theory like quantum mechanics. In coming up with such laws or concepts, an element of luck or blind guessing is involved. Science neither tracks the truth, nor does it produce knowledge from the point of view of the original truth-tracking account. A way to resolve this situation would be to assume that science avoids error with respect to h while simultaneously not guaranteeing the truth of h. According to this version of *weak truth-tracking*, Ξ's belief *weakly* tracks the truth of h insofar as:

3*. $\neg h \mapsto \neg(\Xi$ believes that $h)$,
4*. $h \mapsto \neg(\Xi$ believes that $\neg h)$.

It follows from this weak truth-tracking account that the positive assessment of some hypothesis that was simply hit upon luckily is still considered knowledge insofar as rigorous test procedures preclude errors.[7]

Consider a common context in which brigadier-general Ξ is of the belief that his standard-issue sidearm is in its holster. Skepticism would have it that Ξ dumps this belief because a demon may have set things up so that Ξ believes that his gun is in its holster when in fact this is not the case. Reasoning in accordance with counterfactual epistemology yields the following result: Suppose that the closest possible world to the actual world in which Ξ's gun is not in its holster is a world where no diabolical creature is around. In this case, Ξ would not perceive the gun to be in its holster, as Ξ's senses are still working normally in this world (*ceteris paribus*). Ξ would not entertain the belief that his gun is in its holster.

The counterfactual epistemological account of knowledge also guarantees that if Ξ has taken up the challenge of reading this book, then he knows that he is reading this book when he really is: All the conditions

---

[7] Nozick drops weak truth-tracking without an argument. See Nozick 1993, 682–3 n. 15. I am indebted to Kevin T. Kelly for these observations concerning weak truth-tracking.

1–4 of the definition are met with satisfaction: It is true that Ξ is sitting reading this book, and he believes it to be so. If he were not reading this book, he would not be believing that he is. In the end, if Ξ is sitting reading this book, he will believe that he is reading *Mainstream and Formal Epistemology*:

- Condition 3 ensures that in the closest possible worlds in which Ξ is not reading this book, he does not believe that he is.
- Condition 4 guarantees that in the closest possible worlds in which Ξ is reading this book, he believes that he is.

Everyday knowledge is secured in these contexts.

It is, on the other hand, impossible for Ξ to know that he is not a brain in a vat. Assuming the brain receives the same sensory patterns as it would had it not been dumped in the vat, there would not be anything in the input stream revealing to Ξ that he was not a brain in a vat. In this devious scenario, Ξ is also barred from knowing that he is sitting reading this book on forcing. If Ξ claims to know that he is sitting reading this book, it must follow that, as a prerequisite, he tacitly approves of the hypothesis that he is not a brain in a vat. Given this prerequisite and *modus tollens*, because Ξ does not know that he is not a brain in a vat, he does not know that he is sitting reading this book either.

Now the possible world in which Ξ is a brain in a vat is *ceteris paribus very* distant from the actual world. Failure of knowledge in these cases is not devastating to counterfactual epistemology. It hinges on the relevant possibilities of error. True beliefs are only required in possibilities closer to actuality than any $\neg h$ possibilities: Picture a physicist measuring the voltage drop in some LRC circuit. A student from epistemology class comes to him and asks whether a relevant possibility of error could be that the voltmeter is calibrated incorrectly. The physicist would probably answer 'yes', as calibration problems could lead to a measurement error. But if he was asked whether being a brain in a vat is a relevant possibility of error, the physicist would likely request the student to go back to his course and stop bothering him with silliness.

Gettier paradoxes are situations in which the available evidence might lead to mistake. Knowledge is intimately related to an interest in gaining truth and avoiding error. The method envisioned by Nozick for knowledge acquisition is a reliable method. The method is reliable because of its recursive workings in other worlds close to the actual one. Close worlds in which the belief is true are important, and close worlds in which the belief is false matter likewise. Relevant possibilities of error are belief-dependent. Reliability is categorical on Nozick's account, as a result of the decision procedure operating in all close worlds. In this sense, the proposal is normative: avoiding Gettierization and skepticism require strong epistemic prescriptions to be met.[8] Reliability is a world-dependent property insofar as it is sensitive to which possible world is the actual world. Reliability is a belief-dependent property to the extent that the relevant possibilities of error depend on the belief. A method of inquiry cannot be determined to be *a priori* reliable on the counterfactual account. Reliability is sensitive to which world is actual, and one may not know which world this is.[9]

A question remains pertaining to the convergence criterion entertained by Nozick. The idea of introducing the proximity relation is that when the agent's local epistemic circumstances suffice for the truth of the consequent, inquiry may as well just stop. This feature also shows Nozick's first-person perspective on inquiry. Inquiry with a halting property was called *certainty convergence* in Chapter 2. This is emphasized by another consideration due to Kelly (2000). Consider the following subjunctive conditional:

1. If the universal hypothesis were false, Ξ would not believe it now.

It seems to be the case that (1) would not be true unless the following sentence was also true:

2. If the universal hypothesis were false, Ξ would have observed something different than Ξ in fact has up until now.

---

[8] It is often argued that the counterfactual definition of knowledge requires such strong epistemic prescriptions that mere mortal agents cannot meet them (see Everitt and Fisher 1995).

[9] Dretske and Nozick explicitly relativize reliability to methods, which is crucial in that whether or not they obtain their rejection of closure might depend upon it. Suppose, for example, that methods are individuated externally, an interpretation that even Nozick himself gives some reasons for thinking is the way to go. On this construal, however, it is far from clear that Dretske and Nozick can get their skeptical counterexample to closure, at least if closure keeps the knowledge at issue indexed to the same method throughout. The world in which agent Ξ is a brain in a vat is a world in which, intuitively, Ξ's perceptual faculties are not engaged with the world at all and thus one in which Ξ cannot use these 'methods' to form the belief that he is not a brain in a vat. Accordingly, there is no world in which the target hypothesis ('I, Ξ, am not a brain in a vat') is false, and yet Ξ believes it in the same way in which he believes it in the actual world (given that he believes it on perceptual grounds, of course). Thus, Ξ can know it by the light of sensitivity after all. Moreover, given that Ξ forms his ordinary perceptual beliefs in the same way, he can also know these hypotheses and the relevant entailment to the denial of the brain hypothesis. Thus, sensitivity poses no problem for closure, at least as regards these types of cases. This does not mean that closure (unrestrictedly) holds on this view, but it does mean that the issue is moot. In essence, this point has been made by Williams (1995, Chapter 8) and, more recently, by Black (2002). I am indebted to Duncan M. Pritchard for pointing this out.

Recall the definition of local underdetermination in Chapter 2. According to this definition, had the universal hypothesis been false, the evidence received up to now might have been all the same. No certain answer seems forthcoming pertaining to this epistemic inductive problem. The counterfactual theory of knowledge successfully combats global demons but not local ones.

To adjust counterfactual epistemology to deal with local underdetermination, the convergence criterion may be weakened to a limiting one, thus dropping the halting property. Such a configuration has been discussed by Kelly. What Nozick demonstrates with his epistemology is the possibility of knowledge here and now rather than the guaranteed convergence to the truth in the long run. Given the counterfactual nature of the epistemological paradigm, limiting convergence is not necessarily actual but 'virtual'. This observation elegantly ties counterfactual and computational epistemological considerations together and suggests a new venue of research, as Kelly (2000) explains:

Nonetheless, convergence may be *virtual*, in the sense that allowing the agent's current learning disposition to interact with the current disposition of the system under study for eternity mathematically determines an infinite 'course of inquiry' in which the agent's belief has already stabilized in the actual present. . . . The agent's current learning disposition may then ground the truth of virtual truth-tracking conditionals even though it does not ground the truth of truth-tracking conditionals (e.g. if H were true I would virtually converge to the belief that H). Now knowledge can be modelled as true, virtually stable belief that virtually tracks the truth in the limit in the best achievable sense. (p. 20)

Sticking to convergence with certainty in close worlds, as the counterfactual proposal originally does, may also just be another way of using forcing to evade the problem of induction and trying to turn inductive inference into deductive inference (see Chapter 7).

Counterfactual epistemology has other close encounters with formal epistemologies. Logical epistemology (the kind based on the standard Kripke-semantics and to which the discussion is largely restricted until Chapter 6) has devised a sliding scale for assessing the validity and epistemic strength of knowledge operators. The scale is built up by axioms that in proper combinations make up modal systems of different strength in the following sense: There are propositions valid in one system that are not valid in another system for which fewer (or different) algebraic properties are assumed for the accessibility relation. The differences in strength are determined by which relational properties the accessibility relation between possible worlds is endowed with relative to the knowledge operators' scope. For instance, the reasonable property that a possible world is accessible from itself (i.e., that the relation between possible worlds is reflexive) allows one, given the standard setup of modal propositional logic, to validate axiom T, which, in an epistemic interpretation, amounts to:

$$\text{If } \Xi \text{ knows } h, \text{ then } h \text{ is true.} \tag{4.3}$$

(4.3) is the default epistemic assumption of the vast majority of epistemologies since Plato. It is the second condition of the standard tripartite definition of knowledge, and the first condition of Nozick's definition of counterfactual knowledge.

Validating (4.3), also referred to as the *axiom of veridicality*, together with two other principles discussed later, results in what is known as modal system **T**. Now, if it is further assumed that the accessibility relation is both reflexive and transitive, then it is possible to validate the following axiom:

$$\text{If } \Xi \text{ knows } h, \text{ then } \Xi \text{ knows that he knows } h. \tag{4.4}$$

This is also known as the *K K thesis* or the *principle of positive introspection*. The resulting strength of the knowledge operator is then on the order of the modal system **S4**. Nozick (1981) rejects (4.4) for counterfactual knowledge:

Some writers have put forth the view that whenever one knows, one knows that one knows. There is an immediate stumbling block to this, however. One may know yet not believe one knows; with no existing belief that one knows to do the tracking of the fact that one knows, one certainly does not know that one knows. (p. 246)

An agent may be tracking the truth of *h* without tracking the fact that he is tracking the truth of *h*. There is a stronger epistemic principle:

$$\text{If } \Xi \text{ does not know } h, \text{ then } \Xi \text{ knows that he does not know } h. \tag{4.5}$$

This is referred to as axiom 5, the *axiom of wisdom* or the *principle of negative introspection* in logical epistemology. An agent validating (4.3), (4.4) and (4.5) is said to have epistemic strength on the order of modal system **S5**, requiring an equivalence relation over possible worlds. (4.5) is valid in **S5** but not in **S4**, so **S5** is a genuinely stronger epistemic system than **S4**. Even though the principle of negative introspection is not discussed by Nozick, it seems very likely that he would dismiss it all the same. If an agent is not tracking the truth of h, it does not follow that he will be tracking the fact that he is not tracking h.

Accepting (4.3) while rejecting (4.5) and (4.4) results in a rather weak epistemic logical system. Counterfactual epistemology furthermore rejects the closure principle (4.1). The simplest modal (Kripkean) system, but also the weakest modal system in terms of validity, is obtained by augmenting the standard propositional logic with the following axiom:

$$\text{If } \Xi \text{ knows } h, \text{ then if } \Xi \text{ knows } (h \to h'), \text{ then } \Xi \text{ knows } h'. \qquad (4.6)$$

Known as axiom **K**, this axiom is equivalent to (4.1). It says that knowledge is closed under implication, which counterfactual epistemology denies. The following rule of necessitation is also adopted by logical epistemology:

$$\text{If } h \text{ is a theorem, then } \Xi \text{ knows } h. \qquad (4.7)$$

The rule of necessitation holds on the counterfactual account of knowledge as well. If h is a logical truth in all possible worlds, the fourth verification condition of the counterfactual definition of knowledge is going to ensure that Ξ believes h, and since h never turns out false, the third condition never comes into play. Thus h is true; Ξ believes h; and since h is true in all possible worlds, h is also true in close worlds, so Ξ knows h.

Counterfactual and logical epistemology (of the standard Kripkean kind) may be considered as viewing the importance of the epistemic axioms almost diametrically opposite with respect to the threat from skepticism. A logical epistemologist considers axioms (4.4) and (4.5) as means of blocking the skeptical challenges. An agent may know of his knowledge and sometimes even his ignorance, leaving the skeptic with less room to maneuver. The stronger the system, the less room for error.

On the other hand, it seems that the only logical axiom acceptable to the counterfactual epistemology is the axiom of veridicality (4.3), together with the rule of necessitation (4.7). Accepting the axiom and the rule does not amount to a logical system in any *normal* technical sense of modal logic, *pace* Kripkean semantics. Closure under implication is denied, but closure does not require any algebraic properties to be assumed for the accessibility relation between possible worlds. For this reason, a logical epistemologist of a Kripkean nature usually assumes (4.6) to be valid under normal circumstances. To adequately capture the counterfactual concept of knowledge, however, Kripkean semantics must be abandoned in favor of more general semantic constructions like neighborhood systems, discussed in the latter half of Chapter 6.

In contrast to the epistemic reliabilism of the previous chapter, Nozick does not venture into discussing which human cognitive faculties, skills and methods in fact have the desired reliability properties. Goldman is of the conviction that undisturbed vision, testimony and good memory, perhaps even regression analysis, are prime examples of faculties and methods that meet his stochastic reliabilistic requirement. In order to find an answer to whether vision, analysis and memory are reliable methods, rather than ask an epistemologist, one should probably ask an optician, a mathematician and a cognitive psychologist, as Nozick (1981) claims:

'It is for empirical science to investigate the details of the mechanisms whereby we track, and for methodologists to devise and refine even better (inferential) mechanisms and methods' (p. 287).

Later Nozick (1993) argues that reliability analyses are not for pure philosophers but for computational and logical epistemologists and other technically minded thinkers in philosophy and elsewhere:

In the study of reliable processes for arriving at belief, philosophers will become technologically obsolete. They will be replaced by cognitive and computer scientists, workers in artificial intelligence, and others (p. 76).

Counterfactual epistemology in general accommodates elements of contextualistic epistemology (see next chapter). Dretske's view of closure lets knowledge transfer work across known implications insofar as the implications in question are close or relevant. Knowing that one is sitting down reading this book transfers immediately through the known implications to the 'close' hypothesis that one is not standing on a street corner doing the same. This knowledge will at the same time not run through the known implications to the 'way-off' hypothesis that one is not being fooled by a malicious demon. Dretske's (1970) point seems to be that knowledge of a hypothesis in some common *contexts* assumes by default the falsity of particular 'way-off' and irrelevant possibilities of error. These possibilities of error are skirted, or their falsity presupposed, in many everyday knowledge acquisition contexts. Lewis strongly subscribes to this contextualistic forcing feature in his epistemology.

5

Contextual Epistemology

The concept of knowledge is elusive – at least when epistemology starts scrutinizing the concept too much. According to Lewis's contextual epistemology, all there is to knowledge attribution in a given context is a set of rules for eliminating the relevant possibilities of error while succeeding over the remaining possibilities and properly ignoring the extravagant possibilities of error. Considering demons and brains as relevant possibilities of error is often what makes the concept of knowledge evaporate into thin air

> FORCING   *S knows* that *P* iff *S*'s evidence eliminates every possibility in which not-*P* – Psst! – except for those possibilities that we are properly ignoring.
>
> David Lewis (1996)

Contextualistic epistemology starts much closer to home. Agents in their local epistemic environments have knowledge – and plenty of it in a variety of (conversational) contexts. Knowledge is not only possible, as counterfactual epistemology demonstrates, it is a real and fundamental human condition.

The general contextualistic template for a theory of knowledge is crisply summarized in DeRose's (1995) description of the attribution of knowledge. The description also embodies many of the epistemological themes central to the contextualistic forcing strategy:

Suppose a speaker *A* says, '*S knows* that *P*', of a subject *S*'s true belief that *P*. According to contextualist theories of knowledge attributions, how strong an epistemic position *S* must be in with respect to *P* for *A*'s assertion to be true can vary according to features of *A*'s conversational context. (p. 4)

The incentive to take skeptical arguments to knowledge claims seriously is based on an exploitation of the way in which otherwise operational epistemic concepts, notably knowledge, can be gravely disturbed by sudden changes of the linguistic context in which they figure.

The standards for the possession of knowledge vary from context to context depending on what is at stake. In a course on epistemology, the standards for knowledge possession fixed by the interlocutors (teacher and students) are usually very high. The conclusion that we know very little, if anything at all, may by the end of class be true. In a discussion after class, a student says, 'I know that *Matrix Reloaded* is playing at the theater on 125 E. 86th Street'. The circumstances have now changed, and the standards for knowledge possession in this new, presumably nonskeptical conversational context are lower. The relatively lower standards put us in the comfortable position of maintaining that we know most of what we think we know. Although the standards are admittedly lower, they surely suffice for going to the movies.

Not only may knowledge attributions fluctuate with contexts, they may also be sensitive to who ascribes knowledge to whom. As indicated by DeRose, there is a delicate issue to be addressed pertaining to the strength of the position an agent has to be in for the epistemic commitment to truthfully pan out. This position is context sensitive, not only with respect to the agent in the environment but also with respect to possible ascribers of knowledge to that agent. The first-third person dichotomy is immanent in contextualistic epistemologies.[1]

Finally, the strength of the epistemic position is responsible for turning the contextualistic theory of knowledge into a modal account, according to DeRose. For every local environmental 'time-slice', the epistemic position of the agent remains constant. The epistemic position the agent would need to be in to warrant possession of knowledge, however, is a subjunctively defined spatiotemporal function of the context. To be in a strong epistemic position with respect to some hypothesis h is to have a belief as to whether h is the case and to track this fact not only through the actual world but through close worlds as well. Maintaining that one's belief still tracks the truth over long distances increases the strength of the epistemic position with respect to the hypothesis in question. For belief to become knowledge, it should be 'nonaccidentally' true in the actual world and in close ones as well.[2] This way of realizing the forcing

---

[1] The distinction outlined by Lewis is not equivalent to the current distinction between the two perspectives, as the third-person stance defined in Chapter 2 incorporates 'means-end' considerations. The difference is negligible for now but not later.

[2] See DeRose 1995, 34.

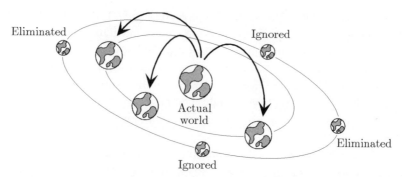

FIGURE 5.1. Modal epistemology requires success in all worlds not either eliminated or ignored.

relation resembles the construction advanced by counterfactual epistemology using sensitivity or tracking (see Chapter 4).

There are garden varieties of contextualism developed by Cohen (1987, 1999, 2000), DeRose (1995, 2000), Lewis (1996), and Williams (1995). Williams (2001) advanced a new version that diverges somewhat from the standard foundation of contextualism. Cohen's contextualism focuses on justificational issues and the structure of supportive reasons for knowledge possession. Both DeRose's and Lewis's accounts serve to spell out the modal contextualistic program in general. Williams's version diverges from this program by individuating contexts in terms of the inferential structure of a context rather than through conversational measures.

Lewis's contextualistic epistemology is particularly engaging, as it balances elegantly between mainstream and formal *modi operandi*.[3] This is not surprising, since Lewis throughout his career was concerned with modal logic, in particular, the logic of counterfactuals (1973), modal ontology (1984) and, almost consequently, contextual epistemology (1996).

As humans, we force for knowledge on a daily basis and obtain it. This means partitioning the set of all possible worlds into relevant, irrelevant and extravagant possibilities of error determined by the current context. To obtain knowledge, we eliminate the relevant possibilities of error, ignore the extravagant ones and succeed over the remaining possible worlds in which the hypothesis in question is true (Fig. 5.1). Everything is dictated by the current context. There are rules for elimination, ignoring

---

[3] Unless otherwise stated the terms 'contextualism', 'contextual' and 'contextualistic' epistemology will be used to denote Lewis's build of contextualism.

and success. On a new definition of knowledge yet to be formulated, these rules are what Lewis's epistemology mostly is about.

To kick off the contextual epistemology, the standard definition of knowledge is abandoned. Justification is neither necessary nor sufficient for the possession of knowledge. Instead of citing clairvoyance as a relevant possibility undermining the sufficiency of justification, as Bonjour did (see Chapter 3), we will find that something less far-fetched suffices: observing some consequences of the *lottery paradox*. Formulated by Kyburg (1961), the lottery paradox shows how otherwise intuitively appealing justificational principles may be rendered logically inconsistent. The paradox rests on the following three assumptions about justification and rational acceptance: (1) One is justified in accepting a conclusion that which is likely to be true, (2) justification is closed under conjunction,[4] and (3) one is never justified in accepting logically inconsistent statements.

Consider next a fair lottery with 1,000 tickets and 1 winning ticket. In such a lottery, the probability of each particular ticket losing is .999 (i.e., it is very high). Based on assumption 1, the high probability of ticket 1 losing should lead to the conclusion that the ticket will lose. This line of reasoning can be repeated for the remaining 999 tickets. Given the assumption of closure under conjunction, one is justified in believing that all 1,000 tickets will lose, which is the same as committing to the belief that no ticket will win. By the rules of the lottery, 1 ticket will win, which *a fortiori* also is a justified belief. One is now faced with being justified in believing the logical inconsistency that no ticket will win and that some ticket will win. This is in conflict with assumption 3, and the lottery paradox is generated.

Some attempts to retain justification but at the same time avoid the lottery paradox focus on showing that at least one of the initial assumptions 1–3 is incorrect.[5] One way out is to reject assumption 1: Justification strong enough to keep the skeptic quiet requires deductive certainty and not likelihoods, no matter how high these likelihoods may be. A justification for belief is not licensed if there is just an infinitesimal chance of a mistake (Dretske 1981).[6]

---

[4] If one is justified in accepting h and justified in accepting h', one is justified in accepting the conjunction $h \land h'$.

[5] For instance, Kyburg (1970) suggests abandoning assumption 2.

[6] A more lenient version maintains that high probablity does confer justification given additional constraints of, say, coherence of belief sets. Justification is not warranted with respect to singular beliefs about losing on individual tickets (see Lehrer 1980 and Pollock 1983).

The way to boost the degree of justification for believing in losing is by increasing the number of tickets in the lottery. The odds of losing may be set arbitrarily high, short of 1.[7] In a one winning ticket setup, there will always remain the chance of winning, though it admittedly grows smaller as the number of tickets increases. An arbitrary increase in the number of tickets implies an arbitrary increase in the degree of justification for believing in losing. But an arbitrarily high degree of justification will not suffice for converting fallible belief about losing into knowledge of losing. Lewis concludes that justification is not sufficient for knowledge.

The conclusion Lewis draws is not quite right unless qualified in some way, as Arló-Costa has pointed out. If one pays homage to Dretske's idea that justification for belief is not warranted as long as there is an infinitesimal chance of a mistake, then increasing the number of tickets arbitrarily will never achieve full justification. Therefore, increasing the number of tickets arbitrarily does not immediately demonstrate that justification is not sufficient for knowledge. What it does show is that an arbitrary increase in the number of tickets is not sufficient for justification, assuming Dretske's condition.

The necessity of justification is also dismissed, but not because of the mainstream Cartesian demon (see Chapter 3). A glance at actual epistemic practice is enough to reveal that justification is not always necessary for knowledge:

What (non-circular) argument supports our reliance on perception, on memory, and on testimony? And yet we do gain knowledge by these means. And sometimes, far from having supporting arguments, we don't even know how we know. We once had evidence, drew conclusions, and thereby gained knowledge; now we have forgotten our reasons, yet still we retain knowledge. (Lewis 1996, 368)

Knowledge is being stripped of its classically distinguishing features by contextual epistemology: True justified belief does not amount to knowledge, knowledge is allowed without justification, and knowledge of something is not always accompanied by belief in something. Lewis cites Radford's (1966) list of cases in which an agent may be said to have

---

[7] Even if one requires a probability of 1 for justification, one has the lottery anyway. This is accomplished by a transfinite version of the paradox (see Arló-Costa 2001b and references there). In this case, one might accept that full justification gives some form of 'risky knowledge' (a term concocted by Kyburg). The main point, however, is that this form of knowledge is incompatible with logical closure, just like Nozick's counterfactual knowledge (see Chapter 4). Various forms of knowledge are actually *in principle* incompatible with different forms of logical closure in the sense of (4.6) as discussed in Chapter 6.

knowledge despite insecurity, lack of confidence, or timidity preventing him from believing what is known.

A substitute for the standard tripartite definition of knowledge is in order. It should explain why what is allegedly known is known infallibly. To the ears of contextual epistemologists, knowledge in light of possibilities of error sounds like a contradiction (see Chapter 2).

Taking infallibility as a basic epistemological condition, for an agent to know a hypothesis, all possibilities of error must be eliminated given the agent's available information. That is, all the possible worlds in which the negation of the hypothesis is true must be eliminated. This forcing relation is achieved through different measures. One measure is simply to ignore the possibilities extravaganza; another is to use the available evidence to force in such a way that the uneliminated possible worlds are determined by perceptual equivalences with the actual world as the fix point (in the spirit of the suggestion by Goldman discussed in Chapter 3). The perceptual experience (and memory) the agent has in the actual world fixes the set of uneliminated possible worlds insofar as the agent's cognitive apparatus functions the same in these worlds. Suppose that a perceptual experience has the propositional content A. The perceptual experience with content A (memory included) eliminates a certain world w' if and only if the content of the experience the agent has in w' differs from A.

Quantifiers are usually restricted to run over some domain of interest. This also goes for the universal quantifier with respect to possible worlds that would lead to error. Every uneliminated world in which the hypothesis holds is restricted to a subdomain of all properly uneliminated worlds. Saying that the surface is 'clean' in a certain conversational context is to properly ignore the microscopic dust particles on the surface. If somebody was to disagree, it would have to be because the new interlocutor in the conversational context means clean in a more restrictive sense. The microscopic dust balls in this case suffice for making the assertion about the clean surface false. Words like 'flat' or 'round' behave in the same way, as does the word 'knowledge'. They are context sensitive.[8]

Alterations of the conversational context occur when a new hypothesis is introduced that for its part is more demanding than any of the other hypotheses currently explicit in the particular context. Such a *nonuniform*

---

[8] The context sensitivity of various words, including 'knowledge', was noted by Lewis much earlier, in 'Scorekeeping in Language Games' (1976).

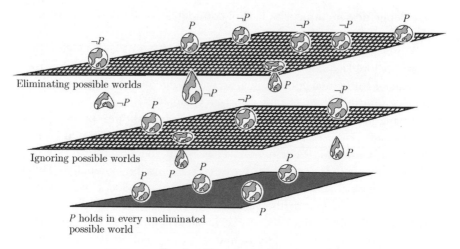

Eliminating possible worlds

Ignoring possible worlds

P holds in every uneliminated
possible world

FIGURE 5.2. Forcing filters in modal epistemology.

introduction implies an increase in the range of possible worlds to be
considered for the attribution of knowledge. The strength of the required epistemic position mentioned earlier is increased accordingly. In
a context in which the usage of 'knowledge' remains *uniform* throughout
the conversation, the range of possible worlds to be considered remains
stable. Given the context-sensitive nature of knowledge, in every context where knowledge attribution is at stake, some uneliminated possible
worlds are not rendered relevant by the *current* context. The universal
quantifier is restricted accordingly.

These considerations essentially pave the way for the colloquially stated
but forceful definition of knowledge of contextualistic epistemology:

S knows that *P* iff *S*'s evidence eliminates every possibility in which not-*P* – Psst! –
except for those possibilities that *we* are properly ignoring. (Lewis 1996, 378)

Knowledge on this definition is forced through a two-step context-
sensitive filtering process – eliminating and ignoring – that leaves the
hypothesis or proposition true in every remaining possible world determined by the agent's evidence and other relevant information (Fig. 5.2).
These are the worlds in which to succeed in order to attribute knowledge.
To carry out the filtration, the agent follows prohibitive rules about which
worlds may not be properly ignored and presumptive rules about which
worlds may be properly ignored while ascribing knowledge to himself
and to others.

The envisioned order of the filtration process is not entirely clear. The phrase 'which of all the uneliminated alternative possibilities may not be properly ignored' (Lewis 1996, 371) suggests eliminating before ignoring. One argument for this order would be that elimination fixes a set of perceptually equivalent possibilities, after which a subset of this set is ignored. Yet ignoring may also supersede eliminating if the question of what is ignored and what is not ignored is connected to the agent's view of the world. In a particular context, it is not a part of agent Ξ's view of the world that he is a brain in a vat, so the elimination is not sensitive to this possibility. The two filtrations may also be so intimately connected that they are virtually indistinguishable during the actual epistemic processing.[9] For expositional purposes, they are separated here.

During the individual knowledge attribution process, the possible world that the agent takes to be the actual state of affairs is never ignored. Because of reflexivity, actuality is always a relevant possible world alternative, although indexical. It follows that falsity may not properly be supposed. If falsity is never to be presupposed, whatever in the end will turn up as knowledge must be true, so the classical condition of truth for knowledge is derived. The rule to never ignore the actual world is referred to as the *rule of actuality*.

Turn next to the ascription of knowledge to others. Lewis's contextualistic definition of knowledge given earlier italicizes 'we'. What *we* may properly ignore is going to be dependent on whose actuality is being referred to in the context in question. Assuming that there is only one actual-world index in play in nonmodal contexts, one should expect that the world considered actual by the agent coincides with the world indexed 'actual' by the ascribers.

In the case of counterfactuals referring, for instance, to what an agent would have known today had he read the paper yesterday, or to whether an agent knew yesterday who he was then, fixing the index of actuality is more complicated. Had the agent read the paper yesterday, he would presumably have known more than he in fact knows today. The agent is ascribing knowledge and ignorance to himself now as the one not having read the paper last night. The ascriber, say, Ξ', of knowledge to agent Ξ has an index of actuality demonstratively different from Ξ's index. The index on actuality for Ξ' is what Ξ' would have been like knowledgewise had he read the paper yesterday. Actuality indices differ for Ξ and Ξ' in this situation. Similarly for the attribution to Ξ of knowing yesterday who

---

[9] I am indebted to Louise Westmark for pointing this out.

he was. For Ξ, reality is defined for his spatiotemporal history up until yesterday; for Ξ', reality is defined for his spatiotemporal history up to today – up to when the question is popped whether Ξ knew yesterday who he was. The two world stories are different. Ξ's actuality yesterday is different from Ξ''s actuality today, similarly for a host of other situations involving iterated modal constructions like knowledge of knowledge, and so on.

The rule of actuality applies both to the ascriber and the ascribed. What may not be properly ignored is the local agent's actuality. Epistemologists considering what Ξ knows from a third-person perspective will attend to whatever possible worlds that Ξ himself attends to as possible and then some. The set of possible worlds ignored by a third-person knowledge attributor for Ξ will properly be a superset of the possible worlds Ξ ignores. An agent may know more than what may be ascribed to him because his actuality in some cases differs from that of any ascriber, and his range of viable worlds does as well. Applying the principle of 'epistemic' charity means that while attributing knowledge to an agent in his local epistemic environment, the third-person ascriber may ignore fewer possibilities than Ξ.

From the actual world, a certain set of alternative worlds are *believed* to be accessible by the agent. These may not be properly ignored either. This is the content of the *rule of belief*: A possible world that the agent believes to obtain may not be ignored independently of whether he is justified in believing that the state of affairs obtains or not. The rule of belief is an epistemic correlate to the ◊-rule in modal tableaux – a sort of existential quantifier rule introducing other worlds in the modal knowledge tree. Not only may such belief-dependent worlds not be properly ignored, but possible worlds that the agent *should* acknowledge to obtain given evidence and other information may not be ignored either. This deontic clause need not be explicitly realized by an agent exhibiting an externalistic bias.

Belief comes in degrees, and some possible worlds will be doxastically more accessible than others given the measure of opinion. Some possible worlds will be tossed out because the measure of opinion pertaining to them is too low – perhaps infinitesimal or even 0. Whatever worlds may not be properly ignored should have a 'sufficiently high' degree of belief attached to them. What degree is sufficiently high is context dependent and will vary with what is at stake. For contexts in which an error would be especially 'disastrous' (Lewis 1996, 373), a quite low measure of opinion may do for not tossing out the possibility. To avoid miscarriage of justice in a court of law, the accused is only convicted when guilt has been proved beyond reasonable doubt. In this context, a very moderate degree of belief is enough to warrant ignoring fewer possible worlds, though some possible worlds are still ruled out. Other contexts are not as serious. A sufficiently high degree of belief will be higher in these contexts, leading to the tossing out of more worlds. The degree of belief for legitimately ignoring worlds requires a justificational story. Justification is in a certain sense reinvited on the way to knowledge.

Having a rule for introducing new worlds calls for a rule of accessibility between the introduced worlds. A world w' that 'saliently resembles' another world w enforces a kind of symmetry. If w may not be properly ignored in virtue of the other rules, neither may w', and vice versa. This accessibility clause is referred to as the *rule of resemblance*, the last of the prohibitive rules. The rule is dangerous and powerful at the same time.

The rule of resemblance is dangerous because if it is not applied carefully, it invites skepticism and global underdetermination back in. The actual world is left uneliminated by the agent's available evidence. It follows that any other uneliminated world resembles the agent's actual world in one important respect, namely, in regard to the agent's evidence. This will continue to hold even in worlds that otherwise are radically different from the agent's actual world, including the demon world. Application of the rule of actuality together with the rule of resemblance leads to the conclusion that these worlds are relevant alternative worlds as well!

There is no obvious remedy to this problem, and it reappears with respect to knowledge closure. Agreeing with counterfactual epistemology that closure over arbitrary contexts amounts to a fallacy driving skeptical arguments, Lewisian epistemology holds that closure is possible locally without skepticism. Knowledge is closed for a fixed context. Knowing that you are reading this book implies that you are reading this book and not being deceived (by a demon or a mad scientist) in this particular uniform context c_1. If the context is nonuniformly changed right after the antecedent conditions obtain to a new context c_2, 'all bets are off' (Lewis 1996, 382):

$$\underbrace{K_\Xi h \rightarrow K_\Xi (h \rightarrow h')}_{c_1} \quad \overset{change!}{\uparrow} \quad \nrightarrow \underbrace{K_\Xi h'}_{c_2} \qquad (5.1)$$

Closure fails because the strength of the epistemic position now required in c_2 to attribute knowledge has been increased way beyond c_1 by the increase in possible worlds at issue dictated by c_2. The range of possible worlds may now include the demon world, which is a whole different context. Knowledge is closed under implication because implication preserves truth in a fixed context, not over arbitrary contexts.

Like Lewis, DeRose presents a contextualistic closure argument that relies on Dretskian sensitivity or Nozickian tracking (discussed in Chapter 4). For closure, the problem is that sensitivity increases the required epistemic position because of the switch in the possible world scope due to the contextual change. For an agent to know that he is not a brain in a vat, sensitivity or tracking demands that if the agent was a brain in a vat, the agent would not believe that he was not so. This takes the issue to another level in terms of epistemic position. The required epistemic position is boosted because the agent has now to believe that he is a brain in a vat in a world where his brain in fact is rigged to an experience-simulating computer. The closest such world is *ceteris paribus* very remote from the actual world. In the actual world, the agent is barred from finding out that his brain is in the tank of fluids and being stimulated. When sensitivity elevates the standards for such hypotheses, it raises them for all other beliefs in the same context. In a world in which the agent is a brain in a vat, the agent will believe that he is reading this book even though he is not. When the agent entertains a proposition and a skeptical hypothesis at the same time, the standards for sensitivity are raised to such an exorbitant level that common hypotheses are unknowable.

There is not any obvious way to ensure that such a contextual change is not taking place. The rules of actuality and resemblance combined immediately permit such a change to occur. The demon world resembles the actual world in salient ways and with respect to the agent's evidence, and it should accordingly not be ignored. Lewis readily admits to an *ad hoc* modification of the rule so as to exclude this resemblance.

Although the rule of resemblance may lead to error in certain circumstances, its forcefulness is demonstrated by its ability to deal with both the lottery paradox and the Gettier paradoxes. The rule reveals why the agent is barred from knowing losing the lottery independently of the arbitrary high odds of losing. Every ticket has a possibility of winning. The possible worlds described by the different winning tickets resemble each other with respect to this feature. By the symmetry of resemblance, all of them should be ignored or none of them should be tossed out. The trouble, then, is that the winning ticket describes a possible world that may not be properly ignored.

Gettier paradoxes are handled in a similar fashion. Smith has ignored the possibility that Jones drives a rented car as much as he has ignored the possibility that Brown is in Barcelona. By assumption, the actual world is not ignored. The Gettier scene world matches the actual world as far as Smith is concerned. The error is committed by Smith's ignoring a world that the accessibility relation of resemblance requires him to take into account. Smith has 'knowledge' for the wrong reasons and consequently does not know, having been too eager to ignore. The story is the same with the papier-maché barns. Seeing a real barn in the country of mixed barns does not license a claim about seeing a real barn. The possibility of seeing a papier-maché version must not be ignored because of the salient resemblance. The Gettier paradoxes are modalized in Lewis's variant of contextual epistemology.

The failure to know of a real barn could also be due to the mode of acquisition (i.e., due to the fact that visual perception is unreliable). This possibility, however, is emphatically denied in Lewis's account. In fact, the possible worlds in which, say, perception, memory and testimony are unreliable may be properly ignored. This is the content of the *rule of reliability*, which, as opposed to the three rules discussed earlier, is a presumptive rule about which worlds may be tossed out or ignored.

It is not entirely clear what sort of reliability is envisioned besides the fact that it has a modal scope. The three cognitive processes (perception, memory and testimony) are described as 'fairly reliable. Within limits we are entitled to take them for granted' (Lewis 1996, 375). This may suggest a variant of reliability with stochastic success over other possible worlds with a high truth ratio. To define 'fairly reliable', Lewis refers in a footnote to Armstrong's (1973) causal theory of knowledge and Goldman's (1967) early theory of a similar nature. The nomic sufficiency account of knowledge utilizes a categorical concept of reliability in terms of success, not a stochastic one (see Chapter 3).

For Lewis, it could be a notion of reliability ranging from stochastic success over other possible worlds to categorical success over other possible worlds. The confusion is not really resolved at any point because 'we do not presuppose, of course, that nowhere ever is there a failure of, say, vision' (Lewis 1996, 375). This could mean with respect to sense of success, but it could also mean with respect to the range of possible worlds. Visual experience and acquired belief based on vision are, at the same time, described in strict accordance with the thermometer model, where the causal dependence covers other possible worlds.

Hallucination is described as an unreliable method of knowledge acquisition except when the hallucinations are so powerful that it is impossible to tell the difference between real perceptual experience and

hallucinated experience. In many contexts, the worlds in which hallucinations are so powerful are ignored. Since hallucination is a real human
condition, it cannot always be tossed out. The rule of reliability may from
time to time be overridden by the rule of actuality, possibly in conjunction
with the rule of resemblance. Whatever reliability is supposed to mean,
it follows, as it did for Nozick's counterfactual epistemological account,
that reliability is a world-dependent property.

Turning to inferential beliefs vindicates the problem. Sampling and
inference to the best explanation compose the *rule of method*. It is a rule
that licences tossing out the possible worlds in which sampling and inference to the best explanation are unreliable nondeductive inference
engines. The general methodological issue concerning inference to the
best explanation is exactly whether it is reliable (stochastically or categorically) for some enumeration of possible explanations reflecting audacity,
simplicity, unification, predictive power, and so on. It could be the case,
moreover, that for some enumerations based on, for instance, simplicity,
consistency and boldness, inference to the best explanation could not
possibly be reliable, neither in some desired stochastic nor categorical
sense.

While Lewis has plenty to offer with respect to global underdetermination, little is said about local underdetermination and the problem of
induction as they relate to methods of inquiry. In fact, it may be that
ignoring worlds in which sampling and inference to the best explanation
are unreliable is just an excuse for forcing one's way out of the problem
of induction (see Chapter 7).

With respect to the methodological notions of success and convergence, it seems that Lewis follows Nozickian lines of thought. Since humans know a lot in everyday contexts, it follows that the local epistemic
environment suffices for the truth of the hypotheses in question. Inquiry
halts, and the agent will know with certainty in the common context given.
This will at least work for assessment construed as inference to the best
explanation and possibly also for genuine discovery mechanisms, even
though they are not discussed.

Two presumptive rules remain to be accounted for. Both seem trivial
yet furnish insight into Lewis's view of the situation in epistemology today. One is a *rule of conservatism* or *convention*. If a certain set of possible
worlds is ignored by the epistemic community to which the agent belongs,
and it is common knowledge among the interacting agents that precisely
these possible worlds are tossed out, then they may be ignored. During routine knowledge attribution, the common and mutually expected

presuppositions are adopted by the members of the epistemic community. Knowledge attribution is partly a socially determined process forced by conventional means to be taken seriously.

This seriousness is reflected in the final *rule of attention*. Which worlds are ignored is context dependent. When ignored in a specific context, these worlds are *really*, not just counterfactually, tossed out and not to be considered. Attending to even far-fetched possible worlds in a different context make them relevant possibilities again. Relevant possibilities of error undercut infallible knowledge claims, and knowledge flies away – becomes 'elusive'. [10]

The prohibitive and presumptive rules of knowledge attribution delicately balance between descriptive and normative epistemology. They are descriptive to the extent that they describe how we have the knowledge we think we have, yet normative to the extent that the alleged knowledge would vanish or never come about if the rules were not followed. They serve as the justification for knowledge claims, yet justification is explicitly dismissed. If justification is tantamount to using guidelines for getting to the truth (i.e., methodology), then justification is normative and may as well be formulated in rules. The application manual for the methodological rules is not fixed once and for all but fluctuates with the context. The rules may also meet with conflict. Conflict resolution involves determining which rule should override other rules for knowledge attribution to take place. Choosing the application of one rule over another may be a matter of social convention or majority vote. Knowledge is accordingly a normative attribution but also a factual human condition.

Buying into too many uneliminated possibilities of error often makes epistemologists end up with buyer's regret. Potential counterexamples to knowledge ascriptions are to be found everywhere in rich domains, making the required epistemic position impossible to reach for anybody. No first persons have knowledge in these particularly demanding contexts, no third persons either. Unfortunately, as a discipline, epistemology is one such demanding context. The foe of epistemology is not really skepticism but epistemology itself:

That is how epistemology destroys knowledge. But it does so only temporarily. The pastime of epistemology does not plunge us forevermore into its special context.

---

[10] Ignoring worlds may from this perspective be seen as a necessary last resort because the available evidence may always be insufficient to block global underdetermination. Ignoring is a precondition for knowledge – love it or leave it and it becomes 'elusive knowledge'.

We can still do a lot of proper ignoring, a lot of knowing, and a lot of true ascribing of knowledge to ourselves and others the rest of the time. (Lewis 1996, 377)

Contextualism may all the same be accused, if not of buying into skepticism, then of being unusually hospitable to skeptical challenges for an epistemology. This accommodation leaves first-person agents as well as third-person ascribers no better off than they were before the advent of contextualism.

On the way to such objections one may initially note a relativization of crucial epistemological concepts. The notion of truth fluctuates with the context. A hypothesis held true by one group of interlocutors may be false for another such that a single hypothesis may be both true and false. 'True' is replaced by 'true for' or 'true in the current context', leaving no general notion of truth behind. Contextualism does not have to take the relativistic bait: 'Ξ knows h' has a definite truth-value fixed by Ξ's current context; 'Ξ knows h in context c' has a definite truth-value across contexts. A general transcontextual notion of truth is preserved.

Preservation of transcontextual truth still accommodates skeptics. Contextualism concedes to skepticism the high epistemic standards with which the skeptical position operates. These epistemic standards are exceedingly harder to meet than those required for everyday attributions of knowledge. Admitting this much to skepticism licences the view that these elevated standards are in fact the correct standards for genuine knowledge ascriptions and acquisitions. When push comes to shove, everyday knowledge attributions do not stand up to these standards, so knowledge attributions are generally bogus, as discussed by Pritchard (2001). Skepticism can never be dodged. Presumptive and prohibitive rules may conflict in such a way that skeptical possibilities like hallucinations become relevant. Applying the prohibitive rule of resemblance merely escapes skepticism by *ad hoc* qualifications. This leaves us again 'caught between the rock of fallibilism, and the whirlpool of skepticism', as Lewis (1996, 367) puts it. Contextualistic epistemology was supposed to come to the rescue.

As bogus as these ascriptions may seem, they may also be as good as it gets. A similar response to skepticism following 'smooth' lines may be found in Levi's (1983, 1991) formal epistemology. To gain truth and avoid error, beliefs carrying the highest 'epistemic utility' should be chosen. The epistemic utility embodies truth as well as content. Significant possibilities of error are forgivable if the agent settles for the belief with the highest epistemic utility in the particular context. This may not exactly add up to real knowledge, but it is good enough for decision and action. The elevation of the skeptical standards for knowledge is immaterial for common epistemic practice. Infallibilism with respect to all worlds cannot be reached anyway, and agents are doing the best they can by quantifying over less and reaching at least a workable impasse with skepticism. That is the epistemic balance: Agents can act on their 'discount' infallible knowledge, but skeptics can do very little with their high standards. Turning the tables, skeptics are the *real* epistemologists.

Denials of skeptical hypotheses cannot be known transcontextually on the modal conception of knowledge. Thus, one objection would be that knowledge is not even possible, much less real. One defense would be simply to admit that the logics of knowledge are rather weak, at least for the third-person knowledge operator and in case of contextual changes. As opposed to counterfactual epistemology's denial of closure (4.6), closure holds for a first-person operator in a uniform context in Lewis's epistemology. Closure may fail from the third-person perspective because the set of worlds to be considered is strictly a superset of the set of worlds the first-person operator has to consider, leaving room for radical context change and failure. There is support to be found for such a defense.

Levi's (1997) epistemological program encompasses a version of the first-person perspective but emphasizes the distinction between *the logic of truth* and *the logic of consistency* rather than the distinction between first- and third-person perspectives. Even though related, the two distinctions are not exactly the same. Levi denies the validity of various epistemic axioms as axioms of an epistemic logic of truth. This crudely means he rejects these axioms as axioms for a third-person knowledge operative. An axiom like the KK thesis (4.4), found to be invalid in counterfactual epistemology, is here valid as an axiom serving the regulative purpose of maintaining consistency for a rational epistemic agent. The logic of truth for an epistemic agent, on the other hand, is not necessarily regulated by a principle like the KK thesis. Lewis seems to follow suit, because knowledge of knowledge introduces a discrepancy of actualities for the first- and third-person operators. Because of the subject-based contextualism enforced by the rule of actuality, the third-person operator is to ignore fewer worlds, leaving more room for error. The agent may perhaps know that he knows, the third person may not necessarily be able to determine that the KK thesis holds for the agent, nor that it holds for himself in regard to the agent in question. The agent in the local environment may have more knowledge than a third person is able to ascribe to him or to the third person himself. If there is a transcontextual third-person logic of knowledge, such a logic is probably rather weak; at least this seems to be the suggestion of Levi and Lewis.

While Lewis may consider a universal third-person logic rather weak, there is nothing in the way of arguing for a much stronger first-person logic. This is in stark contrast to the version of counterfactual epistemology discussed in the previous chapter, in which the first-person logic is quite weak. On the Lewisian epistemological account, (4.3) to (4.7) may be valid in uniform contexts for a first-person knowledge operator. These four epistemic principles are central to logical epistemology, which is the topic of the next chapter.

What makes both counterfactual and Lewisian contextualistic epistemologies in a sense 'formal mainstream' theories of knowledge is that they both admit the significance of epistemic axiomatics for epistemology. Although the formal tools of Kripkean semantics are generally inadequate for capturing Nozick's counterfactual concept of knowledge, the axiom of veridicatlity (axiom T) was seen to hold on the counterfactual account (together with the rule of necessitation). For Lewis, the rule of actuality ensures that axiom T holds, closure holds in uniform contexts, the KK thesis holds, and the rule of necessitation will also immediately hold for a first-person epistemological contextualistic logic. Using the sliding scale devised by logical epistemology to determine validity will make the contextualistic first-person epistemological logic at least have epistemic strength on the order of model system **S4**; perhaps even an **S5** level of strength is acceptable to Lewis under certain conditions, although this issue is not discussed. The third-person logic seems to be no stronger than Nozick's first-person logic, which validates axioms 4.3 and 4.7; as a consequence, the third-person logic is a nonnormal Kripkean modal logic.

One of the new things in Lewis's epistemology is the attempt to provide general rules for the construction of what computer scientists using epistemic logic call 'runs' (vectors of possibilia with a specific range; see Chapter 6). Lewis thought that in order to have a modal theory, one needs to begin with a set of possible worlds. A distinction is made between possible worlds and what he calls 'possibilia', which are composite entities rather than primitives, containing as a part the 'de se' knowledge of an agent. These composite entities complicates Lewis's ontology considerably. For example, how many epistemic possibilities are there? The problem is complicated even more by Aumann's (1994) suggestion to encode sets of agents in worlds, sets of those sets, and so on. Second, the similarity relation between worlds is a sufficiently complicated affair for simple possible worlds. When epistemic states are added, articulating the similarity relation is even harder. Now, Lewis is aware that the rules for ignoring that appeal to the similarity of possibilia are the ones that might be beyond repair. His reaction to this failure is to say, so much the worst for epistemology. Interestingly enough, it may not be so much the worse for logical epistemology.

6

Logical Epistemology

Logical epistemology, also known as epistemic logic, *proceeds axiomatically.* 'Ξ *knows that A' is formalized as a modal operator in a formal language that is interpreted using the standard apparatus of modal logic. This formal epistemological approach also pays homage to the forcing heuristics by limiting the scope of the knowledge operator through algebraic constraints imposed on the accessibility relation between possible worlds.*

> FORCING 'What the concept of knowledge involves in a purely logical perspective is thus a dichotomy of the space of all possible scenarios into those that are compatible with what I know and those that are incompatible with my knowledge. This observation is all we need for most of epistemic logic.
>
> Jaakko Hintikka 2003b

Logical epistemology dates back to Von Wright (1951) and especially to the work of Hintikka (1962) in the early 1960's.[1] Epistemic logics have since then grown into powerful enterprises enjoying many important applications.[2] The general epistemological significance of the logics of knowledge has to some extent been neglected by mainstreamers and formalists alike. The field is in a rather awkward position today. On the one hand, it is a discipline of importance for theoretical computer scientists, linguists and game theorists, for example, but they do not necessarily have epistemological ambitions in their use of epistemic logic. On the

---

[1] It has been pointed out by Boh (1993) and Knuuttila (1993) that the study of epistemic logic may be traced back to at least scholastic philosophy.

[2] See Gochet and Gribomont 2003 for an excellent survey of epistemic logic and its key issues. For another broader survey of the significance of logic for epistemology, see van Benthem 2003. For an encyclopedic overview of epistemic logic, refer also to Hendricks and Symons 2005.

other hand, it is a discipline devoted to the logic of knowledge and belief but is alien to epistemologists and philosophers interested in the theory of knowledge.

Recent results and approaches have fortunately brought the logics of knowledge quite close to the theories of knowledge. One may even identify a set of *logical epistemologies* having essential features in common with the mainstream epistemologies surveyed so far.[3]

Early on, epistemic logic was greatly influenced by the advances stemming from modal logic. Standard systems of modal logic were given epistemic interpretations, and some main technical results of epistemic logic could then be extracted.

Syntactically, the language of propositional epistemic logic is obtained by augmenting the language of propositional logic with a unary epistemic operator K_Ξ such that $K_\Xi A$ reads 'Agent Ξ knows A' for some arbitrary proposition A.[4] This formalization of knowledge is an interpretation of $\Box A$ in alethic logic, reading 'It is necessary that A'. Interpreting modal logic epistemically involves crudely reading modal formulae as epistemic statements expressing attitudes of certain agents toward certain propositions.

The semantics of modal logic is likewise given a novel interpretation. Hintikka [(1962, 2005), 1969] came up with the following semantic interpretation of the epistemic operator:

$K_\Xi A \approx$ *in all possible worlds compatible with what Ξ knows it is the case that A.*

The basic assumption is that any ascription of propositional attitudes like knowledge and belief, requires *partitioning* the set of possible worlds into two compartments: The compartment consisting of possible worlds compatible with the attitude in question and the compartment of worlds incompatible with it.

Based on the partition, the agent is capable of constructing different 'world-models' using the epistemic modal language. He is not necessarily required to know which one of the world-models constructed is the real world-model. All the same, the agent does not consider all these

---

[3] For a complete survey of the epistemological significance of epistemic logic, see Hendricks 2005b.

[4] In a formal language, 'A' will denote the proposition defining a hypothesis h. Instead of hypotheses, throughout this chapter we speak of propositions.

The discussion of epistemic logic is restricted to the propositional case. Epistemic logic has also been developed for first-order languages.

world-models equally possible or accessible from his current point of view. Some world-models may be incommensurable with his current information state or other background assumptions. These incompatible world-models are excluded from the compatibility partition. This may be viewed as another variation of the forcing strategy. In logical epistemology, as in many mainstream epistemologies, it is typically stipulated that the smaller the set of worlds an agent considers possible, the smaller his uncertainty, at the cost of stronger forcing assumptions.

Consider an epistemic logic for a single agent – a *mono-agent system*. The set of worlds considered accessible by an agent depends on the actual world or the agent's actual state of information. It is possible to capture the forcing dependency by introducing a relation of accessibility, R, on the set of compatible possible worlds. To express the idea that, for agent Ξ, the world w' is compatible with his information state or is accessible from the possible world w that Ξ is currently in, it is required that R holds between w and w'. This relation is written Rww', which reads 'world w' is accessible from w'. World w' is said to be an *epistemic alternative* to world w for agent Ξ. Given the above semantical interpretation, if a proposition A is true in all worlds that agent Ξ considers possible, then Ξ knows A. The quantifier restriction on knowledge in logical epistemology is comparable to the quantificational restriction found in Lewis's contextualism (see Chapter 5). Knowledge claims are circumscribed by the compartment of possible worlds in accordance with the epistemic attitude, not the incompatible compartment and not the set of all possible worlds. The context-sensitive quantifier for knowledge in Lewisian epistemology works in a similar way, as all worlds not eliminated in which the proposition of interest is true are restricted to a subdomain of all uneliminated worlds.

Formally, a *frame* $\mathcal{F}$ for an epistemic system is a pair (W, R) in which W is a nonempty set of possible worlds and R is a binary accessibility relation over W. A *model* $\mathbb{M}$ for an epistemic system consists of a frame and a denotation function φ assigning sets of worlds to atomic propositional formulae. Propositions are taken to be sets of possible worlds; namely, the sets of possible worlds in which they are true. Let *atom* be the set of atomic propositional formulae, then $\varphi : atom \longrightarrow P(W)$ where P denotes the powerset operation. The model $\mathbb{M} = \langle W, R, \varphi \rangle$ is called a *Kripke-model* and the resulting semantics *Kripke-semantics* (Kripke 1963). An atomic propositional formulae **a** is said to be true in a world w (in $\mathbb{M}$), written $\mathbb{M}, w \models \mathbf{a}$, iff w is in the set of possible worlds assigned to **a**, that is, $\mathbb{M}, w \models \mathbf{a}$ iff $w \in \varphi(\mathbf{a})$ for all $\mathbf{a} \in atom$. The formula $K_\Xi A$ is true in a world w, that is, $\mathbb{M}, w \models K_{\Xi} A$, iff $\forall w' \in W$: if Rww', then $\mathbb{M}, w' \models A$. The semantics for the Boolean connectives are given in the usual recursive way. A modal formula is said to be *valid* in a frame iff the formula is true for all possible assignments in all worlds admitted by the frame.

There is a formula or axiom that is valid in all possible frames:

$$K_{\Xi}(A \rightarrow A') \rightarrow (K_{\Xi} A \rightarrow K_{\Xi} A'). \tag{6.1}$$

This axiom amounts to the closure condition for knowledge (4.6), discussed previously in Chapters 4 and 5. Counterfactual epistemologists deny closure, and the denial of closure is all for the better, according to them. Accepting closure invites the skeptic right back in the knowledge game, undermining full-fledged infallibility given the unknowability of denials of skeptical hypotheses. Lewisian epistemology only agrees to this conclusion in nonuniform contexts; in uniform contexts, closure holds. Logical epistemology of a Kripkean nature unproblematically accepts axiom 6.1, but for a formal reason.

One rule of inference that is valid in all possible frames is the rule of *necessitation* (**N**):

$$\frac{A}{K_{\Xi} A} \tag{6.2}$$

This rule says that if A is true in all worlds of the frame, then so is $K_{\Xi} A$. The rule was found valid on both the counterfactual and contextual accounts of knowledge.

Neither (6.1) nor (6.2) require any assumptions to be made pertaining to the accessibility relation between the possible worlds considered compatible with the knowledge attitude. It actually turns out that (6.1) and (6.2) are the characterizing axiom and rule for possible world semantics with binary accessibility relations. All Kripke-style modal logics in which (6.1) and (6.2) are valid are called *normal* modal logics. Nozick's logic discussed in Chapter 4 is not normal technically speaking, although it is still a modal logic (see later).

Besides (6.2), other rules of inference are valid in normal modal systems, such as:

$$\frac{A \leftrightarrow A'}{K_{\Xi} A \leftrightarrow K_{\Xi} A'} \tag{6.3}$$

called the *rule of congruence*.[5]

---

[5] There are other valid rules of inference, but for current purposes the ones listed suffice.

There exist a whole range of formulae that are not characterized by all possible frames. Put differently, there are many epistemic axioms that are not valid in all possible frames. These modal axioms may, however, be valid in all frames of a certain subclass of frames.

A nice feature of possible world Kripke-semantics is that many common epistemic axioms correspond to certain algebraic properties of the frame in the following sense: A modal axiom is valid in a frame if and only if the accessibility relation satisfies some algebraic condition. For example, the axiom:

$$K_\Xi A \rightarrow A \tag{6.4}$$

is valid in all frames in which the accessibility relation is *reflexive* in the sense that:

$$\forall w \in W : Rww.$$

Every possible world is accessible from itself. Similarly, if the accessibility relation satisfies the condition that:

$$\forall w, w', w'' \in W : Rww' \wedge Rw'w'' \rightarrow Rww''$$

then the axiom,

$$K_\Xi A \rightarrow K_\Xi K_\Xi A \tag{6.5}$$

is valid in all *transitive* frames. This was denied by counterfactual epistemology but is likely acceptable to contextual epistemology á la Lewis, at least first person.[6] Other axioms require yet other relational properties to be met in order to be valid in all frames.

A nomenclature due to Lemmon (1977) and later extended and refined by Bull and Segerberg (1984) is helpful for cataloguing the axioms typically considered interesting for epistemic logic (Table 6.1).

- Axiom **K**, also called the *axiom of deductive cogency*: If the agent Ξ knows $A \rightarrow A'$, then if Ξ knows A, Ξ also knows A'.
- Axiom **D**, also referred to as the *axiom of consistency*, requires Ξ to have consistency in his knowledge: If an agent knows A, he does not simultaneously know its negation.[7]
- Axiom **T**, also called the *axiom of truth* or *axiom of veridicality*, says that if A is known by Ξ, then A is true.

---

[6] Chapter 8 discusses the KK thesis in more detail.

[7] This axiom also has a deontic motivation in the sense that if an agent is obligated to do whatever A prescribes, he is not at the same time obligated to do $\neg A$.

TABLE 6.1. *Common Epistemic Axioms*

K	$K_\Xi(A \to A') \to (K_\Xi A \to K_\Xi A')$
D	$K_\Xi A \to \neg K_\Xi \neg A$
T	$K_\Xi A \to A$
4	$K_\Xi A \to K_\Xi K_\Xi A$
5	$\neg K_\Xi A \to K_\Xi \neg K_\Xi A$
.2	$\neg K_\Xi \neg K_\Xi A \to K_\Xi \neg K_\Xi \neg A$
.3	$K_\Xi(K_\Xi A \to K_\Xi A') \vee K_\Xi(K_\Xi A' \to K_\Xi A)$
.4	$A \to (\neg K_\Xi \neg K_\Xi A \to K_\Xi A)$

- Axiom 4 is also known as the *axiom of self-awareness, the axiom of positive introspection,* and the *K K thesis.* The basic idea is the same, that an agent has knowledge of his knowledge of A if he has knowledge of A.
- Axiom 5 is also known as the *axiom of wisdom.* Much stronger than axiom 4, it is the thesis that an agent has knowledge of his own ignorance: If Ξ does not know A, he knows that he does not know A. The axiom is sometimes referred to as the *axiom of negative introspection.*
- Axiom .2 reveals that if Ξ does not know that he does not know A, then Ξ knows that he does not know not A.
- Axiom .3 maintains that either Ξ knows that his knowledge of A implies his knowledge of A' or he knows that his knowledge of A' implies his knowledge of A.[8]
- Axiom .4 amounts to the claim that any true proposition *per se* constitutes knowledge. It is sometimes referred to as the *axiom of true (strong) belief.*

These axioms, in proper combinations, make up epistemic modal systems of varying strength depending on the modal formulae valid in the systems given the algebraic properties assumed for the accessibility relation.

The weakest system of epistemic interest is usually considered to be system **T**. The system includes T and K as valid axioms. Additional modal strength may be obtained by extending **T** with other axioms drawn from the above pool and altering the frame semantics to validate the additional axioms. By way of example, while $K_\Xi A \to A$ is valid in **T**, $K_\Xi A \to A$, $K_\Xi A \to K_\Xi K_\Xi A$ and $\neg K_\Xi A \to K_\Xi \neg K_\Xi A$ are all valid in **S5** but not in **T**. System **T** has a reflexive accessibility relation, **S5** has an equivalence

---

[8] Axioms .2 and .3 are perhaps less common than the rest in the list but have nevertheless been entertained recently.

TABLE 6.2. *Relative*
Strength of Epistemic
Systems between **S4** *and* **S5**

KT4	=	S4	
KT4 + .2	=	S4.2	↑
KT4 + .3	=	S4.3	↑
KT4 + .4	=	S4.4	↑
KT5	=	S5	↑

relation of accessibility. Each arrow in Table 6.2 means that the system to which the arrow is pointing is included in the system from which the arrow originates; hence the arrows indicate relative strength. Thus, **S5** is the strongest and **S4** the weakest of the ones listed.

What Hintikka (2003a) recently dubbed first-generation epistemic logic is characterized by the ambition that cataloguing the possible complete systems of such logics would permit choosing the most 'appropriate' or 'intuitive' ones(s).

These 'appropriate' logics often range from **S4** over the intermediate systems **S4.2** to **S4.4** to **S5**. By way of example, Hintikka (1962) settled for **S4**, Kutschera (1976) argued for **S4.4**, while Lenzen (1978, 2003) advocated a system of knowledge at least as strong as **S4.2** and at most as strong **S4.4**. Computer scientists like van der Hoek have proposed to strengthen knowledge to reach the level of system **S4.3** (van der Hoek 1996) and later **S5** (van der Hoek, Ditmarsch, and Kooi 2003) and Fagin, Halpern, Moses and Vardi (1995) assumed knowledge to be **S5** valid. One may at the same time quote Halpern (1995) for the following instructive insight:

> My own feeling is that there is no unique right notion of knowledge; the appropriate notion is application dependent (p. 483).

While the sentiment is certainly to be appreciated, it has recently been argued, as will become apparent, that some systems are more tenable than others both philosophically but likewise for applications.

Reflexivity is the characteristic frame property of system **T**, transitivity is the characteristic frame property of system **S4**, equivalence is the characteristic frame property of **S5**, and so on. From an epistemological point of view, the algebraic properties of the accessibility relation are really forcing conditions (Fig. 6.1).

The cognitive rationale of logical epistemology must be something like this: The more properties the accessibility relation is endowed with, the more access the agent has to his epistemic universe, and in consequence

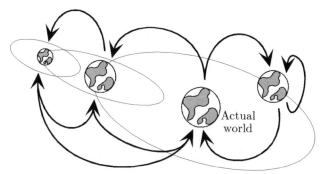

FIGURE 6.1. Logical epistemology requires success in all worlds depending on the algebraic properties of the accessibility relation.

the more epistemic strength he will obtain. Success is required in all possible worlds circumscribed by the accessibility relation entertained, making the notion of reliability in logical epistemology categorical.

Modal epistemic axioms and systems may be viewed as measures of infallibility and replies to skepticism. For instance, knowing your own knowledge is a way of blocking the skeptic, but knowledge of your own ignorance is better still. One motivation for accepting axiom **5** arises in database applications: An agent examining his own knowledge base will be led to conclude that whatever is not in the knowledge base he does not know, and hence he will know that he does not. This idea has close shaves with certainty convergence.

The axiom of wisdom or negative introspection is a sort of closed world assumption. A closed world assumption is a forcing assumption if anything is, 'shutting the world down' with the agent, leaving the skeptic nowhere to go. To know the truth, to know your knowledge and to know your own ignorance, as in **S5**, requires 'full' epistemic access, which is exactly why the accessibility relation must be an equivalence relation. A theorem of **S5** is:

$$\neg A \rightarrow K_\Xi \neg K_\Xi A \qquad (6.6)$$

which states that if A is not the case, then Ξ knows that he does not know A – the 'truly Socratic person', as Girle (2000, p. 157) explains, who knows exactly how ignorant he is.

A bit more ignorance, a bit more skepticism and accordingly a bit more fallibility is allowed in **S4**. Since axiom **5** is dropped and (6.6) is no longer a theorem,

$$\{\neg A, \neg K_\Xi \neg K_\Xi A\} \text{ and } \{\neg K_\Xi A, \neg K_\Xi \neg K_\Xi A\}$$

are not inconsistent in **S4**. It is possible for an agent to be ignorant of the fact that he does not know when actually he does know. Put differently, the agent is allowed false beliefs about what is known.

Yet more ignorance and skepticism are allowed in system **T**, because while,

$$\{ K_\Xi A, \neg K_\Xi K_\Xi A \}$$

is inconsistent in **S4**, this set of epistemic statements is not inconsistent in **T**. The agent may thus know something without knowing that he does. All the same, a restricted kind of positive introspection is still prevalent in system **T**. Given the rule of necessitation (6.2), Ξ knows all the theorems of epistemic logic. By iteration, $K_\Xi K_\Xi A$ is also known. Thus if A is a theorem, Ξ knows that he knows A.

Philosophers have raised the question whether the logic of knowledge makes any epistemological sense. There are at least two ways of answering this question. One is to deny the presupposition that epistemic logic should have broader epistemological pertinence. The discipline is not obligated to hook up with more general epistemological concerns ranging from closure conditions to justification, methodology, reliability and rationality, as Lenzen (1978) argued:

> The search for the correct analysis of knowledge, while certainly of extreme importance and interest to epistemology, seems not significantly to affect the object of epistemic logic, the question of validity of certain epistemic-logical principles. (p. 34)

The other way to answer this charge is to maintain that epistemic logic does carry epistemological significance but in a rather idealized sort of way: One restricts attention to a class of rational agents where rationality is defined by certain postulates. Thus, agents have to satisfy at least some minimal conditions to simply qualify as rational. This is, by and large, what Lemmon (1959) originally suggested. One such condition would be that the assumption that an agent is rational entails that he should know the logical laws. For instance, if the agent knows A and $A \to A'$, he should be able to use modus ponens to infer A'. Now these 'rationality postulates' for knowledge exhibit a striking similarity with the laws of modal and epistemic logic. One may in turn legitimately attempt to interpret the necessity operator in alethic axioms as a knowledge operator and then justify the modal axioms as axioms of knowledge.[9] Although

---

[9] For a more detailed discussion of this approach, see Girle 2000.

Lemmon constructs the rational epistemic agent directly from the axiomatization of the logic, yet another way of justifying the epistemic axioms is by way of meaning: Find a plausible epistemological story to tell about the semantics of epistemic logic.

This line of thought Hintikka pursued from the outset. Hintikka (1962) stipulated that the axioms or principles of epistemic logic are conditions descriptive of a special kind of general (strong) *rationality*. The statements which may be proved false by application of the epistemic axioms are not inconsistent (i.e., their truth is not logically impossible). They are rather rationally 'indefensible'. Indefensibility is fleshed out as the agent's epistemic laziness, sloppiness or perhaps cognitive incapacity to realize the implications of what he in fact knows. Defensibility then means not falling victim of 'epistemic negligence', as Chisholm (1963, 1977) calls it. The notion of indefensibility gives away the status of the epistemic axioms and logics. Some epistemic statement for which its negation is indefensible is called 'self-sustaining'. The notion of self-sustenance actually corresponds to the concept of validity. Corresponding to a self-sustaining statement is a logically valid statement. But this will again be a statement that it is rationally indefensible to deny. So in conclusion, epistemic axioms are descriptions of rationality.

There is an argument to the effect that Hintikka was influenced early on by the autoepistemology of G. E. Moore (1959) and especially Malcolm (1952) and took, at least in part, their autoepistemology to provide a philosophical motivation for epistemic logic. There is an interesting twist to this motivation, which is not readily read out of Moore's autoepistemology. Epistemic principles may be interpreted as principles describing a certain strong rationality. The agent does not have to be aware of this rationality, let alone be able to immediately compute it from the first-person perspective, as Hintikka (1962) argued:

> In order to see this, suppose that a man says to you, 'I know that *p* but I don't know whether *q*' and suppose that *p* can be shown to entail logically *q* by means of some argument which he would be willing to accept. Then you can point out to him that what he says he does not know is already implicit in what he claims he knows. If your argument is valid, it is irrational for our man to persist in saying that he does not know whether *q* is the case. (p. 31)

In Hintikka's logical system, knowledge is closed in the sense of (6.1). The closure is needed for driving the argument through, even if the local agent is not immediately computing it. 'I get by with a little help from my friends' applies here. The man in the local street may turn out to be rational after all when properly advised of directions *actually* available to him, vindicating the first-person interpretation.

There is another argument for closure that Hintikka could make use of. If knowledge is closed in uniform contexts, as Lewisian contextualism has it, then this seems to be exactly what Hintikka could say when presented with the closure challenge and the skeptical invitation. The argument for closure so far rests on autoepistemological and rationality considerations but does not necessarily escape Nozick's argument against closure. Hintikka has all along emphasized the importance of partitioning the set of worlds into the two distinct compartments consisting of the worlds in accordance with the attitude and the ones not. The worlds in accordance with the epistemic attitude may be read in accordance with Lewis's context-sensitive quantifier restriction on knowledge mentioned above. Then, the demon world, the brain-in-a-vat world and other derivatives of global underdetermination are simply excluded from the compatibility partition; these extravagant worlds are not in accordance with the epistemic attitude. Thus, these error possibilities will not disturb the context – in Hintikkian terms, they will not pass over into the compatibility partition – so knowledge is closed for a given compatible partition (i.e., uniform context).[10]

The autoepistemological inspiration is vindicated when Hintikka (1970) argues for the plausibility of the KK thesis as a governing axiom of his logic of knowledge:

This is especially interesting in view of the fact that Malcolm himself uses his strong sense of knowing to explain in what sense it might be true that whenever one knows, one knows that one knows. In this respect, too, Malcolm's strong sense behaves like mine. (p. 154)

Besides the requirement of closure and the validity of the KK thesis, axiom T is also valid, to which neither Moore nor Malcolm would object. A logic of autoepistemology is philosophically congruent with Hintikka's suggestion for a S4 epistemic logic describing strong rationality.

It may be helpful to briefly review the fundamentals of autoepistemology. The common-sense views of Moore upon which autoepistemology is founded deflate the skeptical possibilities of error from various dialectic angles, of which one is particularly pertinent to the current discussion. It is called the argument from *incoherence*. The idea is to demonstrate that skepticism has severe difficulties in formulating its own position

---

[10] This argument is spelled out in greater detail in Hendricks 2004a.

coherently. As with any argument, a skeptical conclusion presupposes knowledge of a set of premises. Moore then points to the fact that merely *asserting* these premises implies at least a doxastic commitment but most likely an epistemic commitment as well. The skeptic cannot retreat to a statement like:

$$\text{There are 9 planets in our solar system but it is not the} \\ \text{case that I believe it.} \qquad (6.7)$$

Statement (6.7) is an instance of what has become known as the *Moore paradox.* Let it be granted that (6.7) only involves an error of omission. All the same, it still sounds self-contradictory when asserted. No formulation of skepticism without incoherence, or in Hintikkian terms, skepticism is an irrational or indefensible epistemological position.

The argument from incoherence is a *first-person perspective* argument. Skepticism is thus rejected along these lines. A first-person perspective is one of the characteristics of autoepistemology. This is also suggested in the label 'autoepistemology' in the Moore paradox: Whatever an agent may know or believe is partly fixed by whether the epistemic or doxastic claim advocated by the agent falls victim to a Moore paradox or not. As long as a thesis concerning epistemic commitments does not result in a Moore paradox, the agent is free to adopt it. As an autoepistemologist, one may, by way of example, say,

$$\text{If I believe that } A, \text{ then I believe that I know that } A \qquad (6.8)$$

which has been called the *Moore principle* and sometimes the *principle of positive certainty.*[11] Formalized, (6.8) amounts to:

$$B_\Xi A \;\rightarrow\; B_\Xi K_\Xi A. \qquad (6.9)$$

According to Moore's theory, there is nothing self-contradictory or incoherent about asserting the principle. No more Moore paradox to the Moore principle than to the widely adopted principle that one knows that one knows if one does, the plausibility of which Malcolm (1952) argues for.

From Moore's first-person autoepistemological perspective, a statement like,

$$A \text{ is the case, but I don't believe } A \qquad (6.10)$$

---

[11] Lamarre and Shoham (1994) explain: 'To the agent, the facts of which he is certain appear to be knowledge' (p. 47).

is a paradoxical Moorean statement. There is, however, nothing paradoxical about,

$$A \text{ is the case, but } \Xi \text{ doesn't believe } A \qquad (6.11)$$

from a third-person perspective. In consequence, what may sound quite implausible from the first-person perspective may sound very plausible from the third-person perspective on inquiry, and vice versa.

The epistemic and doxastic commitments that an agent may hold in the course of inquiry are sensitive to the epistemic environment and what the agent in these local circumstances is both willing and able to defend or maximize. He does not necessarily have an overall skepticism-defeating method at his disposal: The agent is doing the best he can, so is the skeptic, but the skeptic is probably not doing as well as the agent, due to incoherence:

> Whenever knowledge claims are challenged by alleged possibilities of error, the autoepistemological strategy is the attempt to show that, on an individual basis it is not possible to do better than what the agent is in fact doing in the current epistemic environment and that the skeptic is doing at least as bad as the agent but probably even worse.

If autoepistemology may serve as a philosophical basis for at least mono-agent logical epistemology, then it seems that the local epistemic environment suffices for deciding the validity of knowledge claims, after which inquiry should halt. If there is a convergence criterion enforced in epistemic logic described so far, it seems that certainty convergence is a likely candidate, as already observed in connection with the motivation for axiom 5.

Besides Hintikka's partial autoepistemological motivation for epistemic logic, there exists a contemporary 'epistemo-logic' directly inspired by first-person autoepistemology. It is called *autoepistemic logic* and was developed by the computer scientist R. C. Moore (1982, 1985).

To fix the historical setting for the development of autoepistemic logic, it should be observed that Tweety was a fairly popular bird in artificial intelligence and knowledge representation in the 1980s. On the assumption that one knows that Tweety is a bird, one is inclined to say that Tweety flies, because birds usually do, unless some extraordinary circumstances have arisen or possibly will arise. If the agent later learns that Tweety is a penguin or an ostrich, the agent will retract the default assumption that Tweety flies. In general, from a set of axioms or statements Δ, one is able to derive some theorem A, but the same theorem is not possible to derive from a set Δ' where $\Delta' > \Delta$. The set of theorems does not *monotonically* increase with the set of axioms. To handle *nonmonotonicity*, one may try to restrict the application of the axioms in inferences such that A is a theorem if $B_1, B_2, \ldots, B_n$ are not. Thus, the default rule that birds can fly is handled by a rule saying that for a given ξ, 'ξ can fly' is a theorem if 'ξ is a bird' and 'ξ cannot fly' are not.

One approach suggested along these default lines is the default reasoning discussed by Reiter (1980). Default reasoning, or reasoning on *prima facie* assumptions, is based on the principle of drawing plausible conclusions on less than conclusive evidence and in absence of information to the contrary. Thus, if one knows that Tweety is a bird, then this suffices for concluding that Tweety can fly, although the inference falls short of being conclusive. In absence of information to the contrary, one is willing to draw the conclusion, albeit provisionally. The nonmonotonicity is given by the defeasibility of the conclusion if additional information suggesting otherwise is at some point added.

According to McDermott and Doyle (1980), nonmonotonicity is given in a different way. 'Most birds can fly' should be understood as 'For all ξ, if ξ is a bird and it is *consistent* that ξ can fly, then ξ can fly'. The consistency clause is represented as an operator M, and hence it is essentially an inference rule for M that one is after. The concept of consistency entertained suggests that it is consistent to claim A if $\neg A$ is not possible to derive. 'Most birds can fly' is by this consistency condition taken to mean that the only birds that cannot fly are the birds that one can derive cannot fly.

Suppose that one has a theory that has only the axiom just mentioned together with a statement saying that Tweety is a bird. The conclusion that Tweety can fly is a valid inference, or rather, if it is true that Tweety is a bird, and it is true that the only birds that one can derive not to fly actually cannot fly, and one cannot derive that Tweety cannot fly, then it must be true that Tweety can fly.

R. C. Moore points out that this line of reasoning is not default reasoning but rather reasoning about, or introspection of, one's own current knowledge and belief – *autoepistemologically*. In autoepistemic logic, the nonmonotonicity is not given by default and defeasibility. If one is certain that one knows all the instances of birds that cannot fly, then one cannot consistently hold this belief and at the same time accept new instances of birds not being able to fly. The nonmonotonicity is a consequence of the context sensitivity of the autoepistemic claim such that the meaning of the claim is sensitive to the theory in which it figures. Just think of adding an axiom saying that Tweety cannot fly to the example above. Then the consistency operator becomes relative to this new set, and one should not expect to derive the theorem that Tweety can fly.

McDermott and Doyle's nonmonotonic logic suffers from various deficiencies, one of them being that the consistency operator is way too weak. MA is not inconsistent with $\neg A$, which obviously implies that a theory very well may claim simultaneously that A is consistent with the theory yet false. Moore's autoepistemic logic is partly a reconstruction of McDermott and Doyle's proposal that escapes this problem. The idea is to take the autoepistemological part seriously and hence attempt to model the beliefs of what a thoroughly rational introspective agent is willing and able to believe given his current knowledge.

The autoepistemic language is a standard propositional logic augmented with an autoepistemic operator L, read 'it is assumed that...'. Autoepistemic models and interpretations of an autoepistemic theory Δ are simply propositional models and interpretations adapted to the meaning of the operator L. To see this autoepistemic idea in action, suppose an agent is sunk into an epistemic environment characterized by the autoepistemic theory Δ. The environment will provide ascriptions of truth-values to the propositional constants in Δ, and a formula of the form LA will be true relative to the agent if the agent assumes A. Thus, the agent and the environment in which he is sunk directly determine an autoepistemic interpretation of Δ, and this interpretation will again be the autoepistemic model of Δ if all the agent's beliefs are true in this environment.

While the semantics are fairly straightforward, the real autoepistemic characteristic of autoepistemic logic presents itself once one tries to formulate a concept of autoepistemic derivability. This is, of course, a special case of defining nonmonotonic derivability, which in general has turned out to be a fairly sticky problem, as noted by Stalnaker (1996b) Obviously but unfortunately, nonmonotonic rules of inference do not furnish a simple iterative concept of derivability.

Lacking such an iterative structure, Moore applies *fix-point* definitions, which are not algorithms listing the derivable formulas but nevertheless define sets of formulas respecting the 'intentions' of the nonmonotonic rules of inference. The fix-points are given in terms of closure conditions for a rational agent over the autoepistemic theory Δ:

1. If $A_1, A_2, \ldots, A_n \in \Delta$ and $A_1, A_2, \ldots, A_n \vdash B$, then $B \in \Delta$.
2. If $A \in \Delta$, then $LA \in \Delta$.
3. If $A \notin \Delta$, then $\neg LA \in \Delta$.

Theories satisfying these conditions are called autoepistemically *stable*, since apparently no other conclusions would be drawn by a rational agent at any such level. Additionally, a stable autoepistemic theory is *consistent* iff,

4. If $LA \in \Delta$, then $A \in \Delta$.
5. If $\neg LA \in \Delta$, then $A \notin \Delta$.

Condition 4 holds, since if $LA \in \Delta$ but $A \notin \Delta$, then, by condition 3, $\neg LA \in \Delta$, rendering Δ inconsistent. Obviously, condition 5 holds for a similar reason, since if $\neg LA, A \in \Delta$, then $LA \in \Delta$ by condition 2, also rendering Δ inconsistent.

It turns out that the property of stability is equivalent to the property of semantical completeness. Stability, however, provides no guidelines as to what the agent should not believe. For all that has been said, the agent may choose to hold beliefs that are not *grounded* in the epistemic premises, say, U, of an inference. Thus, the stability of the agent's beliefs guarantees that they are complete but does not guarantee that they are *sound* given U. To ensure grounding, it is necessary to fix a rule specifying that the only beliefs the agent will adopt are the ones expressed in U together with the ones prescribed by the stability conditions. In order to satisfy the stability conditions and include U, the autoepistemic theory Δ must include all the tautological consequences of

$$U \cup \{LA \mid A \in \Delta\} \cup \{\neg LA \mid A \notin \Delta\}. \tag{6.12}$$

In other words, Δ is a *stable expansion* of U if and only if Δ is the set of all the tautological consequences of (6.12). Based on the idea of stable expansions, Arló-Costa (1998) has proved a characterization result to the effect that the set of theorems of an autoepistemic logic is axiomatized by **S5**.

Moore's principle (6.8) is a kind of introspection axiom for rational belief or *subjective certainty*. In a combined epistemic and doxastic logical system in which knowledge and belief are approximately equally strong (save for a truth-condition), the agent will (while subjectively reflecting upon his own state of mind with respect to what he believes) be led to believe that he knows the proposition in question if he certainly believes it. Some contemporary logical epistemologists embrace Moore's principle (e.g., Halpern 1995). Early logical epistemologists are more reluctant because they take belief to be fairly weak. As Lenzen (1978) notes,

Remember that the operator B of 'weak' belief covers in particular such presumptions as are expressed by 'a believes (presumes) that Holland will win the next world championship in football'. It ought to be evident that, unless a is a prophet, he does not believe that he knows Holland will win the next championship in football. (p. 80)

Hintikka (1962) likewise dismisses Moore's principle:

Hence . . . and (C.BK) [Moore's principle] are acceptable only when an unrealistically high standard of defensibility is imposed on one's beliefs. The conditions would make it (logically) indefensible to suppose that anyone would have given up any of his present beliefs if he had more information than he now has. And this is clearly too stringent a requirement. (p. 52)

To both Lenzen and Hintikka, belief is a significantly weaker commitment than knowledge. For good reason too: Consider a combined epistemic and doxastic logic in which belief is understood as subjective certainty such that (6.9) holds. Assume also that positive introspection

$$B_\Xi A \;\to\; K_\Xi B_\Xi A \qquad\qquad (6.13)$$

holds for belief, together with negative doxastic introspection,

$$\neg B_\Xi A \;\to\; K_\Xi \neg B_\Xi A. \qquad\qquad (6.14)$$

Even subjective certainty, as strong as it may seem in this system, implies a margin of error: The fact that Ξ is subjectively certain of A does not necessarily imply that A is true. Accordingly, axiom **T** will be dropped for subjective certainty and replaced by the consistency axiom **D**:

$$B_\Xi A \;\to\; \neg B_\Xi \neg A. \qquad\qquad (6.15)$$

On the standard definition of knowledge, knowledge implies belief,

$$K_\Xi A \;\to\; B_\Xi A \qquad\qquad (6.16)$$

which is also an uncontroversially accepted assumption for knowledge and subjective certainty. The logic of subjective certainty is **KD45**. Knowledge will obviously have to be stronger than subjective certainty, so it must validate **S5**. On assumptions (6.9) and (6.13)–(6.16), Lenzen (1978) was able to show that $B_\Xi A$ in the end is equivalent to $K_\Xi A$. So knowledge and belief collapse into each other![12]

Many contemporary epistemic logics do nevertheless consider strong belief, rational belief or subjective certainty to be approximately as strong as knowledge. Assuming belief is taken to be approximately as strong as **S5** knowledge, the equivalence relation over worlds implies some attractive

---

[12] This issue is discussed in Stalnaker 1996a.

formal features, like readily epistemic and doxastic partitions. This does not by itself make up for the result that the logic of knowledge and belief coincide.

The plausibility of the epistemic axioms has occasioned quite stormy debates in the logico-epistemological literature. Axiom K has been under attack, many have found axiom 4 implausible, as Nozick did (see Chapter 4), and so forth. In the eye of the tornado has been axiom 5. A few objections to this axiom will be briefly reviewed.

Hintikka denies its plausibility, as does Lenzen (1978), essentially because introspection alone should not license agents to ascertain whether some proposition in question is known. Under special circumstances, axiom 5 suggests that agents can even decide intractable problems (see Binmore and Shin 1992) and Shin and Williamson (1994). Williamson has launched two objections to models of knowledge and belief validating axiom 5. For S5 knowledge, Williamson disagrees with those who interpret knowledge in a database-like fashion to justify the closed world assumption of axiom 5. Even under the closed world assumption, it does not follow in general that an agent can 'survey the totality of its knowledge'.[13] Second, Williamson recently noted that the result to the effect that knowledge and belief collapse under the strong understanding of belief in a combined system points to the untenability of axiom 5, not to the unacceptable nature of subjective certainty *per se*. Moore's principle is not too extravagant an assumption for rational belief, neither are axioms (6.13), D and (6.16), nor axioms T and 4 for knowledge. That leaves axiom 5 as the culprit responsible for collapsing the two notions, and besides it entails the infallibility of the agent's beliefs: Whatever Ξ believes is true. On these grounds, Williamson (2001) abandons axiom 5 rather than any of the other principles used in the derivation. Voorbraak (1991) makes the unusual move of sacrificing (6.16), thus challenging the intuitions of philosophers since antiquity. That knowledge does not necessarily imply belief is an idea that Lewis was sympathetic with (see Chapter 5).

If S5 assumptions about knowledge and belief are dropped, ideal rationality descriptions and autoepistemological considerations may supply a philosophical foundation and motivation for logical epistemology.[14] The

---

[13] See Williamson 2000, 317.

[14] If G. E. Moore's intuitions can be captured via what is encoded by the stable expansions in autoepistemic logic, then one is inclined to believe that he is committed to axiom 5. For a thorough discussion of autoepistemology and autoepistemic logic, see Arló-Costa 1998.

treatment of logical epistemology as a branch of modal logic is still quite costly, and also for less ambitious logics than **S5**. A further objection to the modal approach to the logic of knowledge is that, even without **S5** stipulations, implausible and unrealistic assumptions about the reasoning powers of agents still prevail. The explanation for this is related to the, by now, notorious principles of closure. The principle of closure axiom **K** (6.1) can under the certain circumstances be generalized to a stronger principle of closure regarding an agent's knowledge, a principle considered still more unacceptable than (6.1) itself. The principle of *logical omniscience* is as follows:

> *Whenever an agent Ξ knows all of the formulae in a set Γ, and A follows logically from Γ, then Ξ also knows A.*

In particular, Ξ knows all theorems (letting $\Gamma = \varnothing$), and he knows all logical consequences of a formula that he knows (letting Γ consist of a single formula). Logical omniscience, incorporates some generally weaker forms of omniscience, such as knowledge of valid formulae: Agent Ξ knows all logical truths (given rule [6.2]); closure under logical equivalence: If agent Ξ knows A and if A and A' are logically equivalent (i.e., $A \leftrightarrow A'$ is valid), then agent Ξ knows A' (given the rule of congruence [6.3]), and so forth.

There are various ways of dealing with logical omniscience. One is to avoid omniscience technically, another is to attempt to make epistemological or cognitive sense of the property. Computer scientists, especially, have opted for the latter, proposing that what is being modelled in epistemic logic is not knowledge *simpliciter* but a related yet different concept. Proposals include reading the basic epistemic operator $K_\Xi A$ as 'Agent Ξ knows implicitly A' (Levesque 1984; Fagin and Halpern 1988), '*A* follows from Ξ's knowledge' (Fagin et al. 1995), 'Agent Ξ carries the information A' (Barwise 1989) or '*A* is agent Ξ's possible knowledge' (Huang and Kwast 1991). Propositional attitudes like these should replace the usual 'Agent Ξ knows A'. Although they differ, the locutions all suggest modeling *implicit knowledge* or what is implicitly represented in an agent's information state (i.e., what logically follows from his actual knowledge).

Furnished with this new interpretation, the epistemic operator really describes cognitive dispositions that potentially could be realized by

On the other hand, Moore may also be disinclined to advocate the axiom of negative introspection, either because it could amount to a Moorean sentence or because it demands too much rationality on the part of the singular agent – there is a difference between doing the best you can and outdoing yourself.

reflecting upon one's current information state. The concept of implicit knowledge is totally detached from a particular agent's actual cognitive capabilities. The agent neither has to compute knowledge, nor can he be held responsible for answering queries based on his knowledge, under the implicit understanding of knowledge. A distinction must accordingly be enforced between what the agent actually knows (his *explicit* knowledge) and his *implicit* knowledge, in the sense just described.

Logical omniscience and its various derivatives no longer present problems under the implicit interpretation of the epistemic operator. Logical omniscience is an epistemological condition for implicit knowledge, but the actual agent may nevertheless explicitly fail to realize this condition. While the axioms and inference rules of epistemic logic may seem unreasonable for the explicit view, they may be acceptable for the implicit view of knowledge.

Technical solutions to logical omniscience are facilitated on the syntactical or semantical level. On the syntactical level, Hintikka (1989) recently suggested placing on deductive arguments suitable syntactical constraints that preserve knowledge.

Interesting philosophical solutions are to be found on the semantical level. The idea here is to introduce some semantical entities that explain why the agent could be accused of logical omniscience but, at the end of the day, is not guilty of it. These entities are called 'impossible possible worlds' by Hintikka (1975). Similar entities, called 'seemingly possible worlds' and represented by urn-models, are introduced by Rantala (1975). Allowing impossible possible worlds in which the semantic valuation of the formulas in a certain sense is arbitrary provides the necessary means for dodging logical omniscience: The logical laws do not pass muster in the impossible possible worlds. When knowledge is evaluated with respect to all possible worlds but the logical laws do not hold in some of them, logical omniscience is simply out. In an impossible possible world, a tautology $A \rightarrow A$ may, as odd as it admittedly sounds, be false. Now, the agent Ξ may all the same view that very world as a possibility, so universally $K_\Xi(A \rightarrow A)$ fails. In consequence, the rule of necessitation (6.2) is invalid in impossible possible world models. Axiom K is the victim of failure as well. Further, both A and $A \rightarrow A'$ may be true and A' simultaneously false.[15] From a strictly logical point of view, the epistemic logics specified by impossible worlds models are not very exciting. No real epistemic statement is valid in a universal way. The validity of

---

[15] The failure of axiom K would satisfy Nozick although he probably would consider impossible possible worlds as weird as demon worlds if not weirder.

the various epistemic principles may, however, be obtained by imposing suitable constraints on these models.

From a forcing perspective, the introduction of impossible possible worlds is a rather curious strategy. The idea is first to inflate the local circumstances of the agent, in the sense that the agent may regard some models of the (real) world as possible, then afterwards deflate the local situation because of the limited reasoning capacities of the agent. The worlds in question are really logically impossible. For example, a logical contradiction cannot be true. An agent may nevertheless not have enough resources to determine the truth-value of that contradiction and simply assume it to be true. He will consider some worlds possible, although logically they are impossible. To avoid logical omniscience, more worlds can be let in, worlds worse than the demon worlds, since the latter are at least logically possible whereas the impossible possible worlds are not.

The debate over whether epistemic logical principles are plausibly describing agenthood or not seems to depend largely on whether one subscribes to a first- or third-person perspective on inquiry. Given an autoepistemological inspiration, epistemic axioms describe a first-person knowledge operator, as Hintikka suggested. If epistemic axioms describe implicit knowledge, as Fagin et al. suggest, then what is being modeled is what follows from actual knowledge independently of agent computations. On the basis of this third-person perspective, agents cannot be held responsible for failing to exercise some reflective disposition. Logical omniscience is a problem from a first-person perspective but not necessarily from a third-person perspective in logical epistemology. Closure principles may be problematic from the point of view of the agent but not necessarily from the point of view of the ones studying the agent. This allows for *very* strong third-person logics, in contrast to both counterfactual epistemology and contextualism.

The same goes for assuming **S5** for knowledge in monoagent systems. It may seem unrealistically strong for a singular agent in his environment, unless his environment is defined solipsistically (e.g., using the closed world assumption). Solipsism is not necessarily a human or a real agent condition but a philosophical thesis – a thesis making idealized sense of standing outside looking at the agent in his, admittedly, rather limited epistemic environment. Stone-hearted solipsism on a first-person basis is hard to maintain coherently, as indicated by this anecdote:

Bertrand Russell was giving a lesson on solipsism to a lay audience, and a woman got up and said she was delighted to hear Bertrand Russell say he was a solipsist; she was one too, and she wished there were more of us. (Thorpe 1983, 224)

A reason for adopting the third-person perspective and paying homage
to **S5** for singular agents is that these assumptions provide some nice
technical advantages or properties. There is now also a philosophical
basis for doing things in this idealized way – epistemic solipsism and no
false beliefs (e.g., infallibilism). Both of these philosophical theses have
little to do with logic but plenty to do with the preconditions for studying
knowledge from any point of view.

The upshot of this discussion is that the distinction between first- and
third-person perspectives is just as important in a formal epistemology
like epistemic logic as it is in mainstream epistemology. For example, criticizing epistemic logic for implying logical omniscience may be a matter
of apples and oranges if the first-person–third-person dichotomy is not
observed.

Besides the interpretational difference, another important difference
between alethic logic and epistemic logic is the addition of the agent Ξ
to the syntax. The interesting epistemological question is what roles are
assigned the agents in first-generation epistemic logic. The agents are the
ones who apparently have knowledge – knowledge that is, say, **S4.3** valid.
That agents have such knowledge is also the natural understanding of
the symbolic notation $K_\Xi A$:

Epistemic logic begins as a study of the logical behavior of the expression of the
form 'b knows that.' One of the main aims of this study is to be able to analyze
other constructions in terms of 'knows' by means of 'b knows that.' The basic
notation will be expressed in the notation used here by 'K_b.' This symbolization
is slightly misleading in that in a formula of the form $K_b S$ the term b for the agent
(knower) is intended to be outside the scope of K, not inside as our notation
might suggest. (Hintikka and Halonen 1998, 2)

There is only one role left to agents in the first-generation epistemic logic.
They serve as indices on the accessibility relation between possible worlds.
Epistemic-logical principles or axioms building up modal systems are
relative to an agent who may or may not validate these principles. Indices
on accessibility relations will not suffice for epistemological and cognitive
pertinence simply because there is nothing particularly epistemic about
being indices. The agents are *inactive* in first-generation epistemic logic
(Fig. 6.2).[16]

If epistemic logics are not to be pertinent to the knower, who are they
to be pertinent to? An agent may have knowledge that is **S4.3** valid. What

---

[16] Active and inactive agenthood was first discussed in 'Active Agents' (Hendricks 2002),
and the current discussion follows the same lines. Reference to the agent is sometimes
dropped in the formalism of epistemic logic such that $K_\Xi A$ becomes KA (read 'It is

FIGURE 6.2. An inactive agent.

bakes the epistemological noodle, however, is *how* the agent has to *behave* in order to gain the epistemic strength that he has. We need to activate the agents in order to make epistemic logic pertinent to epistemology, computer science, artificial intelligence and cognitive psychology. The original symbolic notation for a knowing agent also suggests this: An agent should be inside the scope of the knowledge operator, not outside. Inquiring agents are agents who read data, change their minds, interact or have common knowledge, act according to strategies and play games, have memory and act upon it, follow various methodological rules, expand, contract or revise their knowledge bases, and so on, all in the pursuit of knowledge. Inquiring agents are *active agents* (Fig. 6.3).

This is an interpretation of one of the characteristic features, and great virtues, of what Hintikka (2003a) calls the 'second-generation epistemic logic': The realization that the agents of epistemic logic should play an active role in the knowledge acquisition, validation and maintenance processes. Hintikka (1999a, 2003a) observes this obligation by emphasizing the strategies for his new application of epistemic logic as a logic of questions and answers and the search for the best questions to ask. In this new setting, logical epistemology augmented with an independence-friendly logic constitutes the basis for an interrogative theory of inquiry.[17]

known that A') exactly because of the inactive nature of first-generation agents. See, for instance, Hintikka 2003.

[17] Independence-friendly logic (or IF-logic) is a first-order logic augmented with an independence operator '/'. The slash notation for a quantified statement of the form $Q_2 y / Q_1 x$ expresses the independence of the two quantifiers. This independence may be captured by game-theoretical semantics as informational independence in the sense that the move performed or mandated by $Q_2 y$ is independent of the move performed by $Q_1 x$. Introducing the independence operator then allows for the unequivocal formulation of a range of questions and answers without scope ambiguity, cross-world identity problems, and so on.

FIGURE 6.3. An active agent.

Answers to questions are in essence requests for knowledge, information or epistemic imperatives (Hintikka 2003a, 2003b):

> Another main requirement that can be addressed to the interrogative approach – and indeed to the theory of any goal-directed activity – is that it must do justice to the strategic aspects of inquiry. This requirement can be handled most naturally by doing what Plato already did to the Socratic *elenchus* and by construing knowledge-seeking by questioning as a game that pits the questioner against the answerer. Then the study of those strategies of knowledge acquisition becomes another application of the mathematical theory of games. (Hintikka 2003b, 10–11)

Game theory is about strategies for winning games – and it is an agent who may or may not have a winning strategy vis-à-vis other agents. Van Benthem, Fagin, Halpern, Moses and Vardi, Aumann, Stalnaker and others studying game theory have demonstrated how logical epistemology uncovers important features of *agent rationality*. They also show how game theory adds to the general understanding of notions like knowledge, belief and belief revision.[18] Belief revision theorists like Rott model 'informational economy' or 'conservatism' and consider cognitive economics and the problem of rational choice for *agents* (Rott 2003). Baltag, Moss and Solecki (1999) combine epistemic logic with belief revision theory to study actions and belief updates in games.[19] Another way of adding an active perspective to epistemic logic is pursued in nonmonotonic logic, starting notably with Reiter's default logic and R. C. Moore's autoepistemic logic.

---

[18] Van Benthem (2000a) has also pointed out that there is an epistemic logic hidden in game theory.
[19] The work of Baltag, Solecki and Moss was somewhat preceded by the work of Plaza (1989).

The idea of combining the static first-generation epistemic logic with the dynamics of belief revision theory dates back to the mid-1990s. Alchourrón, Gärdenfors and Makinson's seminal belief revision theory (AGM) from the 1980s is a theory about the rational change of beliefs (expansion, contraction or revision) in the light of new (possibly conflicting) evidence (Alchourrón, Gärdenfors and Makinson 1985; Gärdenfors 1988). In 1994, de Rijke showed that the AGM axioms governing expansion and revision may be translated into the object language of dynamic modal logic. Segerberg, about the same time, demonstrated how the entire theory of belief revision could be formulated in a modal logic.

A bit before but especially around the turn of the millennium, Segerberg (1995) merged static first-generation doxastic logic with the dynamics of belief change into 'dynamic doxastic logic'. Doxastic operators in the logic of belief like $B_\Xi A$ may be captured by AGM. For example, 'A is in Ξ's belief-set T' (or $\neg B_\Xi \neg A$) becomes '$\neg A$ is not in Ξ's belief-set T,' similarly for other combinations of the belief operator with negation. An immediate difference between the two paradigms is that, while AGM can express dynamic operations on belief sets like expansion ('A is in Ξ's belief-set T expanded by D' $[A \in T + D]$), revision ('A is in Ξ's belief-set T revised by D' $[A \in T * D]$), and contraction ('A is in Ξ's belief-set T contracted by D' $[A \in T - D]$), no such dynamics are immediately expressible in the standard language of doxastic logic. On the other hand, action languages include operators like $[\nu]$ and $\langle\nu\rangle$, which prefixed to a well-formed formula A, $[\nu] A$ and $\langle\nu\rangle A$, respectively, on Segerberg's interpretation mean that 'after $[every]$ $\langle some\rangle$ way of performing action ν it is the case that A'. By introducing three new operators $[+]$, $[*]$, and $[-]$ into the doxastic language, the three dynamic operations on belief sets may be rendered as $[+D] B_\Xi A$, $[*D] B_\Xi A$ and $[-D] B_\Xi A$.

After revising the original belief revision theory so that changes of beliefs happen in 'hypertheories' or concentric spheres enumerated according to entrenchment, Segerberg (1999a, 1999b) provided several axiomatizations of the dynamic doxastic logic, together with soundness and completeness results. The dynamic doxastic logic paradigm may also be extended to iterated belief revision[20] (Lindström and Rabinowicz 1997) and may accommodate various forms of agent introspection (Lindström and Rabinowicz 1999).

---

[20] A change in beliefs may either occur once in which case it is a one-shot revision or multiple changes may successively occur in which case it is an iterated revision.

A related approach, devised notably by van der Hoek, Linder and Meyer at approximately the same time as dynamic doxastic logic, establishes a new way of distinguishing knowledge from belief (van der Hoek and Meyer 1995). Actions are responsible for bringing about changes of belief. The distinction between knowledge and belief is not just a matter of paying homage to axiom T or not but involves the dynamic property of defeasibility. Knowledge is indefeasible under the belief-changing operations of expansion, contraction and revision, belief is not. Van Ditmarsch, van der Hoek and Kooi's new 'dynamic epistemic logic' is partly a continuation of this approach that studies how information changes and how actions with epistemic impact on agents may be modeled (van Ditmarsch, van der Hoek and Kooi 2004; van der Hoek et al. 2003).

Attention has so far been restricted to monoagent systems. The logics of knowledge have been developed with a single agent as the object. To get a better feel for the new dynamics and possibilities of modern epistemic logics, the monoagent setup will be expanded to a multiagent setup.

Syntactically, the idea is to augment the language of propositional logic with n knowledge operators, one for each agent involved in the group of agents under consideration. The primary difference between the semantics for a monoagent and a multiagent setup is roughly that, for the latter, n accessibility relations are introduced. A modal system for n agents is obtained by joining together n modal logics where for simplicity it may be assumed that the agents are homogenous in the sense that they may all be described by the same logical system. An epistemic logic for n agents consists of n copies of a certain modal logic. In such an extended epistemic logic, it is possible to express that some agent in the group knows a certain fact, that an agent knows that another agent knows a fact, and so on. It is possible to develop the logic even further: Not only may one agent know that another agent knows a fact, but all agents may know this fact simultaneously. From here it is possible to express that everyone knows that everyone knows that everyone knows, that...That is *common knowledge*.[21]

---

[21] In multiagent systems, implicit knowledge seems to create conceptual problems with respect to common knowledge. If what is being modeled by logical epistemology is the implicit knowledge of the agents, how can this knowledge, and knowledge about the other agents, be common explicit knowledge for the group of agents: Whatever the singular agent knows about himself and others is not necessarily explicit to him. Common knowledge would have to be explicit; otherwise it would seem that the agents base their actions on information they do not really, or at least readily, have available. You have got to be readily informed to make a move.

A convention would hardly be looked upon as a convention if not for common knowledge among the agents regarding its observation, as Lewis noted (see Chapter 5). Other norms, social and linguistic practices, agent interactions and games presuppose a concept of common knowledge. A relatively simple way of defining common knowledge is not to partition the group of agents into subsets with different common 'knowledges' but only to define common knowledge for the entire group of agents. Once multiple agents have been added to the syntax, the language is augmented with an additional operator C. CA is then interpreted as 'It is common knowledge among the agents that A'. Well-formed formulas follow the standard recursive recipe, with a few, obvious modifications taking into account the multiple agents. An auxiliary operator E is also introduced such that EA means 'Everyone knows that A'. EA is defined as the conjunction $K_1 A \wedge K_2 A \wedge \ldots \wedge K_n A$.

To semantically interpret n knowledge operators, binary accessibility relations R_n are defined over the set of possible worlds W. A special accessibility relation, R°, is introduced to interpret the operator of common knowledge. The relation must be flexible enough to express the relationship between individual and common knowledge. The idea is to let the accessibility relation for C be the transitive closure of the union of the accessibility relations corresponding to the singular knowledge operators. The model $\mathbb{M}$ for an epistemic system with n agents, and common knowledge is accordingly a structure $\mathbb{M} = \langle W, R_1, R_2, \ldots, R_n, R^\circ, \varphi \rangle$ where W is a nonempty space of possible worlds, $R_1, R_2, \ldots, R_n, R^\circ$ are accessibility relations over W for which $R^\circ = (R_1 \cup R_2 \cup \ldots \cup R_n)^\circ$, and φ again is the denotation function assigning worlds to the atomic propositional formula $\varphi : atom \longrightarrow P(W)$. The semantics for the Boolean connectives remain intact. The formula $K_i A$ is true in a world w, that is, $\mathbb{M}, w \models K_i A$ for agent i, iff $\forall w' \in W$: if $R_i ww'$, then $\mathbb{M}, w' \models A$. The formula CA is true in a world w, that is, $\mathbb{M}, w \models CA$, iff $R^\circ ww'$ implies $\mathbb{M}, w' \models A$. Varying the properties of the accessibility relations $R_1, R_2, \ldots, R_n$ as described above results in different epistemic logics. For instance, system **K** with common knowledge is determined by all frames, while system **S4** with common knowledge is determined by all reflexive and transitive frames. Similar results can be obtained for the remaining epistemic logics (Fagin et al. 1995).

A dynamic embodiment of multiagent *systems* is to be found in Fagin et al. (1995). In such a multiagent system, each individual agent is considered to be in some *local state*. This local state holds all the information available to the individual agent 'now'. The whole system, as the sum of the local agents, is in some *global state*. A system like this is a dynamic entity given the global state of the system and local states of the involved agents at any particular time. The dynamics may be modeled by defining what is referred to as a *run* over the system, which really is a function from time to global states. In consequence, the run may be construed as an account of the behavior of the system for possible executions. This gives rise to *points*, which are pairs of runs and times. For every time, the system is in some global state as a function of the particular time. The system may be thought of as series of runs rather than agents. What is being modeled here are the possible behaviors of the system over a collection of executions.

A system like the one just described defines a Kripke-structure with an equivalence relation over points. The accessibility relation is specified with respect to possible points such that some point w' is accessible from the current point w if the agent is in the same local state at w and w'. Knowledge is defined with respect to the agents' local states. The truth of a formula is given with respect to a point. If the truth is relative to a point, then there is a question of *when*, which opens up for the introduction of *temporal operators*. One may, for instance, define a universal future-tense operator ('$\Box$' in their notation) such that a formula is true relative to the current point and all later points.[22] The mixture of epistemic and temporal operators can handle claims about the temporal development of knowledge in the system. A multimodal axiom considered in Fagin et al. (1995) reads as follows:

$$K_\Xi A \rightarrow \Box K_\Xi A. \tag{6.17}$$

The axiom says that if an agent Ξ knows A at some particular point, then he will know A at all points in the future. The combined axiom holds under special circumstances.

In multiagent systems like the one just described, it is possible to endow the agents with *epistemic capacities* facilitating special epistemic behaviors. Fagin et al. 1995, have considered 'perfect recall': Interacting agents' knowledge in the dynamic system may increase as time goes by, but the agents may still store old information. An agent's current local state is an encoding of all events that have happened so far in the run. Perfect recall is in turn a methodological recommendation telling the agent to remember his earlier epistemic states.

---

[22] Other temporal operators may be defined as well; see Fagin et al. 1995.

There are other interesting structural properties of agents being studied in the literature on dynamic epistemic logics. In an epistemic logic suited for modeling various games of imperfect information, van Benthem (2000a) refers to such properties as 'styles of playing'. Properties like 'bounded memory', various 'mechanisms for information updates' and 'uniform strategies' have been analyzed by van Benthem (2001);[23] perfect recall and 'no learning' have been studied by van der Hoek et al. (2003) as they relate to the change of knowledge given the execution of certain plans. These and other properties of the agents make them active agents.

The modeling 'record' of second-generation logical epistemology is impressive: multiple epistemic operators, multiple doxastic operators, common knowledge operators, temporal operators, monomodal systems, multimodal systems, dynamic modal systems, epistemic capacities of active agents, and this is not an exhaustive list. There is a vast range of interesting applications and modeling using these advanced epistemic logics. Examples include robots on assembly lines, social and coalitional interactions in 'social software', card games, 'live' situations in economics, miscellaneous linguistic practices, and so on.[24]

The impressive expressiveness of the new epistemic logics reinvites some philosophically problematic issues, notably the **S5** stipulation. It is tricky to argue that it is reasonable to assume **S5** in multiagent setups. But when game theorists, for instance, model noncooperative extensive games of perfect information, an **S5** logic of knowledge is used to establish the backward induction equilibrium (Bicchieri 2003).

For game theory, the untenability of **S5** in multiagent systems is quite severe. The problem concerns the knowledge of action, as Stalnaker has pointed out:[25] It should be possible for a player Ξ to know what a player Θ is going to do. For instance, it should be rendered possible that, in a case where Θ only has one rational choice and Ξ knows Θ to be rational, Ξ can predict what Θ is going to do. This should not imply, however, that it is impossible for Θ to act differently, as he has the capacity to act irrationally. To make sense of this situation, what is needed is a counterfactually

---

[23] For an excellent survey of the logic in games, see van Benthem's (2000b) recent lecture notes.

[24] 'Social software' is a new term coined by Parikh to denote the use of methods from epistemic logic, game theory, belief revision and decision theory to study social phenomena. For more information, see Hendricks et al. 2005a.

[25] This problem was touched upon by Stalnaker (1999a), and I am indebted to him for explaining it to me in detail during a conversation.

possible world such that Θ acts irrationally, but is incompatible with what Ξ knows. Now Ξ's prior beliefs in that counterfactual world must be the same as they are in the actual world, for Θ could not influence Ξ's priors beliefs by making a contrary choice (by definition of the game, Ξ and Θ act independently). Thus it has to be the case in the counterfactual world that Ξ believes he knows something (e.g., that Θ is irrational) that he in fact does not know. This is incompatible with **S5**.

This discussion of the untenability of **S5** is not in any way linked to a view of inappropriateness of modeling a (third-person notion of) knowledge via the axiom of veridicality.[26] One may reasonably argue like Stalnaker and Aumann that knowledge requires truth, referring to a notion of third-person knowledge. The unintuitive results obtained by Aumann and others indicate that there is something wrong in the information model used by economists, which assumes that agents engaged in economic interactions actually have common knowledge rather than common belief. For example, one can infer the impossibility of trade from the assumption that the agents engaged in economic interaction have greater powers than they actually have. Once one endows agents with more realistic epistemic powers, they then are able to agree to disagree, and trade is made possible again. Collins's explanation of what is wrong in Aumann's models is quite plausible. If agents have common belief rather than common knowledge, then they cannot share a common prior, a crucial probabilistic assumption in Aumann's seminal paper 'Agreeing to Disagree' (1976). An intuitive explanation is provided by Collins (1997):

Finally, an opponent might challenge my claim that it is belief rather than knowledge that ought to be central to *interactive epistemology*. My response to this is simply to point out that agents, even rational agents, can and do get things wrong. This is not a controversial claim, just the commonplace observation that rational agents sometimes have false beliefs. The reason for this is not hard to find. It is because the input on which we update is sometimes misleading and sometimes downright false. To demand that everything an agent fully believes be true is not to state a requirement of rationality but rather to demand that the agent be invariably lucky in the course of her experience. Being completely rational is one thing; always being lucky is another.[27]

---

[26] The discussion of game theory, **S5** and the perspectives on inquiry I owe completely to H. Arló-Costa.

[27] The term 'interactive' epistemology was coined by Aumann (1994) to refer to a discipline that contains game theory but also encompasses areas of computer science like distributed artificial intelligence among other fields. I am indebted to H. Arló-Costa for pointing out that the term 'interactive epistemology' was already taken.

Nothing is here said about what it would actually mean to have knowledge in economic exchanges. Perhaps to be always lucky aside from being rational. This entails that the notion of knowledge does require truth in order for it to be intelligible. Collins points out that agents get things wrong all the time, even while being completely rational. Aumann's theorem demonstrates how alien to our everyday endeavors the notion of knowledge is. The notion of rationality can, at most, require that the agent only holds beliefs that are full beliefs, that is, beliefs that the agent takes as true from his first-person point of view.

Disagreement alone does not suffice for altering anyone's view. Each agent will therefore have some type of acceptance rule that will indicate to him whether it is rational or not to incorporate information. Sometimes the agent might lend an ear to an incompatible point of view for the sake of argument, and this might end up in implementing a change of view. When a network of agents is modeled from the outside, endowing these agents with third-person knowledge (as is customarily done in economic models) seems inappropriate. Be that as it may, if the agents are rational, one should assume that their theories are in autoepistemic equilibrium, and this leads to the assumption that the first-person views are each **S5**. These two things are perfectly compatible. But this does not mean that certain type of inputs (the ones that are marked positive by the agent's preferred theory of acceptance) might require perturbing the current autoepistemic equilibrium via additions or revisions. The philosophical results questioning the use of **S5** in interactive epistemology question the fact that economic agents can be modeled *by the game theorist* as having third-person knowledge. These results do not necessarily have a bearing on what one might or must assume about the first-person point of view of each agent.

The first-person point of view is crucial for modeling an autonomous agent, not for modeling a network from the outside. When a robot is walking in a corridor, will it take for granted what is given by its censors? Will it take this information to be true? Will the robot accept it for planning and action? Or will the robot attribute to this information only a threshold of probability, being always in doubt as to whether what appears really is? Jeffrey follows the path of Cartesianism to the end while developing a decision theory where agents are never sure of anything. They only have probable belief, never full beliefs of any sort. One of the mathematical consequences is that agents can never be depicted as doing things. They are depicted instead as trying to do things. When moving my hand across the table, I cannot, according to him, properly say, 'I am going to grab this glass.' The action should be described thus: 'I am trying to get this glass.' There is always an infinitesimal amount of doubt as to whether the agent will actually be able to accomplish what he sets out to do. There can always be some tremor that might end up derailing the agent's intentions. The robot does not see a red door, it merely thinks so; thus it is not fully sure that the door is a door and that the color is not a shade of violet while it is trying to walk. Many despair as to the tenability of such a view. G. E. Moore and Wittgenstein pointed out that, for humans, this kind of paranoid attitude leads to pragmatic contradiction (Moore's paradox).

To a great extent, logical epistemology has been viewed so far as a kind of 'Kripkean epistemology'. To recapitulate, the basic idea is to use models (which are not exactly the ones proposed by Kripke, where there is a distinguished actual world) consisting of a triple comprising a set W of worlds, an accessibility relation R and a valuation φ.

There are two salient formal facts regarding this tradition. First, worlds are taken as primitive unstructured points. Second, the set of points W in each model is given as a primitive, and the accessibility relation R is a relation defined on W. On the other hand, when the model is used to characterize binary modal operators (like counterfactual conditionals), the model is equipped as well with a similarity relation, say, S (which tends to be a total ordering on W) or an entrenchment relation, say, E (which also is usually assumed to have the properties of a total ordering). The relations S, E and R should not be confused. They are formally different, and they have different epistemological or ontological roles. Sometimes S can be used to characterize a binary modal operator, which in turn is used to characterize a knowledge operator (as in Nozick's counterfactual model), but the resulting knowledge operator need not have a characterization in terms of a Kripke model (there might not be any R that can characterize it in a standard Kripke model). Nevertheless, the knowledge operator that thus arises is a modal operator, it just fails to be Kripkean. Logical epistemology is not restricted to Kripkean epistemology.

Recent research in logical epistemology has questioned Kripkean epistemology. First, research in formal epistemology inspired by remarks by Aumann (1994) questioned the fundamental assumption that worlds are primitive points without components. The idea (also elaborated by Bacharach 1997) is to consider worlds as composite entities. For example, it seems quite reasonable to consider worlds as structured $n+1$-tuples containing the nature state and n other coordinates specifying the epistemic states of the n agents – a somewhat similar idea is entertained by modal operator epistemology (see Chapter 8). The nature state can have different encodings, depending on the considered application. In game theory, it could be a strategy, in multiagent systems an environment state of some form, and so on. In fields like economics, knowledge is represented by a partition of worlds. Alternatively, the epistemic state of each agent can be represented by the set of propositions that the agent believes. In turn, each of these propositions is usually constructed as a set of worlds. Obviously, this leads to circularity, and the treatment of this circularity leads to profound reforms of the underlying set theory (Barwise 1988; Barwise and Moss 1996).

There is another alternative, explored by Arló-Costa (2002):

The idea is to associate a *neighborhood* of propositions to each world. The intuition is that the set of propositions in the neighborhood of world w is the set of propositions accepted or believed by a certain agent at w. Now the propositions in question are no longer part of w, they are associated with w. This is enough to break the circularity. At the same time, the solution is expressive enough to keep track of the epistemic states of agents at worlds. (p. 97)

Neighborhood semantics is the type of semantics for modalities recommended by Scott and Montague.[28] As pointed out by Arló-Costa (2001a, 2002), the adoption of neighborhood semantics solves two big problems in formal epistemology at the same time. On the one hand, it tackles the problem of circularity without abandoning standard set theory. On the other hand, non-Kripkean neighborhood models interpreted epistemically (as in Arló-Costa 2002) can be seen as representations of epistemic operators where some of the most salient tenets of logical omniscience are abandoned. Logical closure in the sense of axiom **K** is an instance of logical omniscience, and in neighborhood semantics closure corresponds modularly to a quite intuitive closure condition in neighborhoods that in certain applications fails. Finally, neighborhood semantics also have something elegant to offer with respect to the lottery paradox. Modeling 'It is highly probable that A' using a monadic modal operator, $\boxdot A$, leads to abandoning the rule of adjunctive inference that permits the inferrence of $\boxdot(A \wedge B)$ from $\boxdot A$ and $\boxdot B$ even if this rule is valid in all systems of Kripkean modal logic. It has nevertheless been indicated by Arló-Costa (2001b) and Kyburg and Teng (2002) that there are neighborhood models for this kind of modal operator as well, including well-defined and elegant syntax.

---

[28] For a textbook exposition of neighborhood semantics, see Chellas 1980.

Nozick's counterfactual knowledge operator is axiomatizable and characterizable in terms of a neighborhood (minimal) model of the type recommended by Scott and Montague.[29] In the case of Nozick's counterfactual epistemology, a relation of ontological similarity is used to generate a modal analysis of knowledge that is not (and by its very nature cannot be) Kripkean. There is no accessibility relation available for the knowledge operator, although there are neighborhood models for the corresponding modality. This model presupposes a partition not of the set of possible worlds but of the set of all propositions (understood as sets of possible worlds). In this case, there is an underlying motivation to defeat the skeptic, but the tools used in order to do this go beyond Kripkean epistemology. Thus, the counterfactual knowledge operator is located somewhere in the hierarchy of classical but not normal systems of modal logic.

Recent work in formal epistemology likewise questions the fact that the domain of worlds is given as primitive. This can be seen in different types of formal models. One may view the case of Fagin et al. discussed earlier as the definition of the modal operator relative to the use of 'runs' and 'systems' rather than possible worlds. The authors are well aware that while one can immediately construct an epistemic model when the runs and systems are given, there are no general rules for constructing those runs and systems. Constructing these structures is, as the authors say, 'an art'. One of the main functions of these runs and systems is to *ignore* possible worlds, which here also are composite entities, including a local state and an environment state.[30] There are no general rules for ignoring worlds. Once the run is specified, one can concentrate on the set of worlds in the run sharing the same local state. This provides a similarity relation defined in the universe given by the run. If this process of ignoring and eliminating sounds familiar, it should. This is in essence the process that Lewis popularized among mainstream epistemologists in 'Elusive Knowledge' (1996) (see Chapter 5).[31]

Unnatural doubt is not the way to start, and in much contemporary work in epistemic logic doubt is probably not a strong motivating factor either. Partitioning the possibility space does not necessarily imply a

---

[29] Arló-Costa has been exploring this.

[30] In order to avoid circularity the local state is encoded as a primitive rather than as a set of propositions or a partition. Although this might be useful in some applications, it seems to obscure the true role of the local state as an encoding of the epistemic state of an agent.

[31] I am indebted to H. Arló-Costa for making these points clear to me.

forcing strategy against the skeptic, especially when epistemology is not solely 'defensive' in the Van Fraassenian sense. The computer scientists that build runs are hardly motivated by Cartesian doubt. They are motivated by the desire to avoid exponential explosion, the frame problem and other conundra. Moreover, the partitioning generated by a similarity relation (the 'closest' worlds with respect to a world or a set of worlds, as in Nozick's case) and the partitioning generated by an accessibility relation (once the universe of possibilia is fixed, either by fiat or by art) are two different forms of partitioning.

7

Computational Epistemology

Apart from recent trends in logical epistemology, the epistemologies discussed in the preceding chapter largely neglect the connection between successful learning and knowledge. Computational epistemology is an approach embodying knowledge acquisition studies. It utilizes logical and computational techniques to investigate when guaranteed convergence to the truth about epistemic problems is feasible. Every epistemic problem determines a set of possible worlds over which the inquiring agent is to succeed witnessing a forcing relation.

> FORCING   'Logical reliability theory' is a more accurate term, since the basic idea is to find methods that succeed in every possible world in a given range.
>
> Kelly et al. (1997)

Computational epistemology is not a traditional epistemological paradigm by any means – neither from the mainstream nor formal perspectives treated so far. It does not start off with global conceptual analyses of significant epistemological notions like knowledge, justification and infallibility. It does not follow logical epistemology in locally focusing on axiomatics, validity and strength of epistemic operators. Computational epistemology is not obligated to hold a particular view, or formulate its 'characteristic' definition, of what knowledge is. Given its foundation in computability theory and mathematical logic, computational epistemology is not actually about knowledge but about learning – but learning of course is *knowledge acquisition.*

Knowledge acquisition takes forcing. The forcing is specified by the particular epistemic problem at hand, as Kelly (1998b) explains:

A learning problem specifies: (1) what is to be learned, (2) a range of relevant possible environments in which the learner must succeed, (3) the kinds of inputs

115

these environments provide to the learner, (4) what it means to learn over a range of relevantly possible environments, and (5) the sorts of learning strategies that will be entertained as solutions. A learning strategy solves a learning problem just in case it is admitted as a potential solution by the problem and succeeds in the specified sense over the relevant possibilities. A problem is *solvable* just in case some admissible strategy solves it. (p. 1)

Consider the ornithologist worried about whether all ravens are black. He sets out to settle this question by observing ravens one by one.[1] This takes care of item (1) of the specified learning agenda. In circumscribing this epistemic problem, there will be one possible world in which all ravens are black and other possible worlds in which at least one nonblack raven occurs. All these possible worlds are forced by the problem as observation sequences or inputs the ornithologist must consider relevant or accessible (items [2] and [3]).

If the actual world is such that all ravens are black, the ornithologist should eventually settle for this universal hypothesis, whereas if the actual world is such that at some point a nonblack raven occurs, the ornithologist should eventually stabilize to the conclusion that not all ravens are black. Over the range of relevant possible worlds, two aims of learning or knowledge acquisition have thus been specified, as required by item (4).

The next issue concerns the learning strategies or knowledge acquisition methods the ornithologist should use to arrive at the goals specified or whether the methods he in the end chooses to adopt measure up to the aim of knowledge acquisition – truth (item [5]). There are infinitely many methods that could be considered, but attention is currently restricted to two. One is bold in a Popperian way, while the other is more skeptical in flavor. If the first raven has been observed and been found to be black, the bold method Ξ conjectures that all ravens are black and continues to project this conjecture over the relevant set of possible worlds unless a nonblack ravens occurs. The skeptical method Θ is more cautious, as it observes a demand for infallibility and does not conjecture anything beyond what the evidence entails. In case a nonblack raven appears, Θ concludes that not all ravens are black but refuses to produce a conjecture otherwise.[2]

---

[1] The example is taken from Schulte 2002.

[2] Θ is essentially Pyrrhonian in nature. According to Sextus Empiricus, one should not judge beyond what is immediately given in experience. Judging beyond immediate experience is an error committed by 'dogmatists' and Academic skepticists alike, the latter by claiming 'all things are non-apprehensible', facilitating Sextus's inductive argument against them (Sextus Empiricus 1933, 139).

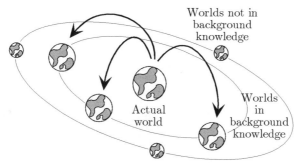

FIGURE 7.1. Computational epistemology requires success in all worlds determined by the epistemic problem (or background knowledge).

The two methods of inquiry, or learning strategies, do not perform the same with respect to arriving at a correct answer about the blackness of ravens. For Ξ, there are two possibilities given the relevant possible worlds determined by the epistemic problem. The actual world may contain only black ravens or may contain at least one nonblack raven. In case the actual world contains only black ravens, Ξ will conjecture that all ravens are black, will never change this conjecture, and will thus converge to the truth about the blackness of ravens. If the actual world is such that a nonblack raven at some point appears, Ξ will conclude that not all ravens are black as soon as the first nonblack raven shows itself. Independently of which world is actual (i.e., independently of how the evidence is presented to the bold method), Ξ will eventually converge to the truth about the blackness of ravens.

This is reliable knowledge acquisition via a learning strategy. Ξ is reliable in the categorical sense, as it succeeds over all the relevant or accessible possible worlds circumscribed by the epistemic problem, also called the *background knowledge* (Kelly 1996). Computational epistemologists call this sort of *a priori* reliability *logical reliability* (Fig. 7.1). Martin and Osherson (1998) emphasize logical reliability as an important component in knowledge studies:

Nonetheless, to the extent that the reliability perspective on knowledge can be sustained, our paradigms concern scientific discovery in the sense of *acquiring knowledge* (p. 13).

If a concept of knowledge has to be imposed on Ξ, it may be something like *reliably inferred stable true belief*, but as Kelly (1996) notes,

A logical reliabilist need not be committed to this or to any other thesis about the nature of knowledge, although logical reliabilism is certainly relevant to such an account of knowledge (p. 34–5).

The skeptical method Θ is not quite so successful in terms of logically reliable knowledge acquisition. Suppose the actual world contains at least one nonblack raven. Then Θ converges to the conclusion that not all ravens are black. If the actual world is inhabited by only black ravens, Θ will never take the risk of conjecturing accordingly, as such a conjecture transcends what is entailed by the evidence. Θ will accordingly fail to output an answer. So, when all ravens in fact are black, Θ will still forever refuse to provide an answer to the question whether all ravens are black.

If not all ravens are black, Ξ and Θ perform equally well. They both conjecture that not all ravens are black following the first encounter of a nonblack raven, and they will do so with certainty. Both methods will signal 'Eureka!' when the first nonblack raven occurs, conclude immediately that not all ravens are black and halt. Now, if the actual world contains only black ravens, then the skeptical Θ will never provide an answer, but the bold Ξ will eventually return the correct answer. Note, however, that Ξ may not signal unambiguously when it has the correct answer ready. The epistemic problem of ravenhood and blackness is solvable but only in the limit. The morale from chapter 2 applies here: To solve the epistemic problem reliably, the limit is needed, since the short run does not suffice for a complete solution, as Θ demonstrates. Rather a complete solution to the epistemic problem in the long run than a partial, or no, solution in the short run.

The epistemic problem of ravenhood and blackness is admittedly a simple learning theoretical example, but it suffices for fleshing out much of the epistemological pertinence of computational epistemology. Forcing is determined by the epistemic problem under consideration as it specifies a set of relevant possible worlds over which to succeed. The forcing relation is not fixed once and for all but varies with the epistemic problem under consideration. Global underdetermination is forced out from the beginning, as an epistemic problem is not specifiable for systematic underdetermination of the hypothesis of interest with the evidence.

The fluctuation of the forcing relation with the epistemic problem in computational epistemological theory bears a bit of resemblance to the workings of the forcing relation entertained in counterfactual epistemology and contextual epistemology. The forcing relation here is sensitive to which world is actual, as the range of close worlds is determined accordingly or in accordance with the particular conversational context. There is a significant difference, however, between counterfactual forcing and computational forcing as they relate to reliability considerations.

Reliability, although categorically defined in close worlds in counterfactual epistemology, was seen to be a world-dependent property because it depends on which world is actual – something one may be unsure about. So a method on the counterfactual account may not be known to be *a priori* reliable (see Chapter 4). If a method is logically reliable in one possible world, it will be so in all relevant possible worlds specified by the epistemic problem. Reliability is a categorically defined, world-independent property of an inquiry method in computational epistemology and may be assessed *a priori* (Kelly 1996, 34). The same sort of difference manifests itself with respect to contextualistic epistemology and computational epistemology, as reliability is a world-dependent property for Lewisian contextualism as well, owing to the indexicality of actuality.

Another difference related to forcing, skepticism and the solvability of epistemic problems is that forcing may be enforced for different reasons in traditional epistemologies and computational epistemology, as Kelly (2000) suggests:

Skeptics propose models of inductive inference and prove that they are unsolvable. The various schools of epistemology advocate different strategies for modifying such problems to make them solvable. The most obvious strategy is to excuse or neglect relevant possibilities of error. This is achieved by assuming that we can succeed . . . ignoring possibilities that have not entered into the scientific debate, ignoring errors in 'distant' possible worlds (i.e. truth-tracking), and eliminating possibilities with hidden structure (empiricism) . . . Weakening the convergence criterion reflects the pragmatist's strategy of dropping the halting condition from the concept of scientific success. (p. 4)

Forcing is initially introduced to get inquiry off the ground, as global underdetermination simply amounts to the impossibility of reliable inquiry, whatever reliability is supposed to mean. This much holds for all the epistemologies introduced so far, computational epistemology included. Now epistemic reliabilism and counterfactual, contextualistic and logical epistemologies all pay homage to the traditional philosophical idea that knowledge should be acquired with certainty (Chapter 2). The local epistemic environment should in one way or the other suffice for settling the truth-value or validity of a knowledge claim, and inquiry may just as well stop once the issue has been settled (Chapters 3–6). If the solution to the epistemic problem cannot immediately be had with certainty, *then* the classical epistemologies use the forcing technique of choice again to boil down the set of relevant possibilities of error in such a way that solutions again can be had with a halting property. Tossing out way-off worlds (counterfactual epistemology), ignoring the possible worlds in which sampling and inference to the best explanation are unreliable inductive engines (contextual epistemology), and so on, are simply excuses for restoring epistemic problems in such a way as to again comply with the philosophical hallmark of certainty convergence. This is Kelly's reason for suggesting weakening the counterfactual epistemological concept of knowledge to a limiting concept in which case convergence becomes virtual rather than actual (see Chapter 4).

The suggestion is that the epistemologies in question, and others outside the tradition as well, are 'relational' in nature (Kelly 2000). This means that epistemic notions like verification, refutation and decision are taken to confer epistemic justification insofar as a logical relation of entailment holds between the propositions of interest. Then, short of full entailment of the solution to the epistemic problem due to local underdetermination, weaker entailment relations will do (the best solution, the simplest solution, the most unifying solution, etc.) in the short run, and forcing will be responsible for this weaker entailment relation obtaining. Forcing in turn becomes responsible for turning inductive inquiry into near deductive inquiry. One proposal is that this possible use of forcing is an evasive maneuver with respect to the problem of induction (Kelly 1999).

Computational epistemology only uses forcing to block global underdetermination (and the epistemic problem itself determines the nature of this relation), not local underdetermination. Solutions to epistemic problems may be obtained all the same if the criterion of convergence is weakened, as shown by the raven example. The paradigm entertains a whole range of different convergence criteria. So far, certainty and limiting convergence have been defined, but other criteria of convergence include n-mind-change convergence and gradual convergence. Convergence with n-mind-change means that the method may retract its conjecture and accordingly change its mind an arbitrary but finite number of times n as long as the method converges by the time the number of mind-changes is used up. Suppose finally that the method is allowed to output rational numbers. Then say that the method converges to an output t *gradually* if for each rational r there exists a time such that for each later time the method's conjectural performance remains within distance r of t.

The epistemic problems solvable with certainty are also solvable with n-mind changes, solvable in the limit and solvable gradually. The converse relation does not hold, however. An epistemic problem gradually solvable is not necessarily solvable in the limit, solvable with n-mind-changes, or

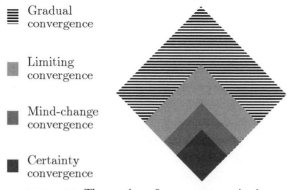

Gradual convergence

Limiting convergence

Mind-change convergence

Certainty convergence

FIGURE 7.2. The nesting of convergence criteria.

solvable with certainty. The hierarchy of convergence criteria is 'nested' in nature (Fig. 7.2).

Whether an epistemic problem has a solution is going to depend not only on possibly weakening the convergence criteria but also on the sense of success. Recall that the skeptical method Θ in a certain sense solves the problem of whether all ravens are black if the actual world is such that not all ravens are black. Θ provides a partial solution to the problem, and this is one sense of success. The bold method Ξ provides a complete solution to the problem. Ξ eventually gets it right either way, independently of whether all ravens are black or not. That is another sort of success, and in this case, the latter rather than the former is desirable. Not all epistemic problems, however, allow for complete solutions.

One way to look at the ornithologist's methodological situation is in the light of hypothesis assessment. Faced with the hypothesis that all ravens are black, the ornithologist sets out to determine whether this hypothesis is true or false given the incoming evidence. Ξ and Θ are now methods of hypothesis assessment.

On the computational epistemological construal, a hypothesis assessment method may be thought of as a mapping from observed evidence in a possible world together with hypotheses into {0, 1} where 1 denotes truth and 0 falsity. This portrayal of assessment gives rise to the following *procedurally* based, as opposed to entailment based, senses of success with respect to the truth/falsity status of hypotheses (Kelly 1996):

- **Verification.** The assessment method may only return the answer 1 if the hypothesis is true in a possible world but refuses to return an answer otherwise.

- **Refutation.** The assessment method may only return the answer 0 if the hypothesis is false in a possible world, but refuses to return an answer otherwise.
- **Decision.** The assessment method may return an answer either way, 1 or 0, depending on whether the hypothesis is true or false in a possible world.

Combining success and convergence criteria allows for a hierarchy of criteria of successful convergence in the assessment case. Refutation with certainty means that there is a time n such that the assessment method announces at n that it is ready to answer and at $n+1$ answers 0 and stops. Verification in the limit means that there is a time n such that for each later time n' the assessment method answers 1,[3] similarly for other combinations of success and convergence for assessment.

The skeptical method in the raven example is a refuter in the sense that Θ returns 0 if the hypothesis is false; the bold method Ξ is a decider, as it returns 1 and verifies the hypothesis if it is true and returns 0 and refutes the hypothesis if it is false. If the actual world includes one nonblack raven, Θ will refute the hypothesis that all ravens are black with certainty but will refuse to answer otherwise. Ξ will refute the hypothesis with certainty for the same reason but verify the hypothesis in the limit if it is true that all ravens are black. As certainty convergence implies limiting convergence, Ξ will decide the whole epistemic problem in the limit.

The point advanced by computational epistemology is that decision with certainty, which epistemology has traditionally held dear, is but one among many criteria of successful convergence. Epistemic problems may have reliable solutions for successful convergence criteria weaker than halting decision, as shown by the workings of Ξ. More and more epistemic problems may come within the scope of reliable inquiry as the conditions of success are weakened.

Another way to look at the ornithologist's methodological situation is as one of discovery. Observing ravens one at a time, he is eventually asked to conjecture a hypothesis about ravens and their color. Ξ and Θ are now methods of hypothesis discovery. A discovery method is construed as a generator which conjectures a hypothesis in response to evidence observed. The discovery method identifies a hypothesis h in a possible world if there is a time n such that for each later time n' the value of

---

[3] See Chapter 2 for the exact definitions of convergence with certainty and limiting convergence.

the discovery method's conjecture is h. This is limiting convergence, but one may equally well define discovery for other criteria of convergence. The following notion of successful discovery may now be formulated (Kelly 1996):

- **Discovery.** The discovery method identifies a true hypothesis in the limit in a possible world if there exists a true hypothesis h and the discovery method limiting converges to h.

Ξ will conjecture that all ravens are black if the first raven observed is black and will stick with this conjecture forever unless a nonblack raven appears, then switch conjectures to not all ravens are black. According to the definition of discovery, this will suffice for reliably discovering in the limit whether all ravens are black. Θ will only discover ravens one at a time.

Reichenbach formulated a classical distinction between the context of justification and the context of discovery. Hempel (1965) later referred to a *logic* of justification but to a *context* of discovery to further emphasize the great divide between the two notions. The idea, still held by some today, is that studying the discovery of new hypotheses from evidence is futile. The reason is the unreliable nature of discovery. Computational epistemology concedes to the tradition that from the point of view of logical reliability analysis there is not much difference between assessment and discovery, as Kelly (1996) notes:

Indeed, assessment can be viewed as a *special case* of discovery, where what is to be discovered is whether h is correct or incorrect. Both in discovery and in assessment, the question is whether the method employed is guaranteed to arrive at a correct result relative to what is assumed in advance. From this point of view, the presumed sharp distinction between assessment and discovery is spurious. (p. 218–19)

Besides, discovery is in a certain sense more important to epistemology than assessment, as Hintikka (2003b) recently concluded:

Surely the first order of business of any genuine theory of knowledge – the most important task both theoretically and practically – is how new knowledge can be achieved, not merely how previously obtained information can be evaluated. A theory of information (knowledge) acquisition is both philosophically and humanly much more important than a theory of whether already achieved information amounts to knowledge or not. Discovery is more important than the defense of what you already know. (p. 9)

This is not the time or the place to survey the numerous results of computational epistemology and thus reveal the delicate interplay between assessment and discovery or the knowledge acquisition power of logical reliable discovery.[4] Suffice it to say that both assessment and discovery may come within the scope of logical reliable inquiry, an insight used in the next chapter to construct a limiting concept of knowledge based on discovery (a concept whose validity and relation to a limiting concept of knowledge based on assessment are also studied in that chapter).

Independently of whether Ξ and Θ are construed as assessment or discovery methods, the raven example goes to show another important point about the methods of knowledge acquisition. Computational epistemology has a very natural way of realizing the second-generation obligation of active agents (see Chapter 6). In fact, the agents are active by definition, as they are the ones to learn and acquire knowledge by being functions assessing hypotheses in the light of incoming evidence or functions conjecturing hypotheses in light of the same.

While the bold method succeeds, the skeptical one fails, and the explanation has to do with the way in which they *behave* in response to the incoming evidence. The skeptical method proceeds timidly and is thus barred from getting to the truth, so whereas the boldness of Ξ makes it succeed in the case of this particular epistemic problem. Boldness is a truth-conducive, or *permissive*, methodological property of the method relative to this particular problem, while timidity is a *restrictive* knowledge acquisition strategy, as computational epistemology would put it (Kelly 1996).

Computational epistemology systematically investigates the feasibility of the norms proposed for truth-conducive inquiry in accordance with the hypothetical methodological imperative: 'if you want to converge to the truth (in a given sense), then use method M' (Kelly 1999a, 80). If justification concerns securing the connection between the belief and truth conditions in order to acquire knowledge, then the study of justification in epistemology is essentially the methodological study of methods' reliable performance (see Chapter 2).

Canons of inductive rationality or justification imposed on methods of inquiry can interfere with reliability. Suppose we call a method for assessing belief in a hypothesis consistent if the belief in the hypothesis is taken back as soon as the hypothesis has been refuted by the observed

---

[4] For discussion of these topics, see Kelly 1987, 1991, 1994, 1996, 1998a; Kelly and Schulte 1996; and Kelly, Schulte and Juhl 1997.

evidence. The consistency recommendation is popular among methodologists such as Bayesians and belief revision theorists, among others. The recommendation sounds like a rational prescription; it does not seem rational to continue to believe in a hypothesis refuted by available evidence. Ideal agents not limited by effective or computational constraints have no problem with the consistency requirement. Even if, for ideal agents, the scope of reliable inquiry is not limited by consistency, for agents computationally bounded, consistency may cause problems:

- Kelly and Schulte proved that for special computable epistemic assessment problems, consistency stands in the way of getting to the truth. There is an epistemic problem that in fact is computably refutable with certainty by a computable method, but no consistent method, even with infinitely effective powers (in the sense that it is hyperarithmetically defined), can even gradually solve this problem in terms of refutation or verification (Kelly and Schulte 1995; Kelly 1996).
- Osherson, Stob and Weinstein (1986) showed that the consistency prescription restricts the set of identifiable recursive enumerable Σ_1^0-sets to the recursive Δ_1^0-sets for effective hypothesis discovery methods. The consistency prescription also has an impact on effective belief revision AGM-identifiers (Hendricks 1997).

Consistency may be a truth-conducive methodological requirement for ideal agents in many cases. It should, however, be advocated cautiously in effective epistemology, as consistency can restrict inquiry carried out by Turing machines or similar canonical computing devices.

There are also positive computational epistemological stories about permissive norms. Kelly, Schulte and Hendricks (1996) showed that when there is a reliable method for solving epistemic problems of a particular kind, there is a method for solving the problems in accordance with the AGM-prescriptions of belief revision. Other positive results concerning belief revision and logically reliable inquiry are provided by Martin and Osherson (1998, 1999). A systematic survey of the reliable performance of variations of the belief revision paradigm is provided by Kelly (1998b).[5]

The distinction between permissive and restrictive architectures of inquiry carries over into modal operator epistemology (see Chapter 8). The object here is to investigate whether different methodological

---

[5] Other positive and negative methodological results about Bayesian learning, identification of first-order structures, and so on, may be found in Kelly 1996.

recommendations are feasible for converging in the limit to the validity of various epistemic axioms discussed in Chapter 6.

It may sound as if all epistemic problems have reliable solutions if the criteria of success and convergence are sufficiently weakened. This is not so. Epistemic problems that are globally underdetermined dump reliable inquiry on the side-walk for all success and convergence criteria. Short of global underdetermination, other epistemic problems may remain unsolvable for any agent, ideal or computational, still others may be partially solvable by ideal agents but not by computable agents. Some epistemic problems are solvable by computable agents but not by finite-state computable agents. It depends on how much local underdetermination is involved. Some problems like whether human cognition is computable, turn out to be verifiable in the limit but not refutable in the limit ideally, while the epistemic problem of whether matter is infinitely divisible is dually refutable in the limit but not in the limit verifiable for any admissible knowledge acquisition strategy, as shown by Kelly (1996).

Underdetermination in computational epistemology becomes a measure for the degree of unsolvability of epistemic problems. Solvability of epistemic problems is determined by the notions of convergence and procedural success. Strengthening or weakening these criteria gives rise to a scale of local underdetermination or inductive skepticism. The epistemic problem offered by the raven example determines a set of possible worlds differing by the way in which the evidence can be *temporally* arranged in these worlds. The bold method succeeds independently of how the evidence is presented temporally, the skeptical method does not. What this shows is that even though the problem is solvable, solvability is in general acutely sensitive to the temporal arrangement of the evidence. An important insight of computational epistemology is that the possible temporal 'entanglement' (Kelly 2000) governing epistemic problems may be expressed in terms of topological and computational complexity measures. The scale of local underdetermination is constructed accordingly. The problem of induction is not just one problem but a hierarchy of problems determined by classes of topological and computational complexity, which in turn reveal the sense in which epistemic problems are solvable.

Computational epistemology has a skeptical side as an unsolvability result shows how every admissible strategy of knowledge acquisition fails. On the other hand, it is also epistemologically or methodologically optimistic if it can be shown that some constructed knowledge acquisition strategy succeeds in solving every solvable epistemic problem of a particular complexity class in the required sense. This prompts the following question: What is it about an epistemic problem that allows it to have reliable solutions? It turns out that solvable epistemic problems have a particular combinatorial structure. The so-called *characterization theorems* of computational epistemology provide necessary and sufficient logical conditions for epistemic problems to have reliable solutions based on their topological or computational complexity. The characterization theorems reveal the structure of the epistemic problems that can be solved for every notion of procedural success with certainty, with *n*-mind-changes, in the limit and gradually. They draw the line between what is solvable and what is not. Characterization theorems have been provided for both ideal and computable assessment and discovery, for the first-order logic paradigm, for finite state automata and for ideal and computable prediction methods (Kelly 1996).

The ornithologist had the choice between two methods, but there are infinitely many other methods to consider, although none of them necessarily is at the ornithologist's disposal. In fact, the two methods considered may not even be at his disposal, for one reason or the other. For idiosyncratic reasons, he may refuse to use the method that succeeds, his local epistemic circumstances may not allow him to use the method, social pressure or conservative trends in his environment may ban the use of a bold method, and so on. For similar reasons, it may be that the skeptical method is unavailable to the ornithologist. If we suppose that both methods are at his disposal, though, he should, assuming he wants to get to the truth of the matter, adopt the method that will succeed. The fact that an epistemic problem is solvable in principle for some notion of success and convergence does not entail that whatever it takes to solve the problem is available to the local inquirer. The fact that an epistemic problem is unsolvable does not necessarily entail that the first-person inquirer recognizes it to be so. Computational epistemology does not adopt a first-person perspective.

Instead of being situated in the epistemic environment, the computational epistemologist is standing outside looking at what it would take to solve the epistemic problem. Recall the list of questions a computational epistemologist will ask: Does there exist a method that can reliably solve the particular epistemic problem? If there is a method currently entertained by the local agent, or a method advocated by some other theory of knowledge, can that method then solve the epistemic problem? If it can, what are the relevant criteria of successful convergence for solvability? Is there a method that will do better in terms of speed? Is there some method that will succeed whenever success is possible for epistemic problems of this particular kind? Can the method currently entertained measure up to the universally successful method? Is there an intrinsic characterization of solvability of the epistemic problem in terms of topological or computational complexity? And so forth. These questions are asked largely independently of the epistemic environment that some agent is sunk into and from the third-person perspective of computational epistemology.

The relation to the first-person is this: If it can be shown *a priori* from the computational epistemological perspective that some method the first-person inquirer is considering adopting is destined to flunk, then there is not much sense in adopting this method, assuming the point of inquiry is to get to the truth. By deciding not to use the doomed method, at least the first-person agent is not guilty of committing error, even when this does not entail gaining truth. Better still, if there is a method available to the agent that *a priori* can be determined to succeed in the relevant sense, then he should rather adopt this alternative method instead. The first-person inquirer will then both avoid error *and* gain truth.

Computational epistemology occupies a rather unique place in the contemporary epistemological debate. It balances delicately between pessimistic skepticism and optimistic epistemology insofar as negative knowledge acquisition results partly vindicate a skeptical position and positive learning results leave hope for a truth-conducive methodology and the acquisition of knowledge.[6] Rather than 'caught between the rock of fallibilism, and the whirlpool of skepticism' by not having a workable infallible definition of knowledge, the computational epistemologists adopt a more 'transcendental' viewpoint regarding knowledge acquisition. Even when knowledge of some epistemic problem cannot be acquired, it is still possible to characterize the combinatorial structure responsible for its unsolvability, and this is *epistemologically* pertinent information to any theory of knowledge, whether it buys into knowledge infallibility or not. Nozick may be read as having demonstrated that infallible knowledge is indeed possible but not how possible. A skeptic may have shown that infallible knowledge in some sense is impossible but not how impossible.

Computational epistemology balances between descriptive and normative features of current epistemological work. Suggesting a course of methodological conduct or demonstrating the infeasibility of another course of conduct is normative, but the goal is to arrive at true

---

[6] While demonstrating one situation or the other, computational epistemology favors definitions, lemmata and theorems over fictions, thought experiments and intuition pumps.

beliefs about the world in a logically reliable way. This seems to be what knowledge and knowledge acquisition are about. Humans may acquire knowledge, and machines, animals and social institutions may learn too (Kelly 1998a). The questions that drive the theory are, how reliable could any of these cognitive systems possibly be and does the systems' dispositions to adopt beliefs in response to observed evidence meet the aim of inquiry set forth? (Schulte 2002). In this light, computational epistemology may be viewed as the mathematical version of normative naturalism or 'naturalism logicized' (Kelly 1999).

With its roots in computability theory, computational epistemology was first put to use in linguistics rather than philosophy, as a tool for modeling language acquisition and a child's abilities and dispositions to converge to a grammar for its natural language (Gold 1965, 1967). Around the same time, Putnam (1963) achieved one of the first computational epistemology results pertinent to methodology and the philosophy of science by demonstrating the infeasibility of Carnap's suggestion for a confirmation theory.[7] More language learnability results came during the 1980s, obtained by Osherson et al. (1986). The emphasis on the philosophical, epistemological and methodological importance of computational epistemology is largely due to Glymour and, even more, to Kelly (1996).

Although it is a logic-influenced epistemology, it does not proceed in the spirit of logical epistemology by formalizing knowledge as an operator in a formal language and categorizing systems of epistemic logics. The paradigm focuses on learning mechanisms and knowledge acquisition methods, naturally connecting three factors that play a major role in contemporary epistemology: learning, active agents and temporality. These three factors may actually be formalized as operators using some parts of the computational epistemological machinery, as the next chapter shows.

---

[7] Putnam's result is discussed in Chapter 2.

8

Modal Operator Epistemology

The epistemological traditions discussed in the preceding chapters have proceeded largely in isolation from one another. Those who find intuitive definitions of knowledge appealing focus narrowly on folksy examples rather than on scientific method. Epistemic logicians have only recently begun to reflect on epistemological interpretations of their calculi, and computational epistemologists do not formalize knowledge as a modal operator. Such is the fragmented state of epistemology today.

Modal operator epistemology is a model of inquiry obtained by mixing alethic, tense and epistemic logics with a few motivational concepts drawn from computational epistemology (Fig. 8.1). It was developed to study the acquisition and subsequent validity of limiting convergent knowledge.[1] The term 'modal operator epistemology' is derived from the idea that it takes multiple modal operators to model inquiry in a pertinent way. Because it is an agent or his method that eventually acquires knowledge, modeling the active acquisition of knowledge involves epistemic logic; because knowledge is acquired over time, temporal logic is required; and because knowledge is forced over a set of relevant possible worlds, alethic logical elements are needed.

Multimodalities have been on the formal epistemological agenda for some time. In 1970, when epistemic logic was still partly in its infancy, Scott (1970) noted,

Here is what I consider one of the biggest mistakes of all in modal logic: concentration on a system with just one modal operator. The only way to have any

---

[1] For further discussion, see Hendricks 1997, 2001, 2002, 2003, 2004a; Hendricks and Pedersen 1998a, 1999a, 2000a, 2000b, 2002. The outline of modal operator epistemology given here follows the outline given in Hendricks 2002. Modal operator epistemology has been developed in close cooperation with Stig Andur Pedersen.

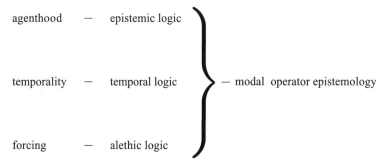

FIGURE 8.1. Modal operator epistemology comprises at least three different logics.

philosophically significant results in deontic logic or epistemic logic is to combine these operators with: Tense operators (otherwise how can you formulate principles of change?); the logical operators (otherwise how can you compare the relative with the absolute?); the operators like historical or physical necessity (otherwise how can you relate the agent to his environment?); and so on and so on. (p. 143)

The focus on monomodal systems in the 1970s was needed to clarify the mathematical foundations of modal logic in general and to get a firm grip on the basic tools needed for the model theory and proof theory of modal logic. Then in the 1980s multimodal systems began to appear under the influence of computer science and artificial intelligence; these combined dynamic, temporal, and epistemic logic. Around 1990, based on this experience, the first significant mathematical theorizing started appearing, focussing on the 'transfer' of properties of component modal systems to the whole and on 'emergent phenomena' of the combined systems.

Today, in branching temporal logic, researchers are mixing alethic and tense logical operators (Zanardo 1996). In the logical epistemology of Fagin, Halpern, Moses and Vardi, epistemic operators are combined with tense logical operators in modeling the knowledge dynamics of an entire system of agents, as discussed in Chapter 6. Sowa's (2000) theory of nested graph models, based on Dunn's semantics for laws and facts combined with a theory of contexts, is a way of simplifying the reasoning tasks in multimodal reasoning and may be adapted to Kripke models, situation semantics, temporal models and variants of these.[2]

---

[2] There are many other examples to choose from, for instance, Pacuit and Parikh 2004. I am indebted to Johan van Benthem for explaining to me the history of multimodalities.

As for mainstream modal epistemologies, epistemic variants of modal logics based on Kripke-semantics begin with possible worlds. Possible worlds are sometimes viewed as largely unanalyzed or even unanalyzable entities complete in their spatiotemporal history. From there, the various modalities are introduced. Another way to obtain multimodalities is to decompose or 'deconstruct' possible worlds and provide them with some explicit structure that allows one to model and study their temporal extensions, their spatial extensions and the agent to which these extensions are epistemically important. In a way, this is what Sowa is doing when levelling contexts. The decomposition of possible worlds in modal operator epistemology follows a 'deconstruction' recipe.[3]

The initial formal setup is adopted from Kelly's (1996) computational epistemology. First, an evidence stream supplies an inquiry method or agent with evidence. An evidence stream ε is an *ω-sequence* of natural numbers, that is, $\varepsilon \in \omega^{\omega}$. It is assumed that the method of inquiry is studying some system with discrete states that may be encoded by natural numbers. In the limit, the method receives an infinite stream ε of numbers. Hence, an evidence stream $\varepsilon = (a_0, a_1, a_2, \ldots, a_n, \ldots)$ consists of *code* numbers of evidence; at each state i of inquiry a_i is the code number of the evidence acquired at this state of inquiry. The lower case Greek letters $\tau, \theta, \zeta, \mu, \varsigma, \upsilon, \ldots$ denote evidence streams.

It is now possible to provide possible worlds with some explicit analyzable structure, leaving the metaphysics largely behind, as formalists have been seen to do:

> *A possible world is a pair consisting of an evidence stream ε and a state coordinate n, that is, (ε, n), where $\varepsilon \in \omega^{\omega}$ and $n \in \omega$.*

The set of all possible worlds $W = \{(\varepsilon, n) \mid \varepsilon \in \omega^{\omega}, n \in \omega\}$. The following notational conventions are used with respect to possible worlds:

- Let all pairs (ε, n), (τ, n'), (θ, m), (ς, m''), $\ldots$, denote possible worlds.
- Let $\varepsilon \mid n$ denote the finite initial segment of an evidence stream, also called the *handle*.
- Let $\omega^{<\omega}$ denote the set of all finite initial segments of evidence streams.
- Let $(\varepsilon \mid n)$ denote the set of all infinite evidence streams that extend $\varepsilon \mid n$, also called the *fan*.

The handle $\varepsilon \mid n$ is the evidence observed by the agent up to state n, that is, $\varepsilon \mid n = a_0, a_1, \ldots, a_{n-1}$. The rest $\varepsilon \backslash \varepsilon \mid n = a_n, a_{n+1}, a_{n+2}, \ldots$, is

---

[3] For alternative approaches to possible worlds semantics, see Hendricks and Pedersen 2005.

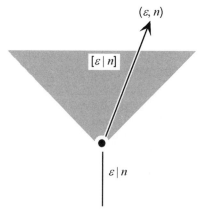

FIGURE 8.2. Handle, fan and possible world.

the evidence that the agent would observe insofar as the world develops according to (ε, n). The set of possible worlds in the fan is defined by

$$[\varepsilon \mid n] = (\varepsilon \mid n) \times \omega.$$

In other words, $[\varepsilon \mid n] = \{(\tau, k) \mid k \in \omega \text{ and } \tau \mid n = \varepsilon \mid n\}$ (Fig. 8.2).

The *world fan* $[\varepsilon \mid n]$ depicts the empirical possibilities the world may turn on as far as the inquiring agent is concerned. Here lies the forcing relation of modal operator epistemology. To acquire knowledge, the agent will eventually have to succeed over the fan of possible worlds that have the same evidential handle as the actual world observed up until 'now', e.g. n (Fig. 8.3). There is an infinity of other worlds running through the handle up until n, but these are not to be considered, as they are not consistent with the agent's observations of the actual world so far (Fig. 8.4). The forcing condition remains fairly weak, because, despite

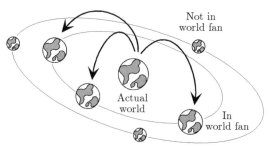

FIGURE 8.3. Modal operator epistemology requires categorical success in all worlds in the world fan.

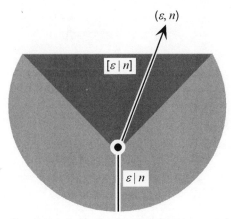

FIGURE 8.4. Forcing over the fan in modal operator epistemology.

the restriction, there will still be plenty of worlds in the fan for the agent to eventually succeed over.[4]

This characterization of evidence streams, state coordinates and possible worlds imposes a branching time structure (Fig. 8.5).

The agent has observed some part of the handle (of the world) for any finite time. From this point on, the world may 'branch' and take on any of the empirical possibilities described by $[\varepsilon \mid n]$, for all the agent knows. Points or moments in time may be construed as finite initial segments of evidence. This in turn points to a branching time structure and a branching temporal logic. The current structure is closely related to standard Ockhamistic semantics (see Braüner, Hasle, and Øhrstrøm 1998a, 1998b.) An Ockhamistic temporal structure is typically given by:

1. O is a nonempty set of moments in time,
2. $\prec$ is an irreflexive and transitive earlier-later relation that is backwards linear:

$$\forall n, n', n'' \in O : (n \prec n' \wedge n'' \prec n') \to$$
$$(n \prec n'' \vee n'' \prec n \vee n = n'').$$

An Ockhamistic model is a triple $(O, \prec, \varphi)$ where φ is a denotation function that assigns truth-values $\varphi(n, a)$ to all pairs where the first argument is an element of O and the second argument a is a propositional variable. It is possible to define a similar Ochamistic temporal structure

---

[4] The fan itself is homeomorphic to the Baire space and thus uncountable.

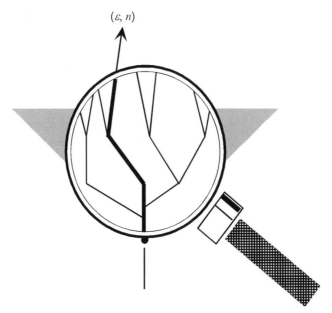

FIGURE 8.5. The branching time structure.

in modal operator epistemology as a pair $(\mathbb{T}, \prec)$ such that

1. $\mathbb{T} = \{\varepsilon \mid n \mid \varepsilon \in \omega^\omega, n \in \omega\}$ and
2. $t_1 \prec t_2$ iff $\varepsilon \mid n = \tau \mid n$ and $n < m$ where $t_1 = \varepsilon \mid n$ and $t_2 = \tau \mid m$.

A moment in time is a finite initial segment $t \in (\mathbb{T}, \prec)$. Hence a moment in time is defined as the course of events up until 'now'. Time is based on events, and the branching time structure is given by events.[5] The evidence stream ε is the actual evidence stream. The state coordinate n, for some specified n, is to be thought of as the 'age' of the actual world (ε, n), that is, n is the time in the branch. The earlier-later relation is defined with respect to finite initial segments.

The structure $(\mathbb{T}, \prec)$ satisfies the requirements above; the relation is irreflexive, transitive and backwards linearly ordered. There exist many other Ockhamistic temporal structures. One example would be a structure that extends into the indefinite past. The current structure, however, has a starting point.

---

[5] The tense structure is defined on the entire tree of finite sequences of natural numbers, where finite initial segments (of events) define moments in time.

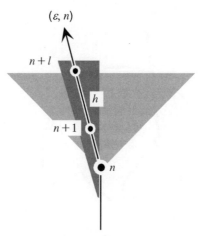

FIGURE 8.6. Truth of an empirical hypothesis in a possible world.

The agents involved in the inquiry process will eventually need some hypotheses to have knowledge of. Hypotheses will be identified with sets of possible worlds. Define the set of all empirical hypotheses as

$$\mathcal{H} = P(\omega^{\omega} \times \omega).$$

So $h \in \mathcal{H}$ iff $h = \{(\varepsilon, n) \mid \varepsilon \in S, n \in N\}$ where $S \subseteq \omega^{\omega}$ and $N \subseteq \omega$. An empirical hypothesis h is said to be *true* in world (ε, n) iff

$$(\varepsilon, n) \in h \quad and \quad \forall l \in \omega : (\varepsilon, n + l) \in h.$$

Truth is inclusion of the actual world (ε, n) in the hypothesis for all possible future stages of inquiry (Fig. 8.6).

Given the branching time structure, a host of different types of hypotheses are definable with respect to their truth-value fluctuations over time. It is currently assumed that the hypotheses of interest are *absolute time-invariant* empirical hypotheses. By Fagin et al. (1995), such hypotheses are called *stable* in truth-value. Absolute time-invariant hypotheses may be viewed as having fundamental features in common with laws of nature. They are temporally and alethically symmetrical or universal, as Earman (1978) explains:

The large majority of the numerous discussions of the concept of a law of nature agree on one point; namely, a law must be universal in space and time (p. 173).

The setup outlined so far, which follows relatively standard branching temporal logic, allows for the introduction of tense and alethic operators.

In the following intuitive way, the tense operators F, G, P and H take their usual meaning.

- The **singular future** operator, Fh, is true in world (ε, n) iff at some time in the future it will be the case that h:

$$(\varepsilon, n) \text{ validates } Fh \text{ iff } \exists k > n : (\varepsilon, k) \text{ validates } h.$$

- The **universal future** operator, Gh, is true in world (ε, n) iff for all times in the future it will be the case that h:

$$(\varepsilon, n) \text{ validates } Gh \text{ iff } \forall k > n : (\varepsilon, k) \text{ validates } h.$$

- The **singular past** operator, Ph, is true in world (ε, n) iff at some time in the past it was the case that h:

$$(\varepsilon, n) \text{ validates } Ph \text{ iff } \exists k < n : (\varepsilon, k) \text{ validates } h.$$

- The **universal past** operator, Hh, is true in world (ε, n) iff for all times in the past it was the case that h:

$$(\varepsilon, n) \text{ validates } Hh \text{ iff } \forall k < n : (\varepsilon, k) \text{ validates } h.$$

- The **temporal necessity** operator, $\boxdot h$, is true in world (ε, n) iff for all times it is the case that h:

$$(\varepsilon, n) \text{ validates } \boxdot h \text{ iff } \forall k \in \omega : (\varepsilon, k) \text{ validates } h.$$

- The **universal necessity** operator, $\Box h$, is true in world (ε, n) iff in all worlds it is the case that h:

$$(\varepsilon, n) \text{ validates } \Box h \text{ iff } \forall (\tau, m) \in \mathcal{W} : (\tau, m) \text{ validates } h.$$

- The **empirical necessity** operator, $\boxminus h$, is true in world (ε, n) iff in all worlds in the world fan it is the case that h:

$$(\varepsilon, n) \text{ validates } \boxminus h \text{ iff } \forall (\tau, m) \in [\varepsilon \mid n] : (\tau, m) \text{ validates } h.$$

It remains to introduce the epistemic operators in this new framework.

With respect to the role of agents, the modal operator theory of knowledge, like second-generation epistemic logic, treats agents as active (see Chapter 6 and 7). The theory has at its base, not as a derivative, the idea that whatever epistemic axioms and epistemic systems are possible to validate for some epistemic operator is *acutely sensitive to the methodological behavior of the agents involved*. This is clear from the fact that agents can be viewed as learning or knowledge acquisition functions, as suggested by

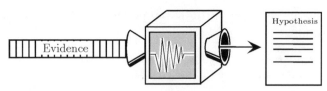

FIGURE 8.7. Discovery methods take finite initial segments of evidence as inputs and return hypotheses.

computational epistemology (see Chapter 7), rather than inactive indices on the epistemic operators of first-generation logical epistemology.

Say that a scientific inquiry method, in particular a discovery method, conjectures hypotheses in response to the evidence received (Fig. 8.7). More specifically, a discovery method δ is a function from finite initial segments of evidence to hypotheses following the computational episte-mological construal of such inquiry engines:

$$\delta : \omega^{<\omega} \longrightarrow \mathcal{H}.$$

The only immediate criterion of rationality imposed on a discovery method is that it is not allowed to conjecture absurdities: For any discovery method δ and for any world $(\tau, n') : \delta(\tau \mid n') \neq \emptyset$. What remains to be de-fined is a criterion of successful convergence for a discovery method.

Successful limiting discovery of a hypothesis h in a possible world (ε, n) means that there is a time k such that for each later n' in all worlds admitted by the world fan $[\varepsilon \mid n]$, the discovery method δ conjectures h: δ discovers h in (ε, n) iff:

$$\exists k \forall n' \geq k \forall (\tau, n') \in [\varepsilon \mid n] : \delta(\tau \mid n') \subseteq h$$

for which the convergence modulus is defined as:

$$cm(\delta, h, (\varepsilon, n)) = \mu k \forall n' \geq k \forall (\tau, n') \in [\varepsilon \mid n] : \delta(\tau \mid n') \subseteq h.$$

This definition of limiting convergent discovery is fairly strong, as it re-quires uniform convergence moduli in all relevant worlds.[6]

The method may be subject to various methodological recommenda-tions, program commands or structural properties imposing epistemic behavior. For a well-known example, say that a discovery method δ is *consistent* iff:

$$\forall (\tau, n') : \big[[\tau \mid n'] \cap \delta(\tau \mid n') \neq \emptyset\big].$$

---

[6] A weaker version of limiting convergent discovery may also be entertained such that there are no uniform convergence moduli over the relevant possible worlds; see, for instance Kelly 1996.

Consistency may be strengthened to another recommendation. The discovery method δ has *perfect memory* iff:

$$if \ (\mu, k) \in \delta(\varepsilon \mid n) \ then$$

$$(\mu \mid n = \varepsilon \mid n) \quad and \quad \forall l \leq k : (\mu, l) \in \delta(\varepsilon \mid n).$$

A discovery method δ is next said to be *consistently expectant* iff:

$$if \ (\mu, k) \in \delta(\varepsilon \mid n) \quad then \quad [k \geq n \quad and \quad (\mu \mid n = \varepsilon \mid n)].$$

Perfect memory and consistent expectation are inconsistent: Suppose $(\mu, k) \in \delta(\varepsilon \mid n)$. If the discovery method has perfect memory, then $\forall l \leq k : (\mu, l) \in \delta(\varepsilon \mid n)$. Now, if the method simultaneously is consistently expectant, then $(\mu, k) \in \delta(\varepsilon \mid n)$ implies $k \geq n$. By perfect memory, $(\mu, n - 1) \in \delta(\varepsilon \mid n)$. Contradiction! Thus, a discovery method cannot entertain perfect memory and consistent expectation at the same time. Methodological recommendations may conflict, as Kitcher (1993) noted, Nozick (1993) emphasized and Lewis pointed out in terms of overriding rules (see Chapter 5).

It is possible to define a variety of limiting concepts of knowledge in modal operator epistemology. It suffices for current purposes to restrict attention to the following concept:

δ may know h in the limit iff there exists a possible world that validates δ's knowledge of h. In other words:

1. *h is true, and*
2. *δ conjectures h after some finite evidence sequence has been read and continues to conjecture h in all future.*

Thus, there is a time n such that for each later time $n' : \delta$ conjectures h at n' in all possible worlds admitted by the world fan in which h is true. If this definition is modified such that the method only conjectures something entailed by the evidence and the world fan, the result is:

(ε, n) *validates* $K_\delta h$ *iff*
1. $(\varepsilon, n) \in h \ and \ \forall l \in \omega : (\varepsilon, n + l) \in h$,
2. $\forall n' \geq n, \forall (\tau, n') \in [\varepsilon \mid n] :$
   (a) $\delta(\tau \mid n') \subseteq h$,
   (b) $(\tau, n') \in \delta(\tau \mid n')$.

This definition of knowledge is very strong, especially given (2b). The discovery method δ is *infallible*:

$$(\varepsilon, n) \in \delta(\varepsilon \mid n).$$

Applied to the definition of knowledge, infallibility implies entailment of the truth by the evidence and the fan of relevant possible worlds, and hence condition 1 of the above definition is obsolete. One may now simply say that (ε, n) validates $K_\delta h$ iff:

$$\forall n' \geq n, \forall (\tau, n') \in [\varepsilon \mid n] : \delta(\tau \mid n') \subseteq h, (\tau, n') \in \delta(\tau \mid n').$$

The $\forall\forall$-quantifier block

$$\overbrace{\forall n' \geq n}^{\text{forcing in time}}, \overbrace{\forall (\tau, n') \in [\varepsilon \mid n]}^{\text{forcing in worlds}} : \delta(\tau \mid n') \subseteq h$$

is referred to as the *forcing* quantifier block. A categorical concept of reliability in all worlds forced by the fan of possible worlds is given in this definition of limiting convergent knowledge. The Gettier paradoxes are handled immediately: There is no way the evidence for (h or h') can be undercut when the evidence simply entails (h or h').

It should be observed that since the agent is a function from finite initial segments of evidence to hypotheses, there is no knowledge without the method conjecturing a hypothesis. Thus, the agent is *actively within the scope of the operator*. The symbolic notation $K_\delta h$ in modal operator epistemology is genuinely faithful to the intended meaning of the knowledge operator. This was found to be a problem for logical epistemology (see Chapter 6).

All the formal expressions are completely formalizable in a modal propositional logic, with some modifications to the standard setup. The syntax includes an infinite supply of propositional variables, brackets, the Boolean operators and the unary modal operators F, G, H, P, $\Box$, $\boxdot$, $\boxminus$, and K_δ. The construction of well-formed formulas follow the usual recursive recipe. A model $\mathbb{M}$ is a triple $\langle \mathcal{W}, \varphi, \delta \rangle$ where $\mathcal{W}$ is a nonempty set of possible worlds, φ is a denotation function from propositional variables into $P(\mathcal{W})$, and δ a discovery function: $\delta : \omega^{<\omega} \longrightarrow P(\mathcal{W})$.

Modal operator epistemology is about adding an active long-run perspective to epistemic logic (with agents treated as learning mechanisms over time) and merging branching alethic-temporal logic with rudimentary themes from computational epistemology. In particular, on top of the model of all branching evidence streams, a formal language is introduced, including epistemic modalities whose indices are learning mechanisms. The idea is then to look for reflections between epistemic axioms in the logic and the structural features of the learning mechanisms through considering the following questions:

- Which epistemic axioms may be validated by an epistemic operator based on the definition of limiting convergent knowledge for discovery methods?
- Does the validity of the various epistemic axioms relative to the discovery method depend on enforcing methodological recommendations or structural features of the learning mechanisms?

The first question is close to the first-generation issue of epistemic logic. The second question is a variant of the second-generation issue, with an emphasis that is derived from computational epistemology and shaped by the distinction between permissive and restrictive architectures of inquiry.

Answers to both questions are pertinent to mainstream and formal approaches alike. Validating epistemic axioms goes to show something about the strength of modal knowledge, skepticism and infallibilism; an answer to the second question reveals something about how agents should handle and act to obtain modal knowledge, defeat skepticism and become infallible – assuming that is an ambition of epistemology.

It is possible to prove the following theorem: '*If knowledge is defined as limiting convergence, then knowledge validates **S4** iff the discovery method has consistent expectations*'.[7] (Hendricks 2001, 203)

The rule of necessitation is immediately valid in modal operator epistemology. Neither axiom T: $K_\delta h \to h$ nor axiom K: $K_\delta (h \to h') \to K_\delta h \to K_\delta h'$ require methodological recommendations for their validity. They are valid given the definition of knowledge as it stands, essentially because of the forcing quantifier block. No need for methodology with respect to these two axioms. But axiom 4: $K_\delta h \to K_\delta K_\delta h$, does require one to entertain a methodological recommendation even if the discovery method is infallible. Axiom 5: $\neg K_\delta h \to K_\delta \neg K_\delta h$ is beyond reach no matter what. It may additionally be shown that perfect memory is an impediment to validating axiom 4.

---

[7] It has thus so far been demonstrated that limiting convergent knowledge is sound with respect to **S4**, but it is still an open question (like in many branching tense logics) with respect to which system it is complete.

TABLE 8.1. *Results for Epistemic Axioms*

	K	T	4	5
Consistency	*	*		
Perfect memory	*	*	−	
Consistent expectation	*	*	+	
Infallibility	*	*		

Key: + Boosting, − Debilitation, * Neutrality.

Methodological recommendations may accordingly be classified as to whether they are:

- *boosting* in the sense that a methodological recommendation is *conducive* to validating epistemic axioms and systems,
- *debilitative* in the sense that the methodological recommendation is an *impediment* to validating epistemic axioms and systems, or
- *neutral* (neither boosting nor debilitative).

Table 8.1 summarizes some of the results obtained regarding method, recommendations and the validity of epistemic axioms.

The idea of studying the conduciveness of methodological recommendations in modal operator epistemology has been adopted from computational epistemology. Albeit in quite a different way, it is still in line with the hypothetical methodological imperative discussed in Chapter 7. The primary aim in modal operator epistemology is not to study the solvability of inductive epistemic problems but to investigate the strength of limiting convergent knowledge in terms of the modal system validated by an epistemic operator. Compared to computational epistemology, the hypothetical methodological imperative of modal operator epistemology is crudely this:

If your goal is to validate modal system **SX**, then use method Ξ.

Like axiom **5**, axiom **4** (the axiom of self-awareness, the axiom of positive introspection or the KK thesis) has a controversial status in contemporary epistemology.[8] In philosophy it was embraced as far back as Plato. In philosophical logic, Hintikka calls the thesis epistemically immune to certain kinds of critique. $K_\Xi A$ virtually implies $K_\Xi K_\Xi A$, and the denial of

---

[8] In the early 1970s, the debate over the KK thesis was particularly intense. In 1970, *Synthese* dedicated a volume to the axiom of positive introspection in which Hintikka and Hilpinen defended and Casteñeda and Ginet attacked.

the *virtual implication* is at variance with rationality and thus 'indefensible'. It was also seen in Chapter 6 how Malcolm's autoepistemology may be read as providing a similar defense for the KK thesis. The 'information partition model' has been widely used among economists, particularly in drawing out the consequences of common knowledge of rationality. See, for instance, Aumann's (1976) famous 'agreeing to disagree result'. That model presupposes the KK thesis.

In Chapter 4, counterfactual epistemology was shown to abandon the axiom of self-awareness because the agent may not be tracking the fact that he is tracking. Denying positive introspection likewise supports James's distinction between absolutism in philosophy and pragmatism. It is not necessarily the case that one will infallibly know when one has converged to the fact that one has converged to the truth. Computational epistemologists like Martin and Osherson (1998) have recently joined the debate:

This does not entail that Ψ knows he knows the answer, since (as observed above) Ψ may lack any reason to believe that his hypotheses have begun to converge (p. 13).

A concept of limiting convergent knowledge has now been introduced, and yet limiting convergence is often cited as one of the primary reasons for not validating the KK thesis. Is it possible to eat one's cake and have it too?

Given that both tense and alethic modalities can be treated in modal operator epistemology together with epistemic modalities, it makes sense to distinguish between two interpretations of epistemic axioms:

- An epistemic (or doxastic or combined) implicational axiom is **synchronic** if the consequent obtains at the very same time the antecedent obtains.
- An epistemic (or doxastic or combined) implicational axiom is **diachronic** if the consequent either obtains later or would have obtained later than the antecedent even if things had been otherwise.

Malcolm's (1952) autoepistemology defends the KK thesis synchronically from a first-person perspective. Other construals of first person knowledge operators validating the KK thesis in a synchronic fashion include R. C. Moore (1995), Fitting (1983) and Arló-Costa (1998). These models yield a stronger logic than **S4**, as they validate **S5**. It seems to be the case that epistemic axioms are usually understood synchronically in both mainstream and formal epistemology. The diachronic interpretation of epistemic axioms has not been discussed much in the literature but seems perfectly legitimate for a model of inquiry incorporating temporality, counterfactuality or both. In modal operator epistemology, axioms K and T are valid synchronically, axiom 4 is valid diachronically and axiom 5 is not valid either way.

With these two interpretations of the epistemic axioms in mind, let us return to the question of how to eat one's cake and have it and the current defense of the KK thesis. Knowledge of a hypothesis means reaching a point of convergence after which the agent beams out his conjecture over all later times and possible worlds in accordance with the forcing quantifier block. Knowledge of a hypothesis h is a subset of the hypothesis h. Knowledge of knowledge of a hypothesis h means reaching a point of convergence but only *after* convergence to knowledge of h has come about. The reason is that knowledge of knowledge of a hypothesis is a subset of knowledge of a hypothesis. In turn, knowledge of knowledge can only happen once knowledge of the hypothesis has arisen. This gives the following inclusion order of the knowledge relations:

$$K_\delta K_\delta h \subseteq K_\delta h \subseteq h. \tag{8.1}$$

To validate the KK thesis, the agent must respect (8.1). Respecting the knowledge inclusion order implies *forcing strategically* to learn the KK thesis.

Consider an agent with perfect memory who remembers the past evidence. The KK thesis is then impossible to validate. Perfect memory requires the agent to start forcing for the KK conjecture at a time l, but this is *before* the point of convergence has obtained for simple knowledge of h. Knowledge of h happens at a later stage $n > l$. If the agent tries to force for the validity of the KK thesis prior to knowledge of h, certain worlds may slip the agent's conjecture: A world (λ, m) required for the validity of the KK thesis veers off from the actual world (ε, n) before the knowledge of h has arisen. As the agent perfectly remembers, he will attempt to 'crawl' below n to get this world (λ, m) in the conjecture required for the validity of the KK thesis. If the agent crawls below n and successfully captures (λ, m), then (λ, m) will be in $K_\delta K_\delta h$ but not necessarily in $K_\delta h$. This violates the knowledge inclusion order (8.1).

Suppose the agent has *consistent expectations*. This methodological requirement ensures that additional convergence and forcing demanded for knowing that one knows takes place at a point in time such that $n' > n > l$ to guarantee that the knowledge inclusion order is not violated. The agent *has* converged to h and so forces already. Knowledge of knowledge first requires forcing for knowledge and then later some more forcing for positive introspection.[9]

This sort of strategic forcing is fairly easy to realize if one is standing outside looking in, that is, if one adopts a third-person perspective on inquiry (as modal operator epistemology does) in which means-ends considerations are independent of the epistemic environment. Consistent expectation may infinitely transcend the reasoning powers of any first-person operative or may for other reasons be unavailable to him. Limiting positive introspection is up to the agent and sensitive to a diachronic interpretation. The KK thesis is not valid due to unwarranted confidence in the status of the agent's own earlier beliefs. Due to consistent expectation, the agent knows already. However, the agent may not necessarily be able to realize that he will come to know that he knows using consistent expectation. Only a third-person operator may be able to realize this – as we just were able.

Any method defined for limiting convergence fails to validate axiom 5 no matter which methodological recommendations are in play. Intuitively, the reason is that the axiom of negative introspection, $\neg K_\delta h \rightarrow K_\delta \neg K_\delta h$, requires the method to turn nonconvergence into convergence. When knowledge is defined by convergence, this is impossible. If knowledge is defined by convergence, then it contrapositively follows that if you have not converged, you do not know.

In sum, when determining the validity and modal strength of epistemic operators in a way pertinent to mainstream and formal epistemology alike, we have to go up into at least three dimensions besides the agent involved (Fig. 8.8).[10]

Modal operator epistemology provides a rich framework for other investigations, of which a few will be reviewed. Some axioms, including temporal and epistemic modalities, turn out to be valid, such as

$$K_\delta h \rightarrow \begin{cases} 1.\ F K_\delta h \\ 2.\ G K_\delta h \end{cases} \qquad (8.2)$$

which is independently scrutinized by Fagin et al. (1995), as noted in Chapter 6. (8.2) is valid essentially because of the forcing quantifier block

---

[9] For the formal argument, refer to Hendricks 2001 and Hendricks and Pedersen 2000a.

[10] The agent is also responsible for additional dimensions counting (1) the nature of the method (assessment, discovery, extrapolation...), (2) success and convergence criteria, and (3) methodological recommendations. These further dimensions are not represented in the 3D plot in Figure 8.8.

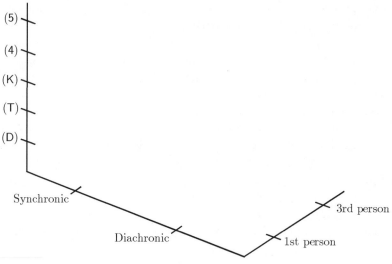

FIGURE 8.8. 3D epistemic strength.

of limiting convergent knowledge together with the assumption of the stable truth-values of the absolute time-invariant empirical hypotheses.[11]

So far attention has been restricted to discovery methods. One may equally well define an assessment method α as a function from finite initial segments of evidence and hypotheses to $\{0, 1\}$ where 0 denotes falsity and 1 denotes truth:

$$\alpha : \omega^{<\omega} \times \mathcal{H} \longrightarrow \{0, 1\}. \tag{8.3}$$

Such a method of justification is the standard one for assessing hypotheses in the light of incoming evidence (Fig. 8.9).

Successful limiting convergence can be defined for assessment such that α decides h in the limit in (ε, n) iff

1. if h is true, then

$$\exists k \geq n, \forall n' \geq k, \forall (\tau, n') \in [\varepsilon \mid n] : \alpha(h, \tau \mid n') = 1$$

2. if h is false, then

$$\exists k \geq n, \forall n' \geq k, \forall (\tau, n') \in [\varepsilon \mid n] : \alpha(h, \tau \mid n') = 0$$

---

[11] Hypotheses fluctuating in a variety of ways in truth-value over time are also possible to define in modal operator epistemology. The prospects of validating epistemic axioms are then somewhat diminished for the current definition of knowledge. see Hendricks and Pedersen 1999a and 1999b.

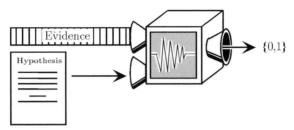

FIGURE 8.9. Assessment methods take finite initial segments of evidence and hypotheses as inputs and return 0 or 1.

with the following limiting convergence modulus:

$$cm(\alpha, h, (\varepsilon, n))$$
$$= \mu k \geq n, \forall n' \geq k, \forall (\tau, n') \in [\varepsilon \mid n] : \alpha(h, \varepsilon \mid n) = \alpha(h, \tau \mid n'). \tag{8.4}$$

The assessment method α verifies h in the limit when h is true and refutes h in the limit when h is false. The assessment method is unlike Nozick's certainty decider (see Chapter 4), a limiting decider, somewhat like the one in Chapter 7.

It turns out that discovery methods can *induce* assessment methods in the following way (Fig. 8.10):

If a discovery method δ discovers h in (ε, n) in the limit, then there exists a limiting assessment method α which verifies h in (ε, n) in the limit.

Assume that δ discovers h in (ε, n) in the limit, and let $cm(\delta, h, (\varepsilon, n))$ be its convergence modulus. Construct α in the following way:

$$\alpha(h, \varepsilon \mid n) = 1 \ iff \ \delta(\varepsilon \mid n) \subseteq h.$$

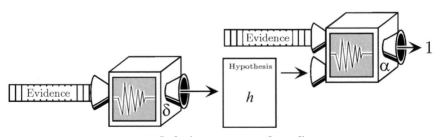

FIGURE 8.10. Inducing assessment from discovery.

If $n' \geq cm(\delta, h, (\varepsilon, n))$, it follows that for all $(\tau, n') \in [\varepsilon \mid n] : \delta(\tau \mid n') \subseteq h$. Consequently $\alpha(h, \tau \mid n') = 1$, and therefore

$$cm(\alpha, h, (\varepsilon, n)) = cm(\delta, h, (\varepsilon, n)).$$

Assessment methods may also induce discovery methods along similar lines. This is interesting because a limiting notion of knowledge defined using an assessment method rather than a discovery method also validates **S4**. This information may in turn be used when *knowledge transmissibility* is studied.

Knowledge transmissibility was first studied by Hintikka (1962). Hintikka investigated whether $K_\Theta K_\Xi h \rightarrow K_\Theta h$ held for his definition of knowledge for different agents Ξ and Θ. In a certain sense, knowledge transmissibility is trivial here because it is essentially the iterated version of axiom T with different agents. As long as the agents index the same possible worlds, knowledge transmissibility holds. In the current scheme of things, knowledge transmissibility is far from trivial because there are agents or methods of different kinds based on either discovery or assessment. Thus, in all generality it must be considered whether

$$K_\Theta K_\Xi h \rightarrow K_\Theta h \qquad\qquad (8.5)$$

is valid for arbitrary inquiry methods $\Theta, \Xi \in \{\alpha, \beta, \gamma, \delta\}$ where γ, δ are discovery methods and α, β are assessment methods. This means a classification of the transmissibility instances which may be paraphrased by the following questions:

- **Uniform Transmissibility**. Is it possible that a discovery method δ having knowledge of the fact that another discovery method γ has knowledge of some hypothesis h may obtain knowledge of this hypothesis h, and similarly for assessment?
- **Nonuniform Transmissibility.** Is it possible that a discovery method δ having knowledge of the fact that an assessment method α has knowledge of some hypothesis h may obtain knowledge of this hypothesis h, and similarly starting with an assessment method?

It turns out, given inducement, that the answers to both of these questions are affirmative. The latter result is interesting in that it, like computational epistemology, partially breaks the back of the dichotomy between assessment and discovery: There is as much a logic of discovery as there is a logic of justification as far as knowledge acquisition is concerned. The different methods may even reliably transmit knowledge to one another.

Successful transmissibility is sensitive to the goal of inquiry. Some philosophers argue that truth is way too ambitious an aim for science. Scientific inquiry may plausibly carry on settling for less, like consistency, simplicity, empirical adequacy, unification, and so on. This making do with less rather than more is partly responsible for the great divide between scientific realism and scientific antirealism in the philosophy of science. One may choose to define other cognitive goals besides truth in the current paradigm. In *The Convergence of Scientific Knowledge* (Hendricks 2001), a goal is defined that is congruent with van Fraassen's (1980) notion of empirical adequacy. According to van Fraassen, truth implies empirical adequacy, but empirical adequacy does not necessarily entail truth. Switching the goal of inquiry from truth to empirical adequacy also changes the epistemic attitude from one of knowledge to one of *acceptance.* It should also be noted that while axiom (8.2) is valid for truth, it is not valid if the goal of inquiry is empirical adequacy. This result of modal operator epistemology also fits well with van Fraassen's ideas about empirical adequacy.

Suppose that an arbitrary method of either assessment or discovery *accepts* some hypothesis. Consider then knowledge transmissibility instances between two methods as in (8.5). Inducement is preserved in both directions, since a discovery method is able to output the hypothesis that the assessment method is currently pointing to. The opposite direction also passes muster because the assessment method is able to verify whatever hypothesis the discovery method is conjecturing. While inducement is preserved, knowledge transmissibility is *not* always preserved. In the uniform case where the methods are of a fixed inquiry type, a discovery method δ may *accept* that another discovery method γ has *knowledge* of h. This does not imply, however, that δ may swap propositional attitudes from acceptance to knowledge of h by watching over what γ does, exactly because empirical adequacy does not imply truth. In the nonuniform case with mixed cognitive goals, the situation is sometimes similar, in that transmissibility also can fail from time to time. An assessment method α may *accept* that another discovery method γ has *knowledge* of h. This does not entail a swap of attitudes in which acceptance is exchanged for knowledge and empirical adequacy is exchanged for truth. The 'cognitive exchange rate' is wrong. While a method may use inducement to communicate convergence, observing stabilization does not necessarily add up to communicating the goal of the inquiry process.

Transmissibility may be construed as a conversation taking place between two agents in which one of the agents is either fully or only partly aware of the information of the other agent. Now, whether the inquiring agent may obtain 'first-hand' information by studying the answering agent's stabilization is highly sensitive to the two agents' sharing the same cognitive goal. Even if the answering agent responds *adequately*, the information passed along may not suffice for the inquiring agent to pick up the *true* message.

Modal operator epistemology observes themes taken from both mainstream and formal epistemologies. Forcing is a mutual concern and is cast in terms of observed evidence and its possible extensions. Justification is a mutual concern but is cast in terms of methodology (method, convergence, success), hypothetical methodological recommendations for reliable truth-conducive inquiry and the validity of modal knowledge. The validity of modal knowledge addresses classical epistemological themes like skepticism and infallibilism. The first- versus third-person distinction is a mutual concern for mainstream and formal epistemologies and quite important in this particular paradigm, as it was for Lewis (see Chapter 5). Some of the formal epistemological results of modal operator epistemology related to the KK thesis are highly sensitive to the enforcement of this distinction. The distinction is, however, not formal but informal; it is a global conceptual distinction, not a local one.

The ambition of the theory is not only to merge themes from mainstream and formal approaches to epistemology but likewise to bring together tools from different formal epistemologies to accommodate more and more mainstream as well as formal concerns, ranging from justification and rationality issues to multimodal systems and learning. Mixing alethic, temporal and epistemic logic with concepts from computational epistemology, combining the axiomatics of modal logic with the learning and knowledge acquisition focus of computational epistemology, emphasizing active agenthood, and so on, are all means to this double end: to open up profitable interaction and exchange between mainstream and formal trends in epistemology. Admittedly, epistemology becomes significantly more complicated with all these additional parameters added in. That is just the way it goes with active agents. We are going to need all the help we can get from mainstream epistemology and formal epistemology alike. *Active agents need a program in 'plethoric' epistemology.*

9

'Plethoric' Epistemology

Epistemology seems to enjoy an unexpectedly sexy reputation these days. A few years ago William Safire wrote a popular novel called *The Sleeper Spy*. It depicts a distinctly post-cold-war world in which it is no longer easy to tell the good guys – or, rather, the good spies – from the bad ones. To emphasize this sea change, Safire tells us that his Russian protagonist has not been trained in the military or the police, as he would have been during the old days, but as an epistemologist.

Jaakko Hintikka (2003b)

9.1 Conceptual Analysis

One often hears that philosophy largely concerns conceptual analysis. Conceptual analysis is enjoying a revival these days after having been put to sleep for a number of years partly due to the stream of naturalism that has fled the philosophical landscape for the past 50 years or so.[1]

In contemporary mainstream epistemology, the goal of these new conceptual exercises is to spell out and elucidate some of the epistemologically significant notions, like knowledge, justification and rationality, that ordinary folk use on a daily basis. An integral part of the elucidation process is to stretch the usage of these concepts to the *max* in order to

[1] Laurence and Margolis (2002) systematically survey the use of conceptual analysis and *a priori* investigations in philosophy and their recent revival. According to the authors, Quine and Putman, notably, convinced philosophers of their limited applicability. Later it seems that at least Putnam (1981) reengaged in more traditional *a priori* conceptual inquiry, a complaint raised by Hacking (1995).

151

reveal their limitations and what these limitations in turn reveal about the nature of human cognition. Seen from this perspective, conceptual analysis is focused on clarifying how words are used in everyday epistemic contexts.

The actual 'stretching' is performed by applying the method of 'consulting intuitions about possible cases,' as Jackson (1994) recently made a case for. Jackson takes conceptual analysis to be an indispensable part of intellectual activity in general. Others, like Bealer (1998), restrict conceptual analysis to philosophical concepts, but the overall ambition is less modest: to argue for the authority and autonomy of philosophy where philosophy has a privileged subject matter accessible only by *a priori* methods – a subject matter that scientific method cannot even hope to reach.

The 'possible cases' are generated, usually not by consulting real-life situations, but most frequently by utilizing yet more intuitions. In a recent book, *The Philosopher's Toolkit* (Baggini and Fosl 2003), which 'takes the beginner through most of the core conceptual tools and distinctions used by philosophers', 'fictions', 'intuition pumps' and 'thought experiments' are described as argumentative tools in philosophical debate. They are described one by one, including their distinctive features, the criteria for their identification and rough guidelines for their use in philosophical discussions. The authors correctly note that it may be hard to tell a fiction from a thought experiment in a given philosophical exchange.

On the difference between thought experiments in science and thought experiments in philosophy the *Toolkit* reads as follows:

The difference between the thought experiments in science and philosophy, however, is that those in science often lead to physical experimentation. For philosophers, however, in most cases physical experimentation is unnecessary because what one is exploring is not the terrain of the physical but the conceptual universe. Reasoning out the leads of our imagination is often sufficient for concepts. (p. 59)

This sentiment does not seem entirely right. Many thought experiments in physics are not immediately amenable to experimentation. Second, there are still rules restricting the use of imagination in a 'conceptual universe', as shown by, for instance, the Gettier paradoxes. Just imagine that Jones does not own a Ford, but Brown is all the same in Barcelona, and from here on out logic kicks in. Using simple logical operations and principles, Gettier uncovered the presuppositions of the intuitions and unequivocally demonstrated the inadequacy of the standard definition of knowledge. But he also uncovered the limitations of the intuitions, which are just as important, as Hintikka (1999a) explains:

More generally, what is wrong with twentieth-century philosophers' use of their alleged intuitions is not so much that they are wrong as that they are limited in their applicability and that their presuppositions are not recognized and spelled out. (p. 138)

While the solutions to the Gettier paradoxes are often modal, the original paradoxes are not themselves modal. The formalism used to generate the counterexamples is strictly extensional. The extensionality of the logical principles involved sets the standards for the applicability of the intuitions and the range of legitimate Gettier paradoxes. Not everything following the Gettierization recipe is a Gettier paradox, especially not if the alleged paradox rests on modal or intensional constructions. The logical principles used to derive the original paradoxes do not necessarily penetrate into modal contexts.

Various additional constraints discussed in the previous chapters have been imposed on knowledge to keep Gettierization from appearing. Nobody has yet suggested abandoning the introduction rule for disjunction, the substitution principle or the introduction rule for the existential quantifier to avoid the Gettier paradoxes. The price would be too high.

Other epistemological conceptual problems reviewed so far include the question of closure of knowledge in counterfactual epistemology, the insufficiency of justification in contextual epistemology, and collapsing knowledge and belief in logical epistemology. The denial of closure provides the skeptic with an answer, and its successful denial is intimately linked to the semantics of counterfactuals. Contextual epistemology views justification as insufficient not because of clairvoyant deliverances but because of the lottery paradox. The conceptual problem of collapsing knowledge and belief in logical epistemology is a consequence of the semantic interpretation, the resulting validity and the implicational relations between the two notions. Nobody has yet suggested dropping the semantics for counterfactuals in relation to the closure issue, denying the existence of the lottery paradox or denouncing the semantics of epistemic and doxastic logics. The price would again be too high.

What all these conceptual problems have in common, taken from mainstream and formal epistemologies alike, is that their production rests on *structure*: logical structure, topological structure, semantic structure, and so on. To abandon this structure is simply too conceptually costly, so alternative routes are pursued instead. 'Reasoning out the leads' of intuitions is still a structured affair and is pursued in order to avoid even more conceptual confusion by abandoning fundamental means of mere reasoning.

Dennett (1980) once coined the term 'intuition pump', referring derogatorily to Searle's 'Chinese Room' argument, which to Dennett hardly constitutes an argument at all – not even an argument by analogy but only a device for boosting the understanding of the issue at hand. Such conceptual stretchings using the method of 'consulting intuitions about possible cases' have also been encountered in this book: Cartesian demons, brains in vats, Alpha Centauri, and to a less extent mirror installations, papier-mâché barns, deranged mothers and identical twins. With respect to some of these possible cases, it is sometimes hard to locate the understanding allegedly boosted by the intuitions, as Dennett and Hofstadter (1982) note: [2]

When philosophical fantasies become too outlandish – involving time machines, say, or duplicate universes or infinitely powerful deceiving demons – we may wisely decline to conclude anything from them. Our conviction that we understand the issues involved may be unreliable, an illusion produced by the vividness of the fantasy. (p. 230)

The lack of conclusion, the unreliability of the conviction, may be related to Hintikka's diagnosis of the unclear and possibly limited applicability, of intuitions: their lack of generalizability combined with a lack of accessibility.

In and by themselves, intuitions are not ready premises for philosophical arguments (Hintikka 1999a) but usually sketches of scenarios, situations or possible worlds that for one reason or the other should be considered relevant in the context given. The relevance of a thought experiment, along with subsequent understanding of its claimed implications, is not unconditional or given merely by a description of the situation itself; it is instead conditional upon a range of determinants, including *ceteris paribus* clauses, proximity relations, similarity conditions and other logical, semantical and topological constructions furnishing criteria of accessibility. If thought experiments and intuition pumps are to be integrated into coherent views, accessibility criteria are the fix points by means of which they must be weighed and evaluated for thrust, relevance and coherence.

---

[2] All the same, Dennett is good for an intuition pump himself from time to time.

9.2   Counterexamples, Intuitions and Structure

An important component in epistemological conceptual analysis is the production of counterexamples like Gettier's. Epistemology, like other areas of philosophy, indulges in advancing theses and then attempting to find counterinstances to make the theses go down in flames. As a form of hypothesis testing, this is a sound practice. 'Consulting intuitions about possible cases' may just produce a counterexample to *something*.[3]

The counterexample must, however, be accessible – just like Gettier's paradoxes. Formal epistemologies are usually aided in this way because accessibility or relevance is dictated by the formal model, and the counterexample is constructed accordingly. Computational epistemology may construct a 'demon strategy' to fool the inquiry method and undermine some knowledge acquisition claim, but the demon operates in the same world, or same set of accessible worlds, as the inquiry method. The 'inductive demon' in computational epistemology, a metaphor for the problem of induction, is simply using the available worlds of evidence admitted by the background knowledge in a way different from what the inquiry method expects. The skeptic also has room to move around in logical epistemology, and this is due to the formal structure of epistemic logic. The skeptic may be forced out of logical systems entirely on pain of diminishing the relevance and plausibility of logical epistemic modeling.

Relevance is dictated immediately through accessibility criteria inherent in the particular formal model. Once the counterexample to a thesis hits in the range of relevant worlds in the formal model of inquiry, that is usually the end of that thesis (Fig. 9.1).

In mainstream epistemology, the use of counterexamples is somewhat less regimented. Perceptual equivalents like identical twins or mirror installations as counterexamples are allegedly more immediately accessible and relevant than brains in tanks of fluids. Whether identical twins on Alpha Centauri are close to the actual world is more difficult to assess. It is not always obvious what counterexamples may be relevantly cited in mainstream epistemological setups. One thing is certain, however, citing global underdetermination as a relevant possibility of error is always an option, on pain of inquiry not leaving the ground. Counterfactual epistemology recognizes this concern by letting the semantics of the counterfactual do the job of determining relevance, leaving the demon

---

[3] For amusing but sagacious fragments of the layman's view of philosophy, philosophical practice and philosophy's broader intellectual environment, see Hendricks 2004b, 2005c, and 2005d.

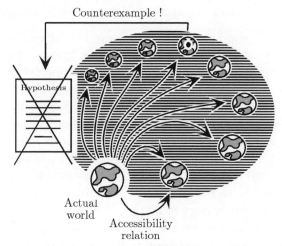

FIGURE 9.1. Relevant counterexample.

world out. If a claim to knowledge holds in the relevant worlds, then a counterexample on Alpha Centauri does not necessarily falsify the theses about knowledge entertained here in the actual world – the very point of forcing (Fig. 9.2). Epistemic reliabilism attempts to distinguish between

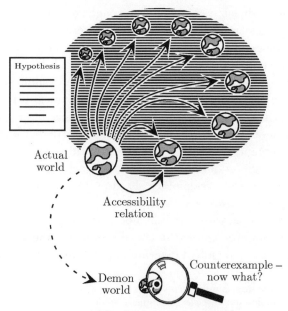

FIGURE 9.2. Irrelevant counterexample.

relevant alternatives in terms of perceptual equivalences but fails to slam the door shut on global underdetermination as a relevant possibility of error. Contextual epistemology slams the door shut in relevant uniform contexts when the presumptive rules (in particular, the rule of actuality and the rule of resemblance) working across the modal universe do not conflict. Logical epistemology can perform a similar reasonable action for single agents, and so on.

Counterfactual semantics gives structure, rules governing eliminating and ignoring possible worlds provide structure, modal semantics provide structure (whether pointwise in the Kripke-style or neighborhood-like in the Scott-Montague–style), and topology is structure. The more lack of structure, the more counterexamples come within the scope of relevance. Here lies the chief danger: not conducting relevant epistemology at all and doing conceptual analysis for the sake of conceptual analysis. Of course, this would not be seen as a danger if one buys into Bealer's and Jackson's view of the intellectual supremacy of philosophy and conceptual scrutinization. The trouble seems to be the means by which the analyses are carried out.

It requires quite *some* intuition to go out to Alpha Centauri to set up a counterexample about deceptive demons who are making the agent believe that everything is normal when it is not or systematically producing images of pink elephants or flying toasters when there are none, and so on. Suppose such a counterexample is constructed relative to some knowledge claim made in the actual world.[4] The question is where the counterexample is to be assessed. On Alpha Centauri, it holds, so it makes little sense to assess it there. Thus, it must be assessed in the actual world, and the only way to do that is by consulting one's intuitions over again. The intuitions stimulated by way-off thought experiments or fictions serve a double purpose: First, they are used as engines to cover the trip to Alpha Centauri, and then they may be used to justify that an error is committed here given a scenario intuited there. In the worst case, it seems to be that using intuitions in this way becomes a self-fulfilling prophecy for counterexamples wherever, leaving very little structure behind.

To consider whether a counterexample is relevant, we need to know what it takes to get out there and back, and, as opposed to a round-trip

---

[4] If the knowledge claim is made on Alpha Centauri, all bets may be off. There is no guarantee that the agent's cognitive apparatus works anything like the way it works in the actual world, nor any guarantee that knowledge means anything like what it is taken to mean in normal circumstances.

ticket, it cannot, without some structural argument, be the same thing.[5] Chances are, in these cases, that the counterexample itself is globally underdetermined, so the intuitions will be too.

Similar skeptical sentiments toward the use of intuitions have been expressed by other philosophers: 'If a view conflicts with intuition, then so much the worse for intuition', Laurence and Margolis claim in response to Davidson's (1986) 'swampman':

> Swampman is a physical duplicate of a normal human being but happens to be created by a freak accident. Intuitively it seems that Swampman has beliefs and desires just as his duplicate does but this conflicts with various accounts of the nature of mental states, accounts that take an organism's history to be crucial to whether it can have contentful mental states. Daniel Dennett says the example is 'not worth discussing'. David Papineau, summarizing his own and Ruth Milikan's earlier responses to the example, says that 'we both gave the same response to the intuition that such a being would, contrary to our theories, have contentful beliefs and desires. Namely, that since we were offering *a posteriori* theories of representation, rather than conceptual analyses of an everyday notion, we were prepared to reject the common-sense intuition that Swampman has contentful states.' (Laurence and Margolis 2002, 22)

9.3   Interactive Accommodations

The examples of conceptual problems cited above have been taken from both mainstream epistemology and formal epistemology. Both approaches may scrutinize epistemological concepts to the limit. Being one of the 'good guys' instead of one of the 'bad guys' in epistemology depends neither on carrying out conceptual analyses nor on being formally minded. It depends on providing structure enough for epistemology to get into the air. Both approaches are in the position to provide such structure and hence accommodate each other's interests. The result can be a fruitful epistemological interaction.

Mainstream epistemology has occasioned formal epistemology. Examples of mainstream epistemology inspiring formal epistemological studies may be found in belief revision theory. The fundamental model suggests an inspiration from the Quineian vibrating web of belief together with entrenchment relations philosophically motivated by Kuhn's paradigmatics and 'scientific revolution', as Gärdenfors (1988) has argued. Recently,

---

[5] Intuitions can hardly be both discovery and assessment engines at the same time if there is no structure revealing what the relation between the two engines are (see Chapters 7 and 8).

Schulte (1999) provided a learning theoretical analysis inspired by Goodman's New Riddle of Induction, scrutinizing the means-ends feasibility of the projection rules and producing new results with respect to speed-optimal reliable inquiry. Autoepistemic logic, which the computer scientist R. C. Moore developed, is in a certain sense the formal embodiment of G. E. Moore's first-person mainstream autoepistemology.

Formal epistemology has also occasioned mainstream epistemology. Lewis's contextual epistemology may be seen as the result of his formal work on counterfactuals, facilitating an admittedly fairly extravagant modal ontology but a sound contextualistic epistemology. Stalnaker's use of belief revision to avoid the Gettier paradoxes is another case in point. Computational epistemology has widened the general understanding of the problem of induction and has questioned intuition-driven norms often proposed for rational inquiry. Logical epistemology systematically addresses the modality of knowledge, sets up measures of its strength and sharpens mainstream discussions of rationality, infallibility, strategies for winning games and other pertinent epistemological issues. Bayesianism has had a profound influence on the epistemological notion of confirmation and coherence (Bovens and Hartmann 2004). Belief revision theory has influenced current philosophical discussions of theory change, and so on.

9.4   Global and Local Approaches

Chapter 2 introduced an initial difference in ambitions between mainstreamers and formalists: global understandings of various epistemic notions versus local understandings of pertinent epistemic ingredients that may or may not sum up to global epistemological notions. Local and global conceptual approaches to epistemology are not mutually exclusive. Global conceptual analyses of epistemic notions may be used to pinpoint and untangle conceptual conflicts arising from local formal analyses.

A global conceptual distinction very feasible for epistemology in general is the distinction between first- and third-person perspectives on inquiry, as demonstrated on numerous occasions already. With this philosophical distinction in hand, it is possible to localize subtle similarities and differences between mainstreamers and formalists. Epistemic reliabilism and counterfactual and contextual epistemology have a fundamentally first-person motivation. The agent's local epistemic circumstances suffice for determining the status of knowledge claims in many contexts. The first-person logic of counterfactual epistemology is very weak on the

Kripke-scale, dismissing concepts like closure, positive introspection and negative introspection and seeming to retain only veridicality and necessitation. The logic of knowledge in contextual epistemology may, on the other hand, be quite strong from the first-person perspective but weak from the third-person point of view. The same concepts including veridicality, necessitation, closure and positive introspection (and possibly also negative introspection), may all be valid on a first-person logic given uniform contexts and the agent's optimal application of the presumptive and prohibitive rules relative to his local environment. More elbow room for error in terms of contextual shifts is left to the third-person inquirer, as he must ignore fewer possibilities than the first-person inquirer to whom he is ascribing knowledge and often entertains a different index of actuality. The third-person logic of contextual epistemology may be as weak as first-person counterfactual logic, even though first-person contextual logic may be as strong as the logics of knowledge advocated by logical epistemology.

Originally, logical epistemology seems to have had a partial first-person motivation, as autoepistemology may be read as providing a philosophical basis for the logic of knowledge. After Hintikka's seminal work, the epistemology of epistemic logic lay dormant for a while (with Hintikka himself as an exception) as the focus changed to: (1) mapping the mathematical properties of the logics of knowledge and belief, and (2) finding venues of application for the logics in computer science, game theory, linguistics, economics, and so on. Cropping up on the way were conceptual problems like the collapse of belief into knowledge, the **S5** assumption about knowledge, and the problem of logical omniscience. While these conceptual problems have had little impact on the technical apparatus and results of epistemic logic, they do bring into question the plausibility of epistemic logic as a logic describing agenthood – any agenthood.

To rectify the situation, conceptual analyses began to appear in logical epistemology, smoothing over, say, the differences between belief and knowledge, claiming epistemic solipsism and closed world assumptions in monoagent systems to make sense of the **S5** assumption and invoking impossible possible worlds and the distinction between explicit and implicit knowledge to cope with logical omniscience. In monoagent systems, it may make sense to suggest a kind of epistemic solipsism as the philosophical foundation for **S5** and to add a stipulation about modeling implicit rather than explicit knowledge to dodge logical omniscience. For multiagent systems, it is somewhat more difficult to maintain epistemic solipsism and the claim about modeling implicit knowledge.

Due to the newly invoked distinction between implicit and explicit knowledge, a change in perspective had to occur to get the new concepts working right in logical epistemology. Explicit knowledge requires the agent to compute knowledge, implicit knowledge does not. What is being modeled on the implicit conceptual understanding is what follows from an agent's knowledge or information state independently of the agent's actual epistemic computation and situation. Hintikka's initial first-person perspective on epistemic logic changed to a third-person perspective in some parts of modern logical epistemology. Logical omniscience is then a problem for the first-person perspective in monoagent systems, not for the third-person model builder of monoagent systems.

This solution still leaves behind a couple of conceptual entanglements. S5 remains an unreasonable stipulation in multiagent systems designed to model game-theoretical scenarios, as Stalnaker (1996a) pointed out. Additionally, acting in the presence of other agents requires the information to be explicitly available to the agents first person, but it may only be implicitly at the agents' disposal. It is not much help to have the knowledge explicitly available on the third-person level if you have to make an informed move on the first-person level featuring other agents trying to beat you as you are trying to beat them.

It is not suggested that the third-person perspective is less feasible than the first-person perspective when it comes to conceptual analyses. They are just different perspectives. If conceptual analysis is partly about stretching the concepts of epistemology as far as they can go, then computational epistemology, modal operator epistemology and logical epistemology are really quintessential examples of this very practice. Analyzing what it takes to solve an epistemic problem independently of an agent's local circumstances, performing *a priori* means-ends analyses, examining the combinatorial structure of solvable epistemic problems in terms of Kelly's complexity-based characterization theorems for different notions of convergence and procedural success, considering the validity of knowledge in the limit, stretching the concept of knowledge all the way to entail logical omniscience, and so forth – are all rigorous ways of doing conceptual analysis.

The analyses are mostly local, as they concentrate on particular ingredients or special interpretations of epistemic notions, which may, together with other ingredients (scrutinized by the same epistemologies or by other theories), add up to a global conceptual understanding of various epistemic notions. Computational and modal operator epistemologies in particular are third-person perspectives concentrating on best or worst cases for agents independently of the local circumstances. This contrasts with other formal epistemologies like Bayesianism and some variants of logical epistemology with a first-person stance. Formal epistemology is as free as any mainstream theory of knowledge to adopt a particular perspective on inquiry and may even incorporate both stances, as Lewis's contextual epistemology does.

In sum, what computational epistemology, modal operator epistemology and logical epistemology furnish are systematic, rigorous and structured ways of conducting exactly what advocates of conceptual analysis claim epistemology is about. The value of local analyses of epistemic concepts for the entire community of epistemologists lies in the regimentation of global intuitions about rationality, justification, reliability and cognitive strength; the fixation of their content and scope; and the creation of systematic manuals for their actual and limiting use. The profit from these interactive accommodations and the value of combining local and global approaches to conceptual analyses are indicated by the many mergers in epistemology.

9.5   Mergers

There have been a great many mergers in formal epistemology lately. Modal logics suitable for epistemology now incorporate alethic, temporal and epistemic logic. Logic and belief revision have merged into doxastic and epistemic dynamic logics. Computational epistemology has been applied to study the logical reliability of belief revision theory. Modal logic and learning concepts from computational epistemology have come together in modal operator epistemology. Game theory incorporates elements from epistemic logic, decision theory, belief revision theory, and so on.

There are similar mergers in mainstream epistemology. Defeasibility theories of knowledge may be utilized to specify conditions intended to sharpen epistemic reliabilism's response to charges of the insufficiency of reliability. Elements from counterfactual epistemology have been utilized to formulate contextualism, nomological reliability has spilled over into contextual epistemology as well, and so forth. Active agents again are appearing.

The mergers in mainstream epistemology are not as common and not always as profitable as the corresponding mergers in formal epistemological theories. The reason tends to be the 'trench wars' in mainstream epistemology, say, between internalism and externalism, coherentism and foundationalism – even epistemology and skepticism. The trench wars are typically counterproductive. From a philosophical perspective, belief revision theory lets foundationalistic entrenchment meet with coherentistic belief change. Epistemic logic, in a certain sense, allows for externalism with respect to implicit knowledge and internalism with respect to explicit and hopefully also common knowledge. Computational epistemology balances between epistemology and skepticism. This is not to suggest that the philosophical distinctions are meaningless. It is to suggest, more modestly, that in fine-grained analyses the distinctions are not obviously enforced, let alone productive in terms of generating new significant technical and philosophically pertinent results.

Here it has not even been considered how epistemology may benefit from consulting 'real-life' situations with cognitive significance, like error management in air-traffic control, uncertainty and epistemic reasoning in complex technological systems, information-gathering engines in web-crawlers – and this list also goes on. For sure, such consultations will occasion more mergers and consequently more plethora in epistemology.

9.6   Plethora

The parameters with respect to which the different epistemologies in this book have been compared (see Chapter 2) balance between global and local approaches to conceptual analysis and also balance between themes usually taken to belong to either mainstream or formal epistemology. Forcing has a global character, exhausting justification in methodology is a more local affair, categorical reliability and stochastic reliability are roughly local, while the first-person/third-person distinction is global. They, all the same, apply equally well to mainstream and formal epistemologies. This is not to suggest that the listed parameters are *the* parameters with respect to which mainstream and formal epistemologies meet, but at least they seem to apply to both approaches. Others will apply as well.[6]

The task bestowed upon 'plethoric' epistemology is to locate these parameters, provide them with rigorous content and structure acceptable to both mainstream and formal camps and then conduct epistemological analyses accordingly. By way of example, Table 9.1 has been steadily

---

[6] For a whole range of different comparisons between mainstream and formal epistemology, see Hendricks 2005a and Hendricks and Pritchard 2005.

TABLE 9.1. *Epistemic Axioms, and Epistemologies*

	CE	COE	LE	MOE
N: $\frac{A}{K_\Xi A}$	1^s	$1^s/3^s$	$1^s/3^s$	3^s
K: $K_\Xi(A \rightarrow A') \rightarrow (K_\Xi A \rightarrow K_\Xi A')$		$(1^s)/(3^s)$	$1^s/3^s$	3^s
T: $K_\Xi A \rightarrow A$	1^s	$1^s/3^s$	$1^s/3^s$	3^s
4: $K_\Xi A \rightarrow K_\Xi K_\Xi A$		1^s	$1^s/3^s$	3^d
5: $\neg K_\Xi A \rightarrow K_\Xi \neg K_\Xi A$		(1^s)	3^s	

Key: CE, counterfactual epistemology; COE, contextual epistemology; LE, logical epistemology; MOE, modal operator epistemology; 1, first-person perspective; 3, third-person perspective; s, synchronicity; d, diachronicity; (), context-sensitive validity.

developed in accordance with mainstream and formal concerns, in accordance with the parameters.[7]

Modal operator epistemology is but one attempt to provide a framework accommodating such epistemological interactions using the parameters. Others will work equally well, as demonstrated by second-generation logical epistemology and computational epistemology. Modal operator epistemology unites themes from these two formal paradigms, partly as an attempt to bring formal epistemology closer to mainstream concerns.

The plethoric epistemological program is not garden variety Quineian naturalized epistemology. While epistemology naturalized is somewhat reductionist in that it seeks to reduce epistemology to a branch of psychology or natural science, plethoric epistemology, in contrast, has a more Hackingian inspiration.

According to Hacking (1995), progress in science is not necessarily measured by approximation to the truth, by unification, by accumulation or by any other classical measure of scientific advancement. The production of new interesting scientific phenomena is the hallmark of a productive science; 'absolute plethora' (p. 218) rather than unity is characteristic of the growth of a scientific research program, similarly in plethoric epistemology. The fact that formalists and mainstream theorists

---

[7] Table 9.1 does not include epistemic reliabilism and computational epistemology. Epistemic reliabilism does not discuss epistemic axioms, and computational epistemology is not obligated to entertain a definition of knowledge (but may all the same have something to offer with respect to the procedural validity of epistemic axioms).

of knowledge may share unilateral forcing heuristics makes for more structured epistemological landscapes.

Perhaps the forcing metaphor is too narrow and too unifying at the same time. Some varieties of formal epistemology are not initially motivated by doubt, although some skeptical challenges may be blocked as a spin-off or a side bonus. From this perspective, the metaphor is too unifying – partitioning is not necessarily forcing. It may also simultaneously be too narrow in that defeating the skeptic is not the only motivation for spending time in epistemology – belief revision, updating, learning are just as important.

Forcing epistemology does not exclude these other epistemological studies and motivations, and some of the epistemologies considered here have exactly these other foci. The metaphor was intended to indicate plethora and certain affinities defined by the epistemo-methodological parameters isolated in the beginning of this book.

Every epistemological paradigm, mainstream or formal, has, as it were, an 'Achilles heel' – something missing, some flaw that can always be pried open by a would-be skeptic or other epistemic pessimist. By bringing the various subsections of the two parallel approaches to epistemology together, one may eventually get *overkill*, given their epistemic overlappings. If an epistemic problem is solvable at all, then one may, by combining the mainstream and formal angles, by the end of the day obtain *overdetermination* in knowledge acquisition and attribution. That would be nice.

Forcing is not unification or reduction but hopefully one among many *methodological* starting points or metaepistemological tools for 'interactive' epistemic plethora in mainstream and formal epistemology.

References

Alchourrón, C. E., Gärdenfors, P., and Makinson, D. (1985). 'On the Logic of Theory Change.' *Journal of Symbolic Logic* **50**: 510–530.

Arló-Costa, H. (1998). 'Qualitative and Probabilistic Models of Full Belief.' In S. Buss, P. Hajék, and R. Pudlák (eds.), *Proceedings of Logic Colloquim'98*. Lecture Notes on Logic **13**.

Arló-Costa, H. (2001a). 'Trade-offs between Inductive Power and Logical Omniscience in Modeling Context.' In V. Akman et al.(eds.), *CONTEXT 2001*. Lecture Notes in Artificial Intelligence **2116**. Berlin and Heidelberg: Springer-Verlag: 1–14.

Arló-Costa, H. (2001b). 'Bayesian Epistemology and Epistemic Conditionals: On the Status of the Export-Import Laws.' *Journal of Philosophy*, **11**: 555–598.

Arló-Costa, H. (2002). 'First Order Extensions of Classical Systems of Modal Logic: The Role of the Barcan Schemas.' *Studia Logica* **71**: 87–118.

Arló-Costa, H. (2003). Non-Adjunctive Inference and Classical Modalities.' *Journal of Philosophical Logic*.

Arló-Costa, H., and Thomason, R. (2001). 'Iterative Probability Kinematics.' *Journal of Philosophical Logic* **46**: 479–524.

Armstrong, D. (1973a). *Belief, Truth and Knowledge*. New York: Cambridge University Press.

Armstrong, D. (1973b). *What Is a Law of Nature?* New York: Cambridge University Press.

Aumann, R. J. (1976). 'Agreeing to Disagree.' *Annals of Statistics* **4**: 1236–1239.

Aumann, R. J. (1994). 'Notes on Interactive Epistemology.' Version 94.06.16. Hebrew University. Recently published in the *International Journal of Game Theory* in two parts.

Bacharach, M. O. L. (1997). 'The Epistemic Structure of a Theory of a Game.' In M. O. L. Bacharach, L.-A. Gerard-Varet, P. Mongin, and H. S. Shin (eds.), *Epistemic Logic and the Theory of Games and Decisions*. Dordrecht: Kluwer Academic Publishers: 303–345.

Baggini, J., and Fosl, P. S. (2003). *The Philosopher's Toolkit: A Compendium of Philosophical Concepts and Methods*. Oxford: Blackwell Publishing.

Baltag, A., Moss, L. S., and Solecki, S. (1998). 'The Logic of Public Announcements, Common Knowledge, and Private Suspicion.' *Paper presented at TARK98*.

Barwise, J. (1988). 'Three Views of Common Knowledge.' *TARK II*, 365–379.

Barwise, J. (1989). 'On the Model Theory of Common Knowledge: The Situation in Logic.' *CSLI Lecture Notes*. Center for the Study of Language and Information: 201–220.

Barwise, J., and Moss, L. (1996). *Vicious Circles: On the Mathematics of Non-Wellfounded Phenomena*. CSLI Publications.

Bealer, G. (1998). 'Intuition and the Autonomy of Philosophy.' In M. DePaul and W. Ramsey (eds.), *Rethinking Intuition*. Oxford: Rowman & Littlefield: 201–239.

Berkeley, G. (1988). *Principles of Human Knowledge/Three Dialogues*. New York: Penguin. (Original work published 1710/1713.)

Bernecker, S., and Dretske, F. (eds.). (2000). *Knowledge: Contemporary Readings in Epistemology*. Oxford: Oxford University Press.

Bicchieri, C. (1993). *Rationality and Coordination*. New York: Cambridge University Press.

Binmore, K., and Shin, H. S. (1992). 'Algorithmic Knowledge and Game Theory.' In C. Bicchieri and M.-L. Dalla-Chiara (eds.), *Knowledge, Belief, and Strategic Interaction*. Cambridge: Cambridge University Press: 141–154.

Black, T. (2002). 'A Moorean Response to Brain-in-a-Vat Scepticism.' *Australasian Journal of Philosophy*, **80**(2): 148–163

Boh, I. (1993). *Epistemic Logic in the Middle Ages*. Oxford: Routledge.

Bonjour, L. (1976). 'The Coherence Theory of Empirical Knowledge.' *Philosophical Studies* **30**: 281–312. Reprinted in M. F. Goodman and R. A. Snyder (eds.), *Contemporary Readings in Epistemology*. Englewood Cliffs, NJ: Prentice Hall, 1993: 70–89.

Bonjour, L. (1980). 'Externalist Theories of Empirical Knowledge.' *Midwest Studies in Philosophy* **5**: 53–73.

Bonjour, L. (1988). *The Empirical Structure of Knowledge*. Cambridge, MA: MIT Press.

Bovens, L., and Hartmann, S. (2004). *Bayesian Epistemology*. Oxford: Oxford University Press.

Boyd, R. (1984). 'The Current State of Scientific Realism.' In J. Leplin (ed.), *Scientific Realism*. Berkeley: University of California Press: 41–82.

Bräuner, T., Hasle, P., and Øhrstrøm, P. (1998a). 'Determinism and the Origins of Temporal Logic.' *Proceedings of the Second International Conference on Temporal Logic*. Applied Logic Series. Dordrecht: Kluwer Academic Publishers:

Bräuner, T., Hasle, P., and Øhrstrøm, P. (1998b). 'Ockhamistic Logics and the True Futures of Counterfactual Moments.' In *Time'98: Proceedings of the Fifth International Workshop on Temporal Representation and Reasoning*. IEEE Press: 132–139.

Bull, R., and Segerberg, K. (1984). 'Basic Modal Logic.' In Gabbay and Guenthner 1984, 1–88.

Castañeda, H.-N. (1970). 'On Knowing (or Believing) That One Knows (or Believes).' *Synthese* **21**: 187–203.

Chellas, B. (1980). *Modal Logic: An Introduction*. Cambridge: Cambridge University Press.

Chisholm, R. (1963). 'The Logic of Knowing.' *Journal of Philosophy* **60**: 773–795.

Chisholm, R. (1977). *The Theory of Knowledge*. 2nd ed. Englewood Cliffs, NJ: Prentice Hall. (First edition published in 1966.)

Chisholm, R., and Keim R. (1972). 'A System of Epistemic Logic.' *Ratio* **14**: 99–115.

Cohen, S. (1987). 'Knowledge, Context and Social Standards.' *Synthese* **73**: 3–26.

Cohen, S. (1999). 'Contextualism, Skepticism, and the Structure of Reasons.' *Philosophical Perspectives* **13**: 57–90.

Cohen, S. (2000). 'Contextualism and Skepticism.' *Philosophical Issues* **10**: 94–107.

Collins, J. (1997). 'How We Can Agree to Disagree.' Columbia University. Version of July 2, 1997. Available at http://collins.philo.columbia.edu.

Curd, M. (1980). 'The Logic of Discovery: An Analysis of Three Approaches.' In T. D. Nickles (ed.), *Scientific Discovery, Logic and Rationality*. Dordrecht: D. Reidel: 201–221.

Davidson, D. (1986). 'Knowing One's Own Mind.' *Proceedings and Addresses of the American Philosophical Association* 60(3): 439–457.

Dancy, J., and Sosa, E. (1992). *A Companion to Epistemology*. Oxford: Blackwell.

De Finetti, B. (1974). *Theory of Probability*. New York: Wiley. (Reprint edition 1990.)

Dennett, D. (1980). 'The Milk of Human Intentionality.' *Behavioral and Brain Sciences* **3**: 140–167.

Dennett, D., and Hofstadter, D. (1982). *The Minds Eye*. Penguin.

DeRose, K. (1995). 'Solving the Skeptical Problem.' *Philosophical Review* **104**: 1–52.

DeRose, K. (2000). 'How Can We Know That We're not Brains in Vats?' *Southern Journal of Philosophy* **38**: 121–148.

Descartes, R. (1981). *A Discourse on Method, Meditations and Principles*. J. Veitch (trans.). Dent.

Dretske, F. (1970). 'Epistemic Operators.' *Journal of Philosophy* **67**: 1007–1022.

Dretske, F. (1981). *Knowledge and the Flow of Information*. Cambridge, MA: MIT Press.

Earman, J. (1978). 'The Universality of Laws.' *Philosophy of Science* **45**: 173–181.

Earman, J. (1992). *Bayes or Bust? A Critical Examination of Bayesian Confirmation Theory*. Cambridge, MA: MIT Press.

Everitt, N., and Fisher, A. (1995). *Modern Epistemology: A New Introduction*. New York: McGraw-Hill.

Fagin, R., and Halpern, J. Y. (1988). 'Belief, Awareness and Limited Reasoning.' *Artificial Intelligence* **34**: 39–76.

Fagin, R., and Halpern, J. Y. (1994). 'Reasoning about Knowledge and Probability.' *Journal of the ACM* **41**(2): 340–367.

Fagin, R., Halpern, J. Y., Moses Y., and Vardi, M. Y. (1995). *Reasoning about Knowledge*. Cambridge, MA: MIT Press.

Fagin, R., Halpern, J. Y., Moses, Y., and Vardi, M. Y. (1996). 'Common Knowledge Revisited.' *Annals of Pure and Applied Logic* **96**: 89–105. (Reprinted in Hendricks et al. 2003.)

Feldman, R. (1985). 'Reliability and Justification.' *The Monist* **68**: 159–173.

Fitting, M. (1983). 'Moore's Non-Monotonic Logic and S5.' CUNY.

Fodor, J. (1985). 'Banish disContent.' In J. Butterfield (ed.), *Mind and Cognition*. Cambridge: Cambridge University Press.

Gabbay, D., and Guenthner F. (1984). *Handbook of Philosophical Logic*. Vol. Z: *Extensions of Classical Logic*. Dordrecht: D. Reidel.

Gärdenfors, P. (1988). *Knowledge in Flux: Modelling the Dynamics of Epistemic States*. Cambridge, MA: MIT Press.

Gettier, E. (1963). 'Is Justified True Belief Knowledge?' *Analysis* **23**(6): 121–123.

Ginet, C. (1970). 'What Must Be Added to Knowing to Obtain Knowing That One Knows?' *Synthese* **21**: 163–186.

Ginet, C. (1985). '*Contra* Reliabilism.' *The Monist* **68**: 175–187.

Girle, R. (2000). *Modal Logics and Philosophy*. Acumen Publishing.

Glymour, C. (1992). *Thinking Things Through*. Cambridge, MA: MIT Press.

Gochet, P., and Gribomont, P. (2003). 'Epistemic Logic.' In D. M. Gabbay and J. Woods (eds.), *Handbook of the History and Philosophy of Logic*. Amsterdam: Elsevier Science.

Gold, E. M. (1965). 'Limiting Recursion.' *Journal of Symbolic Logic* **30**: 27–48.

Gold, E. M. (1967). 'Language Identification in the Limit.' *Information and Control* **10**: 447–474.

Goldman, A. (1967). 'A Causal Theory of Knowing.' *Journal of Philosophy* **64**: 355–372. (Reprinted in Bernecker and Dretske 2000, 18–30.)

Goldman, A. (1976). 'Discrimination and Perceptual Knowledge.' *Journal of Philosophy*, **73**: 771–779. (Reprinted in Bernecker and Dretske 2000, 87–102.)

Goldman, A. (1979). 'What Is Justified True Belief?' In G. S. Pappas (ed.), *Justification and Knowledge*. Dordrecht: D. Reidel: 1–23.

Goldman, A. (1986). *Epistemology and Cognition*. Cambridge, MA: Harvard University Press.

Goldman, A. (1992). 'Epistemic Folkways and Scientific Epistemology.' In *Liaisons: Philosophy Meets Cognitive and Social Sciences*. Cambridge, MA: MIT Press: 155–175. (Reprinted in Kornblith 1994, 291–315.)

Goldman, A. (1996). 'Reliabilism.' *Routledge Encyclopedia of Philosophy*. London: Routledge.

Goodman, M. F., and Snyder, R. A. (1993). *Contemporary Readings in Epistemology*. Englewood Cliffs, NJ: Prentice Hall.

Goodman, N. (1973). *Fact, Fiction and Forecast*. Indianapolis, ID: Bobbs–Merril.

Greco, J. (1999). 'Agent Reliabilism.' In J. Tomberlin (ed.), *Epistemology*. Philosophical Perspectives no. 13. Atascadero, CA: Ridgeview Press: 273–286.

Gundersen, L. B. (2002). *Dispositional Theories of Knowledge*. Ashgate Publishing.

Gutting, G. (1980). 'The Logic of Invention.' In T. Nickles (ed.), *Scientific Discovery, Logic and Rationality*. Dordrecht: D. Reidel: 221–234.

Hacking, I. (1995). *Representing and Intervening*. Cambridge: Cambridge University Press.

Halpern, J. Y. (1991). 'The Relationship between Knowledge, Belief and Certainty.' *Annals of Mathematics and Artificial Intelligence* **5**: 301–322.

Halpern, J. Y. (1993). 'Reasoning about Knowledge.' In A. Kent and J. G. Williams (eds.), *Encyclopedia of Computer Science and Technology*, Vol. 27. New York: Marcel Dekker: 275–296.

Halpern, J. Y. (1995). 'Should Knowledge Entail Belief?' *Journal of Philosophical Logic* **25**: 483–494.

Halpern, J. Y., and Vardi, M. Y. (1988a). 'The Complexity of Reasoning about Knowledge and Time in Asynchronous Systems.' In *Proceedings of the 20th ACM Symposion on Theory of Computing*. 53–65.

Halpern, J. Y., and Vardi, M. Y. (1988b). 'The Complexity of Reasoning about Knowledge and Time, I: Lower Bounds.' *Journal of Computer and System Sciences* **38** (1): 195–237.

Hempel, C. (1965). *Aspects of Scientific Explanation*. New York.

Hempel, C., and Oppenheim, P. (1945). 'A Definition of "Degree of Confirmation."' *Philosophy of Science* **45**: 98–115.

Hendricks, V. F. (1997). *Epistemology, Methodology and Reliability*, Unpublished doctoral dissertation, University of Copenhagen.

Hendricks, V. F. (1999). 'Methodology in Epistemology.' *Danish Yearbook of Philosophy* **34**: 43–64.

Hendricks, V. F. (2001). *The Convergence of Scientific Knowledge: A View from the Limit*. Trends in Logic: Studia Logica Library Series. Kluwer Academic Publishers.

Hendricks, V. F. (2002). 'Active Agents.' ΦNEWS **2**: 5–40. A revised version of the paper is published in a special issue of the *Journal of Logic, Language, and Information*, J. van Benthem and R. van Rooy (eds.), 2003; **12**: 469–495.

Hendricks, V. F. (2003). 'Epistemology Axiomatized.' Paris: UNESCO, November 2003.

Hendricks, V. F. (2004a). 'Hintikka on Epistemological Axiomatizations.' In D. Kolak and J. Symons (eds.), *Quantifiers, Questions and Quantum Physics: Essays on the Philosophy of Jaakko Hintikka*. Kluwer Academic: 3–34.

Hendricks, V. F. (2004b). *Feisty Fragments: For Philosophy*. London: King's College Publications.

Hendricks, V. F. (ed.). (2005a). *Eight Bridges between Mainstream and Formal Epistemology*. Special issue of *Philosophical Studies*. Contributions from H. Arló-Costa, J. van Benthem, L. Bovens, S. O. Hansson, S. Hartmann, V. F. Hendricks, M. Hild, R. Stalnaker, J. Symons, and H. Wansing.

Hendricks, V. F. (2005b). *The Agency: The Epistemology of Epistemic Logic*. In *Texts in Philosophy Series*. London: King's College Publications.

Hendricks, V. F. (2005c). *Logical Lyrics: From Philosophy to Poetics*. London: King's College Publications.

Hendricks, V. F. (2005d). *500CC: Computer Citations*. London: King's College Publications.

Hendricks, V. F., and Faye, J. (1998). 'Abducting Explanation.' In L. Magnani, N. J. Nersessian, and P. Thagard (eds.), *Model-Based Reasoning in Scientific Discovery: MBR'98*. New York: Kluwer Academic Publishers; Plenum Press: 271–292.

Hendricks, V. F., and Malinowski, J. (eds.). (2003). *Trends in Logic: 50 Years of Studia Logica*. Trends in Logic: Studia Logica Library Series. Kluwer Academic Publishers. Contributions from J. van Benthem, W. Buszkowski, M. L. Dalla Chiara, M. Fitting, J. M. Font, R. Giuntini, R. Goldblatt, V. Marra, D. Mundici, R. Leporini, S. P. Odintsov, H. Ono, G. Priest and H. Wansing.

Hendricks, V. F., and Pedersen, S. A. (1997). 'A Note on Innovation and Justification.' *Danish Yearbook of Philosophy* **32**: 87–110.

Hendricks, V. F., and Pedersen, S. A. (1998a). 'Assessment and Discovery in the Limit Scientific Inquiry.' In J. Cachro, S. Hanuszewicz, G. Kurczewski, and A.

Rojszczak (eds.), *Philosophical Dimensions of Logic and Science*. Synthese Library, no. 320. Kluwer Academic: 345–372.

Hendricks, V. F., and Pedersen, S. A. (1998b). 'Discovery, Knowledge and Reliable Limiting Convergence – the $K_a LC$-paradigm.' *Philosophica* **68**: 901–924.

Hendricks, V. F., and Pedersen, S. A. (1998c). 'How Belief and Methodology Imply Knowledge.' In S. Halldén, B. Hansson, W. Rabinowicz, and N. E. Sahlin (eds.), *Festschrift in Honor of Peter Gärdenfors' 50th Birthday*. Lund University: 1–25. Available at http://www.lucs.lu.se/spinning/categories/decision/Hendricks_Pedersen/index.html.

Hendricks, V. F., and Pedersen, S. A. (1999a, February). 'Scientific Respect in Limiting Scientific Inquiry.' Paper presented at the Logic Colloquium, Departments of Philosophy and Computer Science, Carnegie Mellon University.

Hendricks, V. F., and Pedersen, S. A. (1999b, August). *Operators in Philosophy of Science*. Material from this book manuscript was first presented at XI International Congress on Logic, Methodology and the Philosophy of Science, Krakow, Poland.

Hendricks, V. F., and Pedersen, S. A. (2000a, July). 'KK-ing Diachronically.' Paper presented at *LC2000 – European Congress of the Association of Symbolic Logic*, Paris, France.

Hendricks, V. F., and Pedersen, S. A. (2000b). *The Companion to Modal Operator Theory: A Program in Philosophy Online*. Department of Philosophy and Science Studies, Roskilde University, Denmark. Available at http://www.mot.ruc.dk.

Hendricks, V. F., and Pedersen, S. A. (2002). *Moderne elementær Logik*. Forlaget Høst & Søn.

Hendricks, V. F., and Pedersen, S. A. (eds.). (2005). *Forty Years of Possible Worlds*. Special issue of *Studia Logica: An International Journal for Symbolic Logic*. Contributions from H. Arló-Costa, M. Cresswell, A. Brandenburger, P. Blackburn, S. O. Hansson, J. H. Keisler, M. Gehrke, R. Parikh, A. Varzi, and A. Zanardo.

Hendricks, V. F., and Pedersen, S. A. (forthcoming). 'The Fulcrum of Formal Philosophy.' ΦNEWS.

Hendricks, V. F., Pedersen, S. A., and Jørgensen, K. F. (eds.). (2003). *Knowledge Contributors*. Synthese Library no. 322. Kluwer Academic. Contributions from H.v. Ditmarsch, R. Fagin, J. Halpern, J. Hintikka, W. v. d. Hoek, B. Kooi, W. Lenzen, Y. Moses, H. Rott, J. Sowa, M. Vardi, and R. Wójcicki.

Hendricks, V. F., and Pritchard, D. H. (eds.). (2005). *New Waves in Epistemology*. Ashgate Publishing.

Hansen, P. G., Hendricks, V. F. Pedersen, S. A., and Rabinowicz, W. (forthcoming). *Social Software*. Special issue of *Synthese*. Contributions from K. Binmore, W. v. d. Hoek, M. Jiborn, R. Rarikh, W. Rabinowicz, H. Rott, and B. Skyrms.

Hendricks, V. F., and Symons, J. (2005). 'Epistemic Logic,' in Stanford Encyclopedia of Philosophy, Stanford, CA.

Hendricks, V. F., and Symons, J. (2006a). 'Where is the Bridge? Epistemic Logic and Epistemology.' Forthcoming in [Hendricks 2005].

Hilpinen, R. (1970). 'Knowing That One Knows and the Classical Definition of Knowledge.' *Synthese* **21**: 109–132.

Hilpinen, R. (1971). 'Knowledge and Justification.' *Ajatus* **33**: 7–39.

Hintikka, J. (1962, 2005) *Knowledge and Belief: An Introduction to the Logic of the Two Notions.* Cornell: Cornell University Press. Reprinted in 2005, prepared by V. F. Handricks and J. Symons, London: King's College Publications.

Hintikka, J. (1969). 'Semantics for Propositional Attitudes.' In *Models for Modalities.* Dordrecht: D. Reidel: 87–111.

Hintikka, J. (1970). '"Knowing That One Knows" Revisited.' *Synthese* **21**: 141–162.

Hintikka, J. (1975). 'Impossible Possible Worlds Vindicated.' *Journal of Philosophical Logic* **4**: 475–484.

Hintikka, J. (1989). 'Reasoning about Knowledge in Philosophy: The Paradigm of Epistemic Logic.' In J. Hintikka and M. Hintikka (eds.), *The Logic of Epistemology, and the Epistemology of Logic.* Dordrecht: Kluwer Academic: 17–35.

Hintikka, J. (1999a). *Inquiry as Inquiry: A Logic of Scientific Discovery.* Dordrecht: Kluwer Academic.

Hintikka, J. (1999b). 'The Emperor's New Intuitions.' *Journal of Philosophy*: 127–147.

Hintikka, J. (1999c). 'The Theory-Ladenness of Intuitions.' Unpublished paper.

Hintikka, J. (2003a). 'A Second Generation Epistemic Logic and Its General Significance.' In Hendricks et al. 2003.

Hintikka, J. (2003b). 'Epistemology without Knowledge and Belief.' Unpublished paper.

Hintikka, J., and Halonen, I. (1998). 'Epistemic Logic.' *Routledge Encyclopedia of Philosophy*, vol. 1. London: Routledge.

Howson, C., and Urbach, P. (1989). *Scientific Reasoning: The Bayesian Approach.* La Salle, IL: Open Court.

Huang, Z., and Kwast, K. (1991). 'Awareness, Negation and Logical Omniscience.' In J. van Eijck (ed.), *Logics in AI: Proceedings JELIA '90.* New York: Springer-Verlag: 282–300.

Hughes, G. E., and Cresswell, M. J. (1968). *An Introduction to Modal Logic.* London: Routledge.

Jackson, F. (1994). 'Armchair Metaphysics.' In *Mind, Method, and Conditionals: Selected Essays.* London: Routledge: 154–176.

James, W. (1960). 'The Will to Believe.' In *Essays in Pragmatism.* Hafner Publishing Company.

Jeffrey, R. (1992). *Probability and the Art of Judgment.* New York: Cambridge University Press.

Johnsen, O. (1974). 'Knowledge.' *Philosophical Studies* **25**: 273–282.

Kelly, K. (1987). 'The Logic of Discovery.' *Philosophy of Science* **54**: 435–452.

Kelly, K. (1991). 'Reichenbach, Induction and Discovery.' *Erkenntnis* **35**: 123–149.

Kelly, K. (1992). 'Learning Theory and Descriptive Set Theory.' *Logic and Computation* **3**: 27–45.

Kelly, K. (1994). 'Reliable Methods.' In D. Prawitz, B. Skyrms, and D. Westerstahl (eds.), *XI International Congress on Logic, Methodology and Philosophy of Science IX.* Amsterdam: Elsevier: 353–381.

Kelly, K. (1996). *The Logic of Reliable Inquiry.* New York: Oxford University Press.

Kelly, K. (1998a). 'Learning Theory and Epistemology.' In M. Sintonen and I. Niiniluoto (eds.), *Handbook of Epistemology.* Dordrecht: Kluwer Academic.

Kelly, K. (1998b). 'Iterated Belief Revision, Reliability and Inductive Amnesia.' *Erkenntnis* **35**: 11–58.

Kelly, K. (1999). 'Naturalism Logicized.' In R. Nola and H. Sankey (eds.), *After Popper, Kuhn, and Feyerabend*. Dordrecht: Kluwer Academic: 177–210.

Kelly, K. (2000). 'The Logic of Success.' *British Journal for the Philosophy of Science.*

Kelly, K., and Schulte, O. (1995). 'The Computable Testability of Theories Making Uncomputable Predictions.' *Erkenntnis* **42**: 29–66.

Kelly, K., and Schulte, O. (1996). 'Church's Thesis and Hume's Problem.' In M. L. D. Chiara (ed.), *Logic, Methodology, and Philosophy of Science X*. Dordrecht: Kluwer Academic: 159–177.

Kelly, K., Schulte, O., and Hendricks, V. F. (1996). 'Reliable Belief Revision.' In M. L. D. Chiara (ed.), *Logic, Methodology, and Philosophy of Science X*. Dordrecht: Kluwer Academic.

Kelly, K., Schulte, O., and Juhl, C. (1997). 'Learning Theory and Philosophy of Science.' *Philosophy of Science* **64**: 245–267.

Kitcher, P. (1993). *The Advancement of Science.* New York: Oxford University Press.

Klein, P. D. (1971). 'A Proposed Definition of Propositional Knowledge.' *Journal of Philosophy* **68**: 471–482.

Klein, P. D. (1979). 'Misleading "Misleading Defeaters."' *Journal of Philosophy* **76**: 382–386.

Knuuttila, S. (1993). *Modal Logic in the Middle Ages.* London: Routledge.

Kornblith, H. (ed.). (1994). *Naturalizing Epistemology.* Cambridge, MA: MIT Press.

Kripke, S. (1963). 'Semantical Analysis of Modal Logic.' *Zeitschrift für Matematische Logik und Grundlagen der Matematik* **9**: 67–96.

Kraus, S., and Lehman, D. J. (1988). 'Knowledge, Belief and Time.' *Theoretical Computer Science* **58**: 155–174.

Kuhn, T. S. (1973). 'Objectivity, Value and Theory Choice.' Machette Lecture, Furman University.

Kutschera, F. v. (1976). *Einführung in die intensional Semantik.* Berlin: W. de Gruyter.

Kvanvig, J. (2003). 'Simple Reliabilism and Agent Reliabilism.' *Philosophy and Phenomenological Research* **66**: 451–457.

Kyburg, H. E., Jr. (1961). *Probability and the Logic of Rational Belief.* Middletown, CT: Wesleyan University Press.

Kyburg, H. E., Jr. (1970). 'Conjunctivits.' In M. Swain (ed.), *Induction, Acceptance, and Rational Belief.* Dordrecht: D. Reidel.

Kyburg, H. E. Jr., and Teng, C. M. (2002). 'The Logic of Risky Knowledge.' Paper presented at WoLLIC, Brazil.

Lamarre, P., and Shoham, Y. O. (1994). 'Knowledge, Belief and Conditionalization.' In J. Doyle, E. Sandewall, and P. Torraso (eds.), *Principles of Knowledge Representation and Reasoning: Proceedings of the 4th International Conference (KR '94).* Morgan Kaufman: 415–424.

Laurence, S., and Margolis, E. (2002). 'Concepts and Conceptual Analysis.' *Philosophy and Phenomenological Research.*

Lehrer, K. (1970a). 'Believing That One Knows.' *Synthese* **21**: 133–140.

Lehrer, K. (1970b). 'The Fourth Condition for Knowledge: A Defence.' *Review of Metaphysics* **24**: 122–128.

Lehrer, K. (1974). *Knowledge*. New York: Oxford University Press.

Lehrer, K. (1980). 'Coherence and the Racehorse Paradox.' *Midwest Studies in Philosophy* 5: 183–191.

Lehrer, K. (1989). 'Knowledge Reconsidered.' In M. Clay and K. Lehrer (eds.), *Knowledge and Skepticism*. Boulder, CO: Westview Press.

Lemmon, E. J. (1959). 'Is There Only One Correct System of Modal Logic?' *Aristotelian Society*, suppl. vol. **33**: 23–40.

Lemmon, E. J., in collaboration with D. Scott. (1977). *An Introduction to Modal Logic*. Oxford: Blackwell.

Lenzen, W. (1978). 'Recent Work in Epistemic Logic.' *Acta Philosophica Fennica* **30**: 1–219.

Lenzen, W. (2003). 'Knowledge, Belief, and Subjective Probability.' In Hendricks et al. 2003: 17–32.

Levesque, H. J. (1984). 'A Logic of Implicit and Explicit Belief.' In *Proceedings AAAI-84*. Austin, TX: 198–202.

Levi, I. (1983). *The Enterprise of Knowledge*. Cambridge: Cambridge University Press.

Levi, I. (1991). *The Fixation of Belief and Its Undoing*. Cambridge: Cambridge University Press.

Levi, I. (1997). 'The Logic of Full Belief.' In A. K. Peters (ed.), *The Covenant of Reason: Rationality and the Commitments of Thought*. Cambridge: Cambridge University Press: 40–69.

Levy, S. (1977). 'Defeasibility Theories of Knowledge.' *Canadian Journal of Philosophy* 75: 739–742.

Lewis, C. I. (1946). *An Analysis of Knowledge and Valuation*. La Salle, IL: Open Court.

Lewis, D. (1973). *Counterfactuals*. Cambridge, MA: Harvard University Press.

Lewis, D. (1976). 'Scorekeeping in Language Games.' *Journal of Philosophical Logic* 8: 339–359.

Lewis, D. (1984). *On the Plurality of Worlds*. Oxford: Blackwell.

Lewis, D. (1996). 'Elusive Knowledge.' *Australian Journal of Philosophy* 74: 549–567. (Reprinted in Bernecker and Dretske 2000, 366–384.)

Lindström, S., and Rabinowicz, W. (1997). 'Extending Dynamic Logic: Accommodating Iterated Beliefs and Ramsey Conditionals within DLL.' In L. Lindahl, P. Needham, and R. Sliwinski (eds.), *For Good Measure*. Uppsala Philosophical Studies no. 46. 123–153.

Lindström, S., and Rabinowicz, W. (1999). 'DDL Unlimited: Dynamic Doxastic Logic for Introspective Agents.' *Erkenntnis* 50: 353–385.

Malcolm, N. (1952). 'Knowledge and Belief.' *Mind* **61**: 242. Reprinted in M. F. Goodman and R. A. Snyder (eds.), *Contemporary Readings in Epistemology*. Englewood Cliffs, NJ: Prentice Hall, 1993: 272–279.

Martin, E., and Osherson, D. (1998). *Elements of Scientific Inquiry*. Cambridge, MA: MIT Press.

Martin, E., and Osherson, D. (1999). 'Scientific Discovery Based on Belief Revision.' *Journal of Symbolic Logic*.

McDermott, D., and Doyle, J. (1980). 'Non-monotonic Logic.' *Artificial Intelligence* **13**(1): 41–72.

McGee, V. (1994). 'Learning the Impossible.' In J. Bell and B. Skyrms (eds.), *Probability and Conditionals*. Cambridge: Cambridge University Press.

Moore, G. E. (1959). 'Certainty.' In *Philosophical Papers*. London: Allen and Unwin/Unwin Hyman. Reprinted in M. F. Goodman and R. A. Snyder (eds.), *Contemporary Readings in Epistemology*. Englewood Cliffs, NJ: Prentice Hall, 1993: 257–271.

Moore, R. C. (1982). 'A Formal Theory of Knowledge and Action.' In J. R. Hobbes and R. C. Moore (eds.), *Formal Theories of a Commonsense World*. Norwood: Ablex.

Moore, R. C. (1985). 'Semantical Considerations on Non-Monotonic Logic.' *Artificial Intelligence* **25**: 75–94.

Moore, R. C. (1995). *Logic and Representation*. CSLI Lecture Notes 39.

Moses, J. Y., and Shoham Y. O. (1993). 'Belief as Defeasible Knowledge.' *Artificial Intelligence* **64**: 299–322.

Nozick, R. (1981). *Philosophical Explanations*. Cambridge, MA: Harvard University Press.

Nozick, R. (1993). *The Nature of Rationality*. Cambridge, MA: Harvard University Press.

Osborne, M., and Rubinstein, A. (1994). *A Course in Game Theory*. Cambridge, MA: MIT Press.

Osherson, D., Stob, M., and S. Weinstein (1986). *Systems That Learn*. Cambridge, MA: MIT Press.

Peirce, C. S. (1958). *Charles S. Peirce: Selected Writings*. P. Wiener (ed.). New York: Dover.

Pacuit, E., and Parikh, R. (2004). 'A Logic for Communication Graphs.' CUNY.

Plantinga, A. (1993). *Warrant and Proper Function*. New York: Oxford University Press.

Plaza, J. (1989). 'Logics of Public Communications.' In *Proceedings of the Fourth International Symposium on Methodologies for Intelligent Systems*.

Pollock, J. (1983). 'Epistemology and Probability.' *Synthese* **55**: 231–252.

Popper, K. (1975). *The Logic of Scientific Discovery*. Hutchinson and Co.

Pritchard, D. H. (2001). 'Contextualism, Skepticism, and the Problem of Epistemic Descent.' *Dialectica* **55**: 327–349.

Pritchard, D. H. (2002a). 'Contemporary Skepticism.' *Internet Encyclopedia of Philosophy*.

Pritchard, D. H. (2002b). 'Recent Work on Radical Skepticism.' *American Philosophical Quarterly* **39**: 215–257.

Putnam, H. (1963). ' "Degree of Confirmation" and Inductive Logic.' In A. Schilpp (ed.), *The Philosophy of Rudolph Carnap*. LaSalle, IL: Open Court.

Putnam, H. (1981). *Reason, Truth, and History*. New York: Cambridge University Press.

Quine, W. V. O. (1975). 'Mind and Verbal Dispositions.' In S. Guttenplan. (ed.), *Mind and Language*. Oxford: Clarendon Press: 83–95.

Radford, C. (1966). 'Knowledge – by Examples.' *Analysis* **27**: 1–11.

Ramsey, F. P. (1931). 'Knowledge.' In R. B. Braithwaite (ed.), *The Foundations of Mathematics and Other Essays*. New York: Harcourt Brace.

Rantala, V. (1975). 'Urn Models: A New Kind of Non-Standard Model for First-Order Logic.' *Journal of Symbolic Logic* **4**: 455–474.

Reiter, R. (1980). 'A Logic for Default Reasoning.' *Artificial Intelligence* **13**: 81–132.

de Rijke, M. (1994). 'Meeting Some Neighbours: A Dynamic Modal Logic Meets Theories of Change and Knowledge Representation.' In J.v. Eijck and A. Visser (eds.), *Logic and Information Flow*. Cambridge, MA: MIT Press.

Rott, H. (2003). 'Economics and Economy in the Theory of Belief Revision.' In Hendricks et al. 2003.

Russell, B. (1956). *Logic and Knowledge: Essays 1901–1950*, R. C. Marsch (ed.). London: Allen and Unwin.

Sankey, H. (1999, May 14). 'A Realist Approach to Method and Truth.' Lecture delivered to the Department of Philosophy and Science Studies, Roskilde University, Denmark.

Santayana, G. (1955). *Skepticism and Animal Faith: Introduction to a System of Philosophy*. New York: Dover.

Schmitt, F. (1981). 'Justification as Reliable Indication or Reliable Process.' *Philosophical Studies* **40**: 409–417.

Schulte, O. (1999). 'The Logic of Reliable and Efficient Inquiry.' *Journal of Philosophical Logic* **28**: 399–438.

Schulte, O. (2000). 'Inferring Conservation Principles in Particle Physics: A Case Study in the Problem of Induction.' *British Journal for the Philosophy of Science* **51**: 771–806.

Schulte, O. (2002). 'Formal Learning Theory.' *Stanford Encyclopedia of Philosophy*.

Scott, D. (1970). 'Advice on Modal Logic.' In K. Lambert (ed.), *Philosophical Problems in Logic*. Dordrecht: D. Reidel: 143–173.

Segerberg, K. (1995). 'Belief Revision from the Point of View of Doxastic Logic.' *Bulletin of the IGPL* **3**: 535–553.

Segerberg, K. (1999a). 'The Basic Dynamic Doxastic Logic of AGM.' *Uppsala Prints and Preprints in Philosophy* **1**.

Segerberg, K. (1999b). 'A Completeness Proof in Full DDL.' In R. Sliwinski (ed.), *Philosophical Crumbs: Essays Dedicated to Ann-Mari Henschen-Dahlqvist on the Occasion of her Seventy-fifth Birthday*. Uppsala Philosophical Studies no. 49. 195–207.

Sextus Empiricus (1933). *Outlines of Pyrrhonism*, Vol. 1. R. G. Bury, (trans.). Cambridge, MA: Harvard University Press.

Shin, H.-S., and Williamson, T. (1994). 'Representing the Knowledge of Turing Machines.' *Theory and Decision* **37**(1): 125–146.

Shope, R. K. (1983). *The Analysis of Knowing*. Princeton, NJ: Princeton University Press.

Sosa, E. (1985). 'Knowledge and Intellectual Virtue.' *The Monist* **68**: 224–245.

Sosa, E. (1991). 'Methodology and Apt Belief.' In *Knowledge in Perspective: Selected Essays in Epistemology*. Cambridge: Cambridge University Press: 245–256.

Sowa, John F. (2000). *Knowledge Representation: Logical, Philosophical, and Computational Foundations*. Pacific Grove, CA: Brooks/Cole.

Sowa, John F. (2003). 'Laws, Facts, and Contexts: Foundations for Multimodal Reasoning.' In Hendricks et al. 2003.

Stalnaker, R. (1968). 'A Theory of Conditionals.' In N. Rescher (ed.), *Studies in Logical Theory*. Oxford: Blackwell: 98–112.

Stalnaker, R. (1983). *Inquiry*. Cambridge, MA: MIT Press.

Stalnaker, R. (1996a). 'Knowledge, Belief and Counterfactual Reasoning in Games.' *Economics and Philosophy* **12**: 133–163.

Stalnaker, R. (1996b). 'What Is a Non-monotonic Consequence Relation?' *Fundamenta Informatica* **3**: 8–21.

Stalnaker, R. (1999). 'Extensive and Strategic Form: Games and Models for Games.' *Research in Economics* **53**: 291–293.

Swain, M. (1981). 'Justification and Reliable Belief.' *Philosophical Studies* **40**: 389–407.

Swinburne, R. (1968). *Space and Time.* Oxford: Oxford University Press.

Talbott, W. J. (1990). *The Reliability of the Cognitive Mechanism.* New York: Garland Publishing.

Thorpe, W. H. (1983). *Beyond Reductionism.* Irvington Publications.

van Benthem, J. F. A. K. (2000a). 'Logic and Game Theory: Close Encounters of the Third Kind.' In I.v. Loon, G. Mints, and R. Muskens, (eds), *Proceedings of LLC99.* CSLI Publications.

van Benthem, J. F. A. K. (2000b). *Logic in Games.* Electronic lecture notes. Available at http://turing.wins.uva.nl/˜johan/.

van Benthem, J. F. A. K. (2001). 'Dynamic-Epistemic Logic of Games.' In G. Bonanno (ed.), *Proceedings of LOFT4, Bulletin of Economic Research.*: 14–31

van Benthem, J. F. A. K. (2003). 'Fifty Years: Changes and Constants in Logic.' In Hendricks and Malinowski 2003, 35–56.

Van Ditmarsch, H., van dar Hoek, W., and Kooi, B. (2004). 'Playing Cards with Hintikka: An Introduction to Dynamic Epistemic Logic., ΦNEWS **6**: 6–32.

van der Hoek, W. (1996). 'Systems for Knowledge and Belief.' *Journal of Logic and Computation* **3**(2): 173–195.

van der Hoek, W., Ditmarsch, H., and Kooi, B. (2003). 'Concurrent Dynamic Epistemic Logic.' In Hendricks et al. 2003.

van der Hoek, W., and Meyer, J.-J.Ch. (1995). *Epistemic Logic for AI and Computer Science.* Cambridge Tracts in Theoretical Computer Science No. 41. Cambridge: Cambridge University Press.

van Fraassen, B. (1980). *The Scientific Image.* Oxford: Clarendon Press.

van Fraassen, B. (1989). *Laws and Symmetry.* Oxford: Oxford University Press.

Von Mises, R. (1956). *Probability, Statistics and Truth.* New York: Dover.

Von Wright, G. H. (1951). *An Essay on Modal Logic.* Amsterdam: North-Holland.

Von Wright, G. H. (1984). Philosophical Papers. Vol. 2: *Truth, Knowledge and Modality.* Oxford: Blackwell.

Voorbraak F. (1991). 'The Theory of Objective Knowledge and Rational Belief., In *Logics in AI: Proceedings of the European Workshop JELIA '90.* New York: Springer Verlag: 499–515.

Weinberg, S. (1992). *Dreams of a Final Theory: The Scientist's Search for the Ultimate Laws of Nature.* New York: Vintage.

Williams, M. (1995). *Unnatural Doubts.* Princeton, NJ: Princeton University Press.

Williams, M. (2001). 'Contextualism, Externalism and Epistemic Standards.' *Philosophical Studies* **103**: 1–23.

Williamson, T. (2000). 'Tennant on Knowable Truth.' *Ratio* **13**, (2): 99–114.

Williamson, T. (2001). 'Some Philosophical Aspects of Reasoning about Knowledge.' In J. van Benthem (ed.), *Proceedings of the 8th Conference on TARK.* San Francisco: Morgan Kaufman: 115–121.

Williamson, T. (2002). *Knowledge and Its Limits.* Oxford: Oxford University Press.

Zanardo, A. (1996). 'Branching-time Logic with Quantification over Branches: The Point of View of Modal Logic.' *Journal of Symbolic Logic.* **61**: 1–39.

Øhrstrøm, P., and Hasle, P. F. (1995). *Temporal Logic. From Ancient Ideas to Artificial Intelligence.* Dordrecht: Kluwer Academic.

Index